THE SECURITY DILEMMA AND THE
END OF THE COLD WAR

The Security Dilemma and the End of the Cold War

Alan Collins

KEELEUNIVERSITY**PRESS**

St. Martin's Press
New York

First published in the United Kingdom by
Keele University Press
22 George Square, Edinburgh

and in North America by
St. Martin's Press, Scholarly and Reference Division
175 Fifth Avenue, New York, N.Y. 10010

Printed in Great Britain at the University Press, Cambridge

British Library Cataloguing-in-Publication Data
A CIP record for this book is available from the British Library

ISBN 1 85331 195 2

Library of Congress Cataloging-in-Publication Data
Collins, Alan.
 The security dilemma and the end of the Cold War / Alan Collins.
  p.   cm.
 Includes bibliographical references and index.
 ISBN 0-312-17672-4 (cloth)
 1. Security, International. 2. International relations. 3. Cold
War. 4. Soviet Union—Foreign relations—1985–1991. I. Title.
JZ5595.C65   1997
327.1′01—dc21   97-21636
                                                          CIP

Contents

Introduction:
Controversies and Caveats

Discussion about the security dilemma revolves around at least three controversies. The first, and the most important, is whether it actually exists at all. Is the security dilemma a figment of academics' imagination? Opponents raise two distinct objections to it. First, they argue that there are other reasons, usually more tangible, that provide a better explanation of state behaviour. Second, that the outcome was the result of an accurate assessment of the situation, not, as with the security dilemma, a mistaken one. While part I of this study will provide a detailed explanation of what the security dilemma is, it is necessary here to explain briefly what the term describes in order to address this challenge.

The security dilemma arises when states inadvertently create insecurity in one another as they seek to gain security. Thus, paradoxically, the policies they pursue have the opposite effect to that intended; rather than generating security, they fuel their own insecurity. Since the effect is unintended, the security dilemma can be thought of as a tragedy in which states that mean no harm to one another (they have benign intent) can actually generate fear in each other that they do mean harm. With the states uncertain of each other's intent, they continue to pursue the paradoxical policies they perceive as strengthening their security. By falling victim to this spiralling process of insecurity, the statesmen are faced with a choice of either continuing to accumulate arms and heightening the tensions in their relations, or unilaterally curtailing their weapon acquisition and risk the dangers of leaving themselves vulnerable to an attack. Their inability to determine accurately the intentions of one another prevents them from appreciating that the latter choice, by not threatening the other's security, provides an escape from this dilemma.

The attempt to acquire security usually involves the acquisition of arms, and it is because hostile powers also require these to achieve their aims that the security dilemma is often used to explain arms races.[1] The security dilemma is seen as being part of the action–reaction explanation of an arms race, and it is because this model attracts criticism, and other more tangible explanations exist for an arms race, that the existence of the security dilemma is questioned.[2] The action–reaction model quite simply posits that as states acquire arms, they alter the military balance; this action then requires a reaction from neighbouring states to equate the balance. While this model and the security dilemma are similar, they are not synonymous; some of the criticisms of this model are therefore not relevant to the security dilemma. This is the case with the issue of timing. In both the model and the security dilemma, the action of the first state receives a response, and it is this response that sets off the spiralling process. A clear action, reaction and counteraction should be discernible. However, the action–reaction model has attracted criticism because the Cold War superpower relationship did not follow this pattern. Buzan notes that: 'rather than interacting with each other in a discernible sequence of stimulus and response, the two superpowers ... engaged in the paradoxical business of *anticipatory* reaction' (emphasis in original).[3] While this might create a problem for the model, this is not the case with the security dilemma. The latter is based upon states' uncertainty creating the belief that the other intends them harm. This fear of each other can be manifest in various ways, whether by the acquisition of new weaponry or changes in force deployments or strategic doctrine. Once this process has begun, anticipatory reactions are in accordance with the security dilemma. The key for the security dilemma is that the reactions, whether anticipatory or not, are generated because of the states' fear of each other. It would therefore be expected that once that fear lessened, so would the intensity of the arms race – as happened between the two superpowers after the Cold War. This does not mean that the action–reaction sequence is irrelevant to the security dilemma – indeed, quite the opposite – it is just not as rigid a sequence as that expected in the action–reaction model.[4] However, even if the security dilemma can avoid this criticism levelled at the action–reaction model, it can only share the criticism that there are other – more tangible – reasons to explain an arms race.

These reasons focus on the domestic factors that drive an arms race and can be divided into two: the domestic structure model and the technological imperative. The former is concerned with the military-industrial complex and how this has a momentum of its own, while the latter focuses on how new weapon systems invariably contain an innovation which, by upsetting the military balance, requires a response from other states. The key point here is that these reasons for an arms race and the existence of a security dilemma are not mutually exclusive. For instance: while the security dilemma might explain the need for a state to react to another state, the magnitude, the timing, or the type of response might be better explained by these domestic factors. Of course, the domestic structure model and the technological imperative might also explain the need to react, but it is unlikely that the fear element of the security dilemma is irrelevant. Indeed, according to Beatrice Heuser, during the Cold War the 'most important factor [influencing NATO strategy] was the perception of Soviet threat'.[5] Thus it is suggested that while other factors can also explain why states might engage in an arms race, they are not necessarily incompatible with the security dilemma explanation; all three can operate at the same time.

The second challenge to the security dilemma's existence arises because it posits a scenario that has developed from misperceptions. It is evident from the brief explanation of the security dilemma given above that its dynamics are often not recognised as the reason behind another state's weapon acquisition. Statesmen with no territorial ambitions know that they are no threat and so do not consider that their actions could be misinterpreted and cause another state to increase its weapons. Instead, the spiralling process of tension and insecurity is blamed on the other state for harbouring aggressive intentions; an intent that is indicated by its willingness to arm. The lack of awareness on the part of decision-makers that their policies are part of the problem, rather than a solution, not only exacerbates the security dilemma, but also makes recognising it more difficult. This receives greater attention in part II, when the superpowers' relationship during the Cold War is examined to highlight the existence of the security dilemma. It is sufficient here to note that while malign intent is seen as the explanation behind the opposing state's actions, the security dilemma is, even if unintentionally, dismissed as an explanation. To claim that the Cold War was a security dilemma is contentious, therefore, because it presupposes that it occurred not as a result of an aggressive communist state or an imperialist/capitalist group of states, but rather as a result of their misinterpretation of each other's actions. The first caveat is that to claim that the Cold War was a tragedy, as both misperceived a malign intent from each other, is clearly contentious. Given the different interpretations that can be garnered from documentary evidence, the issue will probably never achieve a definitive answer; while this remains the case, the arguments about the existence of the security dilemma will persist.

The second controversy concerns the issue of the security dilemma's escape. This controversy arises because, for some writers, the security dilemma is an inherent feature of the anarchical international system. Hence Bradley Klein's comment that 'the international security dilemma is poised by international anarchy',[6] and John Herz's statement that:

> because this is the realm where the ultimate power units have faced, and still are facing each other as 'monades' irreducible to any further, higher ruling or coordinating power, the vicious circle of the power and security dilemma works here with more drastic force than in any other field.[7]

It is the belief that anarchy is a permanent feature of international relations that explains why, according to Jervis, 'the security dilemma cannot be abolished, it can only be ameliorated'.[8] In other words, so long as anarchy exists so will the security dilemma. If this anarchy was subject to change, however, then the issue of the security dilemma's escape becomes debatable. Where states have created security regimes and thereby introduced codes of conduct for their relationship, authors have claimed that the security dilemma becomes ameliorated or mitigated. That is, the dilemma's dynamics become lessened as the states lessen their uncertainty about each other's actions. Some authors have even suggested that, should that lessening continue, the possibility of escape increases. Hence Nicholas Wheeler and Ken Booth's claim that 'the theory of security communities and the practice of international politics among liberal-democratic states suggests that the security dilemma can be escaped, even in a setting of sovereign states'.[9] There is therefore a divergence of opinions in the literature over the issue of escape, and a caveat needs to be inserted. Unless stated otherwise, where escape is mentioned in the following chapters this will be the view of the writers under examination. Given that the Cold War has ended, it might seem logical to assume that the security dilemma which lay at its heart was escaped. As will be seen in the concluding chapters, this is not necessarily the case.[10]

The final controversy concerning the security dilemma is whether the situation it describes is actually a dilemma at all. This debate not only focuses on whether the process under examination is a dilemma; it also touches on the escape issue. Whether the situation the term describes is a dilemma or a paradox or even just a problem is, in many respects, unimportant. However, when the issue of mitigating the security dilemma is addressed, then correctly identifying a security dilemma as opposed to a security problem is of great importance. In recent times the security dilemma has been broadened in its application; the examination of this in part I will begin by addressing whether the security dilemma is a 'dilemma'. The relevance of this controversy to the escape issue is purely linguistic. A dilemma occurs where there are no satisfactory solutions to a problem, which suggests that escaping a dilemma is impossible. This is perhaps what Alexander Wendt is referring to when, in writing about something else, he states: 'security dilemmas are not acts of God: they are effects of practice. This does not mean that once created they can necessarily be escaped (*they are, after all, "dilemmas"*), but it puts the causal locus in the right place' (emphasis added).[11]

The book is divided into three parts: the security dilemma and mitigation; the Cold War; Gorbachev and mitigation. The first part is comprised of three chapters. Chapter 1 is a review of how the security dilemma has been used in the literature and how the security dilemma can operate between states. Chapter 2 examines a new type of security dilemma introduced in the mid-1980s and classified as 'state-induced' by Wheeler and Booth in the early 1990s (in particular, this chapter is concerned with determining if this is an accurate expansion of the term and what effect this might have on mitigation). The final chapter of this part examines whether states can mitigate or even escape the security dilemma. This entails an examination of both military options and broader cooperative approaches to realising security. The former determines if mitigation is possible by states procuring discernibly defensive weapons and adopting defensive force postures. The latter elucidates the idea of common security and whether the creation of security regimes and a minimum deterrence strategy provides a compatible method of mitigation.

Part II, while unlikely to provide conclusive proof that the Cold War was a security dilemma, nevertheless does seek to highlight its operation both at the Cold War's origins and during its existence. Chapter 4 concentrates upon the inherent difficulties experienced by the United States and the Soviet Union in determining one another's intentions; their conspicuous inability to appreciate that their actions might have appeared aggressive; and their inclination to assume hostility on the part of each other. Chapter 5 relates an analysis of the military strategies adopted during the Cold War to the theoretical exposition in Chapter 3. It is suggested that the development of nuclear strategies during this period exacerbated the security dilemma by leading both East and West to adopt a war-fighting approach.

The final part is divided into three chapters. Chapter 6 investigates the claim that the mitigation of the security dilemma became possible because Gorbachev was sensitive to its existence, and that while economic reasons may explain the need for change, they alone do not explain why change occurred in the way that it did. The chapter also notes that although the West may have won the Cold War, this was due to Gorbachev's initiatives rather than the policies that the West had been pursuing since 1949. Chapter 7 examines the Gorbachev era from the perspective of the theoretical discussion expounded in Chapter 3. The questions raised are: did new thinking resemble a common security approach and did Gorbachev try to induce western reciprocation? Did Soviet military doctrine begin to adopt defence postures that were discernibly defensive and adopt a nuclear strategy that would lessen the arms race and, by implication, aid security dilemma mitigation? Was Gorbachev able to induce western reciprocation? Finally, were these efforts responsible for mitigating the security dilemma and, as a result, did they play an important role in bringing the Cold War to an end? The final chapter examines the years after the end of the Cold War and concludes that since the West failed to reciprocate in a positive fashion to Gorbachev, the security dilemma remained. Instead of escaping the dilemma, it was mitigated to such an extent that it lay dormant. However, in the aftermath of the early 1990s euphoria, there are signs that the relationship between Russia and the West is falling foul to a re-emerging security dilemma. With the failure to manage the end of the Cold War so that a security community could be established (something akin to Gorbachev's common European home), the current period illustrates the difficulties in creating security regimes (Partnership for Peace) while one member (Russia) is growing increasingly suspicious of the other's intentions.

Notes

1. See Barry Buzan, *People, States and Fear: an agenda for international security studies in the post-Cold War era* (Hemel Hempstead: 2nd edn, 1991), pp. 314–19.
2. For a thorough analysis of arms racing, see Barry Buzan, *Introduction to Strategic Studies: military technology and international relations* (London: 1987), part II. For the action–reaction model, see pp. 76–93.
3. Ibid., p. 87.
4. Buzan notes the relevance of this sequence to the superpowers' Cold War relationship when he writes (ibid): 'it seems clear from the rhetoric, the rivalry, and the military policies of the two superpowers that they are without doubt, and in an important way, acting and reacting to each other'.
5. Beatrice Heuser, 'The Development of NATO's Nuclear Strategy', *Contemporary European History*, 4/1 (1994), p. 38.
6. Bradley S. Klein, *Strategic Studies and World Order* (Cambridge: 1994), p. 21.
7. John Herz, *Political Realism and Political Idealism: a study in theories and realities* (Chicago: 1951), p. 200.
8. Robert Jervis, 'Security Regimes', *International Organization*, 36/2 (1982), p. 178.
9. Nicholas Wheeler and Ken Booth, 'The Security Dilemma', in John Baylis and N. J. Rengger (eds), *Dilemmas of World Politics: international issues in a changing world* (Oxford: 1992), p. 55.
10. For more details on the escape controversy, see ibid., pp. 51–8; see also Buzan, *People, States and Fear*, pp. 319–24.
11. Alexander Wendt, 'Constructing International Politics', *International Security*, 20/1 (1995), p. 77.

I

The Security Dilemma
and Mitigation

Chapter One

Security Dilemma

Of all the dilemmas in world politics, the security dilemma is quintessential. It goes right to the heart of the theory and practice of international politics.[1]

It is this 'quintessential' concept that is the focus of attention in this study. In essence, it describes a situation in which two parties create fear in the other that they mean harm – when, in reality, they only seek to protect themselves. First termed the 'security dilemma' by John Herz in 1951,[2] the situation it describes can be traced back to the writings of the Greek historians Thucydides and Xenophon in the 4th century BC. Thucydides claims that 'what made war inevitable was the growth of Athenian power and the fear which this caused in Sparta',[3] while Xenophon captures the tragedy of a scenario in which two peoples can go to war despite neither wanting such an outcome:

> I observe that you are watching our moves as though we were enemies, and we, noticing this, are watching yours, too ... I know, too, of cases that have occurred in the past when people, sometimes as the result of slanderous information and sometimes merely on the strength of suspicion, have become frightened of each other and then, in their anxiety to strike first before anything is done to them, have done irreparable harm to those who neither intended nor even wanted to do them any harm.[4]

According to Herz and Robert Jervis, the security dilemma can also been found at work in the 19th and 20th centuries. In the 19th century, 'competition for colonies', writes Jervis, 'was fuelled by the security dilemma'.[5] Herz concurs, noting that: 'whatever contributed (or was suspected of contributing) to the strengthening of any power anywhere in the world was considered as of immediate security concern to the others, who therefore would try to oppose or make up for it by their own increase in power or influence.'[6] Jervis also claims that a security dilemma existed between France and Germany between the two world wars of the 20th century,[7] and according to Herz, the bipolarity of the Cold War gave 'the security dilemma its utmost poignancy'.[8] It is the longevity of the security dilemma that helps to explain why it is considered quintessential, and why some writers do not believe it can be escaped. However, before examining the issue of escape, it is essential to understand the workings of the security dilemma; this is the objective of this chapter and the succeeding one.

Defining the Security Dilemma

What does 'dilemma' mean?

The term is of Greek origin and, literally interpreted, means two or double (*di*) assumptions or propositions (*lemma*). Thus, dilemma is created where there are two propositions and the existence of ambiguity or uncertainty over which proposition is the best.[9] There appears to be widespread agreement that these propositions are incompatible. Hence Walter Skeat writes that a dilemma is 'an argument in which one is caught between two difficulties'.[10] These propositions, or difficulties, tend to be further interpreted as being equally unfavourable. Hence Dr Ernest Klein defines a dilemma as 'a choice between two unpleasant alternatives',[11] and Dr C. T. Onions as 'a choice between two equally unfavourable alternatives'.[12] The *Chambers Twentieth-Century Dictionary* summarises the term's development by defining dilemma as:

> a form of argument in which the maintainer of a certain proposition is committed to accept one of two propositions each of which contradicts his original contention: a position where each of two alternative courses (or of all feasible courses) is eminently undesirable.[13]

The term 'dilemma' is thus particularly interesting because its usage suggests that the problem encountered has no satisfactory solution; all the choices available appear undesirable. The following example from a game of chess can be used to explain how a dilemma can occur.

In a game of chess, if player A can challenge a bishop and a rook of player B with one piece (a knight for example) which is itself invulnerable to attack, B is faced with a dilemma. Since B is unable to prevent A from taking one of his pieces, B is faced with the undesirable choice of saving either his bishop or his rook. In other words, B cannot choose a satisfactory solution; the only solution available to him is an unsatisfactory one. B is therefore in a dilemma.[14]

A security dilemma would seem to exist where the policy pursued by a state to achieve security proves to be an unsatisfactory one. By definition, if the achievement is unsatisfactory, then the policy that the state chose failed to realise all that state's security concerns or created new concerns. The state must therefore still be insecure. The state is in a paradox: by falling foul of the security dilemma, any solution the state chooses is unsatisfactory and is thus not a solution at all. The result of the security dilemma is that security cannot be realised. This has led Wheeler and Booth to assert that: 'in an ordinary sense, a security dilemma would seem simply to refer to situations which present governments, on matters affecting their security, with a choice between two equal and undesirable alternatives.'[15] However, when the concept has been used by writers of international relations, this has not always been the meaning they have attributed to the security dilemma. 'In the literature on international politics', Wheeler and Booth argue, 'the term has come to have a special meaning.'[16]

How has the security dilemma been defined?

The definitions of the security dilemma that are employed by writers on the subject have been quite diverse. This has not only created a large degree of ambiguity as to what a security dilemma is, but also as to whether the situation they are referring to is actually a dilemma. These definitions or prerequisites can be broadly categorised as follows: decrease in the security of others; decrease in the security of all; uncertainty of intention; no appropriate policies; required insecurity. The first four relate to one another and form a coherent explanation of a traditional security dilemma. The fifth definition is relatively new and is examined in its own right in Chapter 2. The ambiguity of the security dilemma is compounded when these categories are interchanged in referring to the concept.

Decrease in the security of others

In defining the security dilemma, some writers tend to focus on what occurs as a result of the operation of the security dilemma. Hence Charles Glaser writes: 'the US faces a "security dilemma" [when] it cannot increase its security without reducing Soviet security'.[17] Glaser explains how this occurs elsewhere in his writings, when he defines the security dilemma as 'a situation in which the military forces required by a state to protect itself threaten the forces other states need to protect themselves; in that situation states seeking security cannot avoid threatening each other's military capabilities'.[18] Robert Jervis also defines the security dilemma in this manner. He has written that a security dilemma occurs when 'most of the ways in which a country seeks to increase its security have the unintended effect of decreasing the security of others';[19] he confirms this elsewhere by writing: 'many of the policies that are designed to increase a state's security automatically and inadvertently decrease the security of others'.[20] Barry Buzan likewise comments: 'In seeking power and security for themselves, states can easily threaten the power and security aspirations of other states.'[21] The emphasis of these definitions is on how the state inadvertently decreases the security of its neighbours via the actions it takes.[22] This is an extremely important feature of the security dilemma, since the unintentional effect of decreasing the security of others does not indicate that the state has malign intent – it just appears that it does. Thus, although other states may regard the action as aggressive, this is actually a misperception of benign intent. These first references to the security dilemma therefore highlight that benign intent lies at the core of the security dilemma; the incompatibility that states perceive is illusory. What is peculiar about these references is that they do not relate to the definitions of a dilemma given earlier. Thus, although this is an important feature of the concept, it is not on its own a sufficient description of the security dilemma; the security dilemma is more than just the decrease of security in other states.

Decrease in the security of all

In this instance, the definitions centre on the self-defeating nature of the security dilemma. Robert Lieber notes that, by increasing their power, states 'do not necessarily increase their own security, because their neighbours and rivals also resort to the same means. Indeed, this arming tends to make all states less secure, since it increases the level of potential threat to which all are exposed.'[23] In other words, the emphasis in Lieber's definition is on the reciprocity that is inherent within the security dilemma. In analysing the relevant literature, one finds that this emphasis is a common occurrence. Charles Reynolds refers to the security dilemma as 'the existence of a number of sovereign states each providing for [their] own defence and in so doing [they] creat[e] a general and permanent condition of insecurity for all'.[24] Barry Posen also notes this self-defeating aspect when he defines the security dilemma as a situation in which 'what one does to enhance one's own security causes reactions that, in the end, can make one less secure'.[25] Bruce Blair comments that:

> One state's gain in security achieved through growth in its armaments is another state's loss. The second state is compelled to fortify its strength, which then rebounds to the first state's disadvantage. That spurs another round of arms expansion. The cycle repeats itself endlessly, leaving all sides worse off than they were at the start.[26]

It is this failure to achieve security that explains Jervis's comment that the 'unintended and undesired *consequences* of actions meant to be defensive constitutes the "security dilemma"' (emphasis added).[27] The point of this feature is that victims of the security dilemma actually make their situation worse through the policies they pursue. In other words, the decision-makers appear unable to empathise with each other; although they may recognise a decrease in security, they fail to appreciate that it is because of their policies rather than despite of them. Since these definitions centre on the feature of self-contradictory policies rather than on a choice between undesirable alternatives, the situation would seem to resemble a paradox rather than a dilemma. Thus, as with the first category, while this is an important feature of the security dilemma, there appears to be some doubt that it is able to describe a dilemma on its own.[28]

Uncertainty of intention

The authors who focus on the role of uncertainty are seeking to explain why states fall victim to the security dilemma. Here the focus of attention moves away from explaining the results or consequences of a security dilemma to explaining the origins of this phenomenon. Hence Herbert Butterfield writes:

> You know that you yourself mean him no harm, and that you want nothing from him save guarantees for your own safety; [yet] it is never possible for you to realise or remember properly that since he cannot see the inside of your mind, he can never have the same assurance of your intentions that you have.[29]

In other words, the focus of attention moves to why states perceive hostility and why statesmen fail to appreciate that their benign actions may appear threatening to others. The attention therefore centres upon the interaction between the states. Hence, according to Wheeler and Booth:

> A security dilemma exists when the military preparations of one state create an *unresolvable uncertainty* [emphasis added] in the mind of another as to whether they are for 'defensive' purposes only (to enhance its security in an uncertain world) or whether they are for offensive purposes (to change the status quo to its advantage).[30]

Unresolvable uncertainty is thus an extremely important feature of the security dilemma since, as will be shown later, it explains why states fall victim to its effects. Indeed, it is such an important feature that Wheeler and Booth consider it to be the defining characteristic of the security dilemma, the dilemma's special meaning. This is a contentious claim; while unresolvable uncertainty is an important piece of the security dilemma jigsaw, to regard it as the defining characteristic challenges the definitions noted earlier. The contention here is that, rather than being the defining characteristic, unresolvable uncertainty is a necessary condition for a security dilemma. However, to understand this concept fully, a fourth characteristic must now be explored.

No appropriate policies

This definition relates much more closely to the dictionary definitions of dilemma than the other three categories. The emphasis here is on the hopelessness of the state's situation. It is to this feature of the security dilemma that Richard Smoke refers when he writes:

> The idea of the 'security dilemma' holds, in essence, that one nation will feel insecure if it makes no effort to protect its security, but that any effort to do so must threaten the security of one or more nations

... Thus the first nation faces a dilemma: it will be insecure if it doesn't act and insecure if it does.[31]

Geoffrey Wiseman makes a similar reference to the security dilemma when he writes:

This process where states constantly arm themselves in an upward spiral against adversaries arming on worst-case assumptions creates a dilemma for decision makers who are required to choose between two equally unfavourable alternatives: to become locked into the cycle of arms accumulation or to reject it and expose the country to the dangers of military inferiority.[32]

The emphasis is therefore placed on the perception that, no matter what option is chosen, an unsatisfactory solution is the only result. Thus it is the perceived lack of a desirable outcome that makes this situation a dilemma. It is important to note that it is not necessary for the state to be aware that its position is hopeless for this to be a dilemma.[33] Indeed, unless the decision-makers were sensitive to the security dilemma, it is unlikely that continuing to accumulate arms will appear inappropriate: while it is likely that an arms race which exacerbates a deteriorating relationship will be considered undesirable, it may still be considered the only means of guaranteeing security. This is an important feature of the security dilemma, since it reveals why states continue to pursue what appear clearly to a third party to be inappropriate policies. This can be seen in the comments made by the American President, Theodore Roosevelt, in 1904 regarding Britain and Germany. Roosevelt noted that the Kaiser:

sincerely believes that the English are planning to attack him and smash his fleet, and perhaps join with France in a war to the death against him. As a matter of fact, the English harbour no such intentions, but are themselves in a condition of panic terror lest the Kaiser secretly intend to form an alliance against them with France or Russia, or both, to destroy their fleet and blot out the British Empire from the map! It is as funny a case as I have ever seen of mutual distrust and fear bringing two peoples to the verge of war.[34]

Despite the self-defeating nature of the policies Britain and Germany were pursuing, they were perceived as appropriate. This fourth feature of the security dilemma therefore becomes more complex than Smoke and Wiseman suggest. If the policies that Britain and Germany were pursuing were the cause of their problem, then – logically – if they both altered their policies, they could overcome this difficulty. Thus, rather than there being no appropriate policies, the option of rejecting arms becomes the means of escaping the spiral of decreasing security and heightening distrust. Since there exists an appropriate option, can this situation really be termed a dilemma?

The answer lies in understanding the participants' perception of the situation. It can be termed a dilemma because the means of escape will be considered extremely risky by the participants, who perceive each other to be aggressive. The other state has benign intent, so a third party will see the escape option as appropriate, but the participant cannot be certain of this benign intent and so it cannot know this. To the participants, the escape option appears just as unfavourable; to all intents and purposes, the participants are faced with a dilemma, despite the existence of an appropriate policy option. It will be clear from this answer that to understand the dynamics of the security dilemma, it is necessary to consider the four features as a whole.

While it is certainly true that the literature on the security dilemma creates much ambiguity by focusing on different aspects of the concept – indeed, in some instances the term 'paradox' appears to be a more accurate description – all these differing interpretations of the security dilemma do 'connect' to form a situation that can accurately be regarded as a dilemma. Thus, while some of the definitions appear flawed individually, together they do form a coherent explanation of a scenario that is a dilemma. This will be demonstrated by using a hypothetical example in which states A and B will fall victim to a security dilemma. This example will also help to explain why some writers believe the security dilemma can be mitigated.

The Security Dilemma in Operation

The first time that two states encounter one another, they have no reason to assume that their security is endangered; they can only infer each other's intentions from the actions that are taken. Alexander Wendt argues that 'social threats are constructed, [they are] not natural'.[35] He uses the hypothetical example of aliens visiting earth to suggest what might happen in the first encounter. What is interesting is that even in the non-threatening scenario, the expected human response was to place military forces on alert. In other words, while determining the intent of the other, it is prudent to prepare for the worst.[36] Of course, such preparations can send the wrong signal and be regarded as a threatening move, though this does not necessarily have to be the case. If both states A and B (humans and aliens) mean no harm to one another, then how these first moves are interpreted will determine if they fall victim to a security dilemma. As Wendt acknowledges: 'The first social act creates expectations on both sides about each other's future behaviour: potentially mistaken and certainly tentative, but expectations nonetheless.'[37] Wendt is correct to note that 'we do not *begin* our relationship with the aliens in a security dilemma'.[38]

Let us assume that when states A and B make contact, B places its military forces on alert and A observes this increase in military activity. This military activity may be the result of B warning A that its military forces are properly trained to defend its territory. Although a reasonable explanation, it may not be true; B's increase in military activity could be because it is preparing a force to invade A. In other words, the uncertainty regarding the intent behind B's military manoeuvres has led to uncertainty regarding B's foreign policy intentions. Such an incident occurred during NATO's command post exercise – Able Archer83 – held between 2 and 11 November 1983 to practise nuclear release procedures.[39] According to KGB defector Oleg Gordievsky, the resulting military manoeuvres created very real concerns in the Kremlin that the exercise might be a cover for a surprise attack. It is this uncertainty regarding these two aspects of statecraft that leads Wheeler and Booth to claim that 'security dilemmas arise from a perennial problem in interstate relations, namely the inherent ambiguity of some military postures and some foreign policy intentions'.[40] Since A cannot be certain as to B's intentions – both explanations for B's actions are plausible – how will A react?

State A has done nothing to provoke this increase in military activity by state B, therefore A is likely to conclude that B is deploying its forces for hostile reasons.[41] This is a crucial point in understanding the dynamics of the security dilemma. A has been unable to determine B's intentions accurately and has assumed the worst.[42] There are many reasons why A may have reached this pessimistic conclusion. It may be that the states were once enemies and B's military activity might be the first move in the resumption of hostilities.[43] Even if the states were not enemies, it may be that B can only feel secure if it expands its territory.[44] It could be that A had thought itself safe from danger and, as such, would be quicker to assume hostility on the part of B. Arnold Wolfers makes this point when he writes: 'nations tend to be more sensitive to threats that have either experienced attacks in the recent past or, having passed through a prolonged period of an exceptionally high degree of security, suddenly find themselves thrust into a situation of danger'.[45] In actual fact, the real intentions of B need not be aggressive for A to assume hostility; A will automatically be insecure because B now has the military capability to do harm. Of course, just because it can do harm does not mean that B will do harm. However, there are a number of cognitive dynamics which make this distinction hazy. If A is ideologically opposed to B, or if it adopts worst-case analysis, or zero-sum thinking, or enemy imaging, or indeed any number of what Wheeler and Booth refer to as 'permanent aggravating factors', then accurate threat perception is severely impeded.[46] The distinction between capability and intent is not quite so definite.

These permanent aggravating factors can be seen at work in the relation-ship between the Allies at the end of the Second World War. With the near collapse of their common foe, the poor relations that had existed between the western democracies and the Soviet Union prior to the war began to influence their assessment of each other's intent. When the USA and UK discussed surrender terms with the German troops in Italy, they rejected a Soviet request to have Soviet officers present; Soviet forces had not been involved in the Italian campaign. Stalin, however, was becoming fearful that his allies were seeking a separate peace with Hitler so that they could turn on the real enemy – communist Russia. Such suspicion of malign intent where none exists fuels the security dilemma. For the USSR, the talks were far from preliminary military matters and it demanded that they be broken off. When Harriman, the US Ambassador to the USSR, delivered the reply: 'there appears to be a misunderstanding on the part of the Soviet Government ... [and] we will proceed with the matter along the lines already indicated', suspicions increased. Molotov, Soviet Foreign Affairs Commissar, responded by stating: 'in the present case it is not a question of incorrect understanding of the objective of this contact or of misunderstanding – it is something worse'. The 'something worse' was collusion. Molotov accused Britain and America of negotiating with Germany 'behind the back of the Soviet Government'.[47] According to Vojtech Mastny, this 'imaginary danger continued to obsess Moscow despite compelling evidence of Western loyalty to the alliance'.[48] Such enemy imaging cannot but negate accurate threat assessment and so drive the security dilemma.

A further problem for state A is that even if it decides that state B does not intend to do harm now, there is no guarantee that this will remain so. Therefore, due to the lack of any protector in international society, A, having assumed hostility, is likely to respond to B's action by increasing its own military capabilities. The likelihood of this pessimistic outcome is supported by Barry Posen, who notes that even if statesmen are sensitive to the security dilemma, 'the nature of their situation compels them to take the steps they do'.[49] 'Compel' may be too deterministic, but the implication that most statesmen who are sensitive to the security dilemma may be unable to avoid it is probably correct. To mitigate or avoid the security dilemma requires a special type of statesman, aided by favourable conditions.

By choosing this action, state A can be said to be 'playing safe'. If state B was seeking to invade, then A's action might deter B; however, even if deterrence fails, A, by increasing its military capabilities, may still be able to defend itself successfully. If, on the other hand, B was conducting military exercises and had no intention of attacking A, then, by playing safe, A perceives itself as being no worse off by raising its own military profile. By playing safe, A believes it has chosen an appropriate option and secured a satisfactory solution. Since A knows it is a status quo power, it is unlikely to consider that, by arming, it is also going to appear threatening to B. This is what Jervis is referring to when he writes: 'because the state believes that its adversary understands that the state is arming because it sees the adversary as aggressive, the state does not think that strengthening its arms can be harmful'.[50] Indeed, because statesmen know that they harbour no aggressive intent, they are likely to conclude that a state which reacts negatively to their action is hostile to them. This aspect of the security dilemma is captured in the following exchange between Senator Connally, the Chairman of the Senate Foreign Relations committee, and Dean Acheson during the committee's hearings on the North Atlantic Treaty:

> *The Chairman*: Now, Mr Secretary, you brought out rather clearly ... that this treaty is not aimed at any nation particularly. It is aimed only at any nation or any country that contemplates or undertakes armed aggression against the members of the signatory powers. Is that true?
> *Secretary Acheson*: That is correct, Senator Connally. It is not aimed at any country; it is aimed solely at armed aggression.
> *The Chairman*: In other words, unless a nation other than the signatories contemplates, meditates or makes plans looking toward, aggression or armed attack on another nation, it has no cause to fear this treaty.
> *Secretary Acheson*: That is correct, Senator Connally, and it seems to me that any nation which claims that this treaty is directed against it should be reminded of the Biblical admonition that 'The guilty flee when no man pursueth'.
> *The Chairman*: That is a very apt illustration. What I had in mind was, when a State or Nation passes a criminal act, for instance, against burglary, nobody but those who are burglars or getting ready to be burglars need have any fear of the Burglary Act. Is that not true?
> *Secretary Acheson*: Very true.
> *The Chairman*: And so it is with one who might meditate and get ready and arm himself to commit murder. If he is not going to indulge in that kind of enterprise, the law on murder would not have any effect on him, would it?
> *Secretary Acheson*: The only effect it would have would be for his protection, perhaps, by deterring someone else. He wouldn't worry about the imposition of the penalties on himself, but he might feel that the statute added to his protection.[51]

The inference from this exchange is that only those states (e.g., the Soviet Union) which intend to break the laws, or act aggressively, need fear this treaty – the implication being that any state that feels it is threatened by this treaty must have aggressive intentions. Thus any action by a state that felt threatened to increase its security would be providing evidence of its aggressive designs. Interestingly, Henry Wallace, who was representing the Progressive Party of America, highlighted the workings of the security dilemma perfectly, even noting that the treaty could bring about that which it was supposed to prevent.

> *The Chairman*: Need anybody fear this treaty unless they contemplate an armed attack on another Nation?
> *Mr Wallace*: Yes: I think they do have definite reason to fear it.
> *The Chairman*: You think Russia, then, is afraid of this treaty; is that right?
> *Mr Wallace*: I do; very much so. I think there is grave danger that following these tactics we will, in effect, make Russia ...
> *The Chairman*: Attack us?
> *Mr Wallace*: Make her into the very thing that we have said she is; that is, we will make her into a wild and desperate cornered beast.[52]

Not all statesmen are blind to the security dilemma, but, as Robert Jervis recognises, they often 'represent a minority position that is not taken seriously by most decision makers'.[53] The success of playing safe can only be ascertained, therefore, by knowing the reaction of state B to state A's increase in military activity.

At this point, let us assume that B did not intend to attack and the increase in military activity that A observed was simply a military exercise. State A has assumed hostility even though none was intended by state B. How does B react? B is in exactly the same situation as A was in earlier; B cannot be certain of A's intention. B will therefore also play safe – that is, raise its military profile – it is the logical and prudent action to take. References to the security dilemma at this stage fall within the category of decreasing the security of others. A did not intend to create a security concern for B, and thus B's understandable concern is an inadvertent and unintentional consequence of A's action. In other words, the unintentional effect of A's action is B's uncertainty regarding A's intention.

This exchange between the two states will have quite a profound impact on their relationship. The result of playing safe is that they will become suspicious and mistrustful of each other. For instance, the second increase in military capabilities by B is more likely to convince A that B has aggressive designs. If B did not intend to attack, why increase its military capabilities again? A's inability to appreciate B's position, and vice versa, is fundamental to understanding the security dilemma. Since they did not know the other's intention, they embarked upon understandable, but self-defeating, policies. Uncertainty of intent is thus a crucial ingredient since it explains why A felt threatened by B, and vice versa. It is not surprising, therefore, that certain authors consider uncertainty to be of paramount importance. Thus Wheeler and Booth claim quite emphatically:

If the threat posed by one state to another, be it inadvertent or deliberate, is accurately perceived by the potential or actual target state, then
the situation cannot be classified as a security 'dilemma'. It is simply a
security 'problem', albeit perhaps a difficult one. Whatever the actual
intentions of the state engaging in the military preparations, it is the
unresolvable uncertainty in the mind of the potential or actual target
state about the meaning of the other's intentions and capabilities which
creates the 'dilemma'.[54]

Whether Wheeler and Booth are right to place such importance on
uncertainty – to the extent that it becomes the defining characteristic of
a dilemma – is contentious. At this stage, however, it is clear that unresolvable uncertainty is a necessary condition for the choice of self-defeating
or inappropriate policies.

As the relationship between the states deteriorates, it may result in war.
Since both are suspicious of each other's motives, and therefore regard
the actions of the other as potentially threatening, both will believe that
they need to show resolve in their relations with each other. By showing
such resolution, they hope to deter one another from initiating hostilities.
In the field of defence, this will mean displaying the ability and willingness
to wage war. Jervis notes that even 'issues of little intrinsic value become
highly significant as indices of resolve'.[55] Therefore, although it was a
change in military activity that set in motion this chain of events, a further
deterioration of relations could be the result of something far less threatening and obscure.[56] The more that states A and B increase their military
capabilities and seek to gain the upper hand, the more insecure they feel
and the greater their feelings of mistrust and suspicion. By playing
safe, they perceive that they are gaining security, whereas in actual fact
they are fuelling their insecurity. John Herz captures this aspect when he
defines the security dilemma as 'a condition, a feeling of insecurity,
deriving from mutual suspicion and mutual fear, [which] compels these
units to compete for ever more power in order to find security, an effort
which proves self-defeating because complete security remains ultimately
unobtainable'.[57]

It is quite possible that the insecurity spiral which the two have created
will lead to the outbreak of hostilities. Jervis writes: 'statesmen ... rarely ...
consider seriously the possibility that such a policy will increase the danger
of war instead of lessening it'.[58] This is a very important aspect of the
security dilemma. Since statesmen know that they do not intend harm, they
fail to empathise with the opposition. The inability of statesmen to
appreciate that their own actions to achieve security actually create insecurity for others lies at the heart of the security dilemma. This explains
Butterfield's claim that each side is only 'conscious of its own rectitude,
so [it becomes] enraged with the other for leaving it without any alternative

to war'.[59] In the hypothetical example posited above, states A and B have become enemies even though they may never have intended any harm to each other. As Herz comments: 'it is one of the tragic implications of the security dilemma that mutual fear of what initially may never have existed may subsequently bring about exactly that which is feared the most.'[60] This could be an outbreak of hostilities leading to the defeat of state A or B or even both.

This is the classic security dilemma at work and is a representation of Jervis's spiral model.[61] The two states were engaged in a struggle over security, yet their security was not under threat since both had benign intent; their conflict was based upon a false, illusory incompatibility. Wheeler and Booth refer to this type of security dilemma as an 'inadvertent security dilemma', or 'system-induced' security dilemma. That is, the security dilemma has occurred not by state design, but because of the anarchic nature of the society in which states exist.

It becomes evident from this scenario that if states were able either to determine each other's intent accurately or provide for their own defence without creating fear in each other, the dynamics of the security dilemma could be broken. Herein lie two means to escape/mitigate a security dilemma. If either state had been able to deploy its forces in a non-provocative manner, then neither would have inadvertently created insecurity in the other. The dynamics of the security dilemma would have been negated. Unfortunately, neither state in the hypothetical example was able to exhibit such defensiveness, even though providing for their defence was their only goal (see note 41). Snyder refers to this aspect of the security dilemma as a 'structural security dilemma' and, as happened in the hypothetical example, he suggests that because they perceive one another as a threat, a war can occur: 'a status quo state may choose to attack another status quo state, even though both would prefer a stable compromise to war'.[62]

The second method of mitigation centres not on the force postures that states adopt, but rather on their misperception of one another's intent. If their uncertainty about each other's intention could be reduced so that they became more confident in assessing each other's intent, then choosing an appropriate policy option (to cooperate, reduce arms) becomes that much easier. In the hypothetical example, this would mean both states believing that the other had benign intent (see note 42). Unfortunately, the accurate determinination of intent is extremely difficult, especially where there exists a fear of hostility. These two means of mitigation are examined in Chapter 3.

The system-induced security dilemma highlights the different features, or stages, to which writers on the subject refer when defining the term. This not only helps to explain why there are different definitions, but also reveals the connection between the four categories and, therefore, why the scenario can be termed a dilemma. The crux of the connection is Wheeler and Booth's special meaning – unresolvable uncertainty. However, while this is extremely important, it would be misleading to consider it the sole defining characteristic of a security dilemma. It is more accurate to consider the four different meanings that are used in the literature as revealing three characteristics that must be present in order for a security dilemma to operate. These are: that all parties must have benign intent; they will be uncertain of each other's intent; and, finally, because policy options are undesirable/inappropriate, they are also self-defeating and paradoxical. The linkage between these characteristics can be seen in the hypothetical example, but their importance is such that it bears repetition.

It is because states cannot determine the intentions of other states accurately that policy options are created which are, or appear to be, undesirable. This is an extremely important point to understand with regard to the security dilemma. States do not know what others intend and therefore cannot know what action would be appropriate. With the lack of any guarantor in international society (it is an anarchical society), the most prudent option is for them to provide for their own security via an arms build-up. Unknown to either state is the fact that this is the inappropriate option, since neither actually intends harm. This uncertainty explains why they choose to play safe. This option is undesirable, however, because it inadvertently decreases the security of the other state and eventually, once the other state responds, nullifies the advantage gained by the first state. It is this self-defeating/paradoxical aspect of the security dilemma to which Arnold Wolfers refers when he calls it a vicious circle in which 'the efforts of one side provoke countermeasures by the other which in turn tend to wipe out the gains of the first'.[63] This reciprocation is the dynamics of the security dilemma; in addition to nullifying the relative gains that states accrue, it also lessens their security, as they become convinced that the other does mean harm. Their unresolvable uncertainty leads them to become suspicious and fearful of one another.

Unresolvable uncertainty is thus very important, but, as mentioned earlier, to consider it the sole defining characteristic of a security dilemma, as Wheeler and Booth do, is misleading. This is an extremely important point since, if it is inaccurate, then certain scenarios may manifest uncertainty but not be security dilemmas. Since we are concerned with the security dilemma, it is essential to clarify the role of uncertainty. States are victims of a security dilemma when they can choose either not to continue the arms race and risk being taken advantage of by a state they perceive as an enemy, or continue the arms race and witness the continuing deterioration in relations and feelings of insecurity. Since they regard each other as hostile, the first option would seem untenable. Hence Herz refers to the mutual suspicion and fear as 'compelling' the states to compete for power, and Jervis refers to this increasing insecurity as 'automatic'.[64] This mutual fear is the result of both states being uncertain of the other's intent, and explains why they are faced with a choice of undesirable alternatives.[65] It is this latter requirement that makes the situation a dilemma, not uncertainty. Herz makes this point when he refers to man's basic dilemma as the choice between attacking his fellow man or doing nothing and running the risk of being attacked. For Herz, the dilemma is the need to make the choice, while 'it is his uncertainty and anxiety as to his neighbours' intentions that *places* man in this basic dilemma' (emphasis added).[66] Uncertainty therefore creates the conditions for a security dilemma, but it is the perceived lack of desirable options that actually makes it a dilemma. The need to make this distinction becomes clearer in another type of security dilemma, examined in the next chapter, which Wheeler and Booth refer to as a 'deliberate security dilemma', or 'state-induced' security dilemma.

Conclusion

The security dilemma, while a relatively new term, describes a scenario that has been witnessed by ancient historians through to contemporary political scientists. The very nature of the security dilemma is one of tragedy. The emphasis is on how, when states take defensive measures to protect themselves, they can inadvertently signal to neighbouring states that they might harbour expansionist goals. The scenario represents a deteriorating relationship based upon misperception, where, because the statesmen must provide for their state's own security, a spiralling process of tension and arms procurement occurs. It is a tragedy; neither intends the other harm but, because they do not know this, their relationship deteriorates. This reveals the security dilemma's first characteristic: the participants must have benign intent. Thus, while the relationship might manifest great hostility, neither actually intends to initiate an attack, so their intent is benign.

The second characteristic is the unresolvable uncertainty that statesmen face when trying to determine the intentions of other states. Since the other state has benign intent, the security dilemma will not operate if statesmen act on this premise. However, if statesmen cannot accurately determine the intent of other statesmen, then their uncertainty can lead them to plan for the worst-case scenario. It is suggested that because the accurate determination of the intent of other states is extremely difficult, statesmen will take actions (e.g., the procurement of weapons) that are considered prudent to protect their state's interests. However, this 'playing safe' option can prove to be self-defeating, since it can create uncertainty in the other state about the intentions of the arming state. Thus it is unresolvable uncertainty which puts the dynamics of the security dilemma into operation. The security dilemma could not operate without this second characteristic; therefore unresolvable uncertainty can be considered a necessary condition.

The final characteristic centres on the options available to the statesmen while in the security dilemma. They can either continue to procure arms and thus heighten tension and exacerbate the arms race, or refrain from matching the build-up of weapons by the other state and leave their own state vulnerable to an attack. The options available appear to be undesirable, and it is this perception of their situation that creates the dilemma. To an outsider or third party, who knows that the states do not harbour malign intent, the option not to arm is the correct option. However, since the participants do not know this and, due to 'permanent aggravating factors' such as enemy imaging, are unlikely to believe it, the option to arm and continue the spiralling process of insecurity appears the prudent option. This prudent option is actually self-defeating and thus the policy is paradoxical. The final characteristic therefore is that, while perceived as appropriate, the policies pursued are actually self-defeating and can be considered paradoxical.

These three characteristics – benign intent; unresolvable uncertainty; self-defeating/paradoxical policies – will be used in the next chapter to examine the use of the term 'security dilemma' to describe a scenario that differs from the classic interpretation in a subtle but crucial manner. For now, though, the security dilemma should be seen as representing a process in which state actions, far from increasing security, actually fuel their own insecurity.

Notes

1. Nicholas Wheeler and Ken Booth, 'The Security Dilemma', in John Baylis and N.J. Rengger (eds), *Dilemmas of World Politics: international issues in a changing world* (Oxford: 1992), p. 29.
2. John Herz, *Political Realism and Political Idealism: a study in theories and realities* (Chicago: 1951), p. 3.
3. Robert Lieber, *No Common Power: understanding international relations* (New York: 1991), p. 6; Robert Jervis, 'Realism, Game Theory, and Cooperation', *World Politics*, 40/3 (1988), p. 317. For more details, see Thucydides, *History of the Peloponnesian War*, trans. Rex Warner (London: 1970), p. 25.
4. Gideon Y. Akavia, 'Defensive Defense and the Nature of Armed Conflict', *The Journal of Strategic Studies*, 14/1 (1991), p. 29. For more details, see Xenophon, *The Persian Expedition*, trans. Rex Warner (London: 1972), p. 123.
5. Robert Jervis, *Perception and Misperception in International Politics* (New Jersey: 1976), p. 66.
6. John Herz, *International Politics in the Atomic Age* (New York: 1966), p. 240.
7. Robert Jervis, 'Security Regimes', *International Organization*, 36/2 (1982), p. 361.
8. Herz, *International Politics*, p. 241.
9. Eric Partridge claims that, logically, a dilemma is an ambiguous proposition: Eric Partridge, *Origins* (London: 1990), p. 156.

10. Revd Walter W. Skeat, *An Etymological Dictionary of the English Language* (Oxford: 1946), p. 169.
11. Ernest Klein, *A Comprehensive Etymological Dictionary of the English Language* (Amsterdam: 1966), p. 449.
12. C. T. Onions, *The Oxford Dictionary of English Etymology* (Oxford: 1966), p. 268.
13. *Chambers Twentieth-Century Dictionary* (Edinburgh: 1972), p. 361.
14. It could be argued, of course, that since a rook has a higher value than a bishop, player B will save the rook. Although this might be true, the resulting loss of the bishop is not a desirable or satisfactory outcome for B. It could be argued that B will resort to a counter-attack in order to save both pieces – indeed, there are many manoeuvres B might be able to perform to save both pieces and ultimately gain a satisfactory outcome. However, in this simplistic example, such actions are not available to B.
15. Wheeler and Booth, 'The Security Dilemma', pp. 29–30.
16. Ibid., p. 30.
17. Charles L. Glaser, *Analyzing Strategic Nuclear Policy* (Princeton: 1990), p. 72.
18. Charles L. Glaser, 'Political Consequences of Military Strategy', *World Politics*, 44/4 (1992), pp. 506–7.
19. Jervis, 'Realism', p. 317.
20. Jervis, 'Security Regimes', p. 358.
21. Barry Buzan, *People, States and Fear: an agenda for international security studies in the post-Cold War era* (Hemel Hempstead: 2nd edn, 1991), p. 295. Buzan prefers the term 'power–security dilemma': see p. 324 n1.
22. A similar definition has been used by Jack Snyder, but it contains a crucial difference. Snyder refers to the security dilemma as arising where states believe that their security requires the insecurity of others. In other words, there is nothing inadvertent about the other state's decrease in security. Snyder's definition is very different to the accepted understanding of the concept and will form the basis of the examination in Chapter 2: Jack L. Snyder, 'Perceptions of the Security Dilemma in 1914', in Robert Jervis, Richard Ned Lebow and Janice Gross Stein (eds), *Psychology and Deterrence* (Baltimore: 1985), pp. 153–79.
23. Lieber, *No Common Power*, pp. 5–6.
24. Charles Reynolds, *Modes of Imperialism* (Oxford: 1981), p. 24.
25. Barry Posen, 'The Security Dilemma and Ethnic Conflict', *Survival*, 35/1 (1993), p. 28.
26. Bruce G. Blair, *The Logic of Accidental Nuclear War* (Washington: 1993), p. 28.
27. Jervis, *Perception*, p. 66.
28. At this point, the term 'dilemma' may appear to be a misnomer and the concept under discussion is really a paradox. While this may seem correct, I intend to explain how these different definitions relate to one another and thus show that 'dilemma' is the correct term. As such, I will continue to refer to the concept as a security dilemma rather than a security paradox. I am indebted to Nick Wheeler and Ken Booth for introducing me to the idea of a security paradox. This concept is being developed by them in a forthcoming book on the security dilemma.
29. Herbert Butterfield, *History and Human Relations* (London: 1951), p. 21.
30. Wheeler and Booth, 'The Security Dilemma' , p. 30.
31. Richard Smoke, 'A Theory of Mutual Security', in Robert Smoke and Andrei Kortunov (eds), *Mutual Security: a new approach to Soviet–American relations* (London: 1991), p. 76.
32. Geoffrey Wiseman, *Common Security and Non-Provocative Defence: alternative approaches to the security dilemma* (Canberra: 1989), p. 1.
33. A useful analogy in explaining this can be made with the chess game. Player B knew that he would lose one piece, regardless of what he did. If B had been unaware of his predicament, then he would still have lost one piece and been in a dilemma. The only difference is that B would only have been aware of the dilemma after he lost either his rook or bishop. This also works in reverse; if A was unaware of his advantageous

position, then B has a good chance of saving both pieces. However, B would not realise this and perceive that he was in a dilemma, thus the thought that went into his next move would be built upon this premise. Player B, for all intents and purposes, is in a dilemma.

34. Quoted from Jervis, *Perception*, p. 74.

35. Alexander Wendt, 'Anarchy is What States Make of It: the social construction of power politics', *International Organisation*, 46/2 (1992), p. 405.

36. In keeping with the aliens theme, a useful analogy can be made with what could be called the *Star Trek* phenomenon. The mission of the crew, amongst other things, is to discover and contact alien life-forms in a peaceful fashion. Yet the vessel chosen for this peaceful mission is the latest battleship, armed with an array of sophisticated weapon systems. In other words, when encountering something for the first time, it is considered prudent to carry a big stick.

37. Wendt, 'Anarchy is What States Make of It', p. 405.

38. Ibid., p. 407. Wendt refers to the security dilemma as the state decreasing the security of others as it seeks security. He argues that, when the first social contact takes place, neither participant has yet undertaken an action which can be considered threatening – a security dilemma is not in operation. However, if the criterion of uncertainty is used to define dilemma, then Wendt is wrong, since the participants are uncertain of each other's intention even before the first action. Wendt's comment is thus contentious; however, the argument here is that unresolvable uncertainty is not the defining characteristic, and thus I agree with Wendt's assertion that states do not begin their relationship in a security dilemma.

39. See Christopher Andrew and Oleg Gordievsky, *KGB: the inside story of its foreign operations from Lenin to Gorbachev* (London: 1991), pp. 582–605.

40. Wheeler and Booth, 'The Security Dilemma', p. 30.

41. The reaction of state A to state B's deployment could be affected by the 'defensiveness' of the forces and by whether A believed defence to hold an advantage over offence as a means of waging war. In this example it is assumed that state B and state A's weaponry exhibit offensive and defensive characteristics; in addition, neither state is certain which method of waging war (defence/offence) is advantageous. The importance of this in mitigating/escaping the security dilemma is explained in Chapter 3.

42. This reveals a second method whereby the security dilemma could be mitigated. State A has assumed hostility because it was *uncertain* of state B's intent. If it were possible for A to determine B's intent with greater accuracy, then A will have a greater capacity for choosing the appropriate option – mitigate the dilemma. Of course, being able to determine B's intent is extremely difficult; the means by which this might be accomplished is the focus of analysis in Chapter 3.

43. For example, France was aware after World War I that Germany might seek to reverse the verdict of 1918. It was this fear of Germany that led France to seek such a punitive peace at Versailles, a system of alliances that encircled Germany and the erection of the Maginot Line. For further details, see David Arnold, *Britain, Europe and the World 1871–1971* (London: 1973), pp. 237–40.

44. The cause of the Iraqi invasion of Kuwait in August 1990 is regarded by many commentators as a desire for the resources held in that territory. Interestingly, not only was Kuwait a brethren Arab nation, but it had also provided finance for Iraq during the Iraq–Iran war. See Janice Gross Stein, 'Deterrence and Compellance in the Gulf, 1990–91', *International Security*, 17/2 (1992), pp. 150, 155–9.

45. Wolfers suggested that the United States fitted this pattern after 1945: Arnold Wolfers, *Discord and Collaboration: essays on international politics* (Baltimore: 1962), p. 151.

46. Wheeler and Booth, 'The Security Dilemma', p. 40.

47. *Foreign Relations of the United States – European Advisory Commission; Austria; Germany*, vol. III, 1945, pp. 736, 737.

48. Vojtech Mastny, *Russia's Road to the Cold War: diplomacy, warfare and the politics of Communism* (New York: 1979), p. 272.

49. Posen, 'The Security Dilemma and Ethnic Conflict', p. 28.

50. Jervis, *Perception*, p. 69.

51. Senate Committee on Foreign Relations, *Hearings: North Atlantic Treaty*, 81st Congress, 1st Session, 1949, p. 17.

52. Ibid., p. 448.

53. Jervis, *Perception*, p. 89.

54. Wheeler and Booth, 'The Security Dilemma', p. 31.

55. Jervis, *Perception*, p. 58.

56. For instance, the dismissal of General Glubb by Jordan's King Hussein on 1 March 1956. This was regarded by Eden as a deliberate affront to Britain, contrived by the Egyptian leader Nasser. The dismissal in itself is a minor event, yet its timing is seen as one of the factors that caused the deterioration in Anglo-Egyptian relations that would culminate in the Suez Crisis. For Eden's view of the dismissal, see Anthony Eden, *The Memoirs of Sir Anthony Eden – Full Circle* (London: 1960), pp. 347–50.

57. Herz, *International Politics*, p. 231.

58. Jervis, 'Security Regimes', p. 360.

59. Butterfield, *History*, p. 21.

60. Herz, *International Politics*, p. 241.

61. Jervis, *Perception*, pp. 62–7.

62. Snyder, 'Perceptions of the Security Dilemma', p. 160. The structural security dilemma emphasises how a belief in the advantage of the offensive can exacerbate the fear of attack and create a security dilemma. This is further examined in Chapter 3, when these elements are analysed as mitigators.

63. Wolfers, *Discord and Collaboration*, p. 159.

64. Herz, *International Politics*, p. 231; Jervis, 'Security Regimes', p. 358.

65. The options will only appear undesirable to those sensitive to the security dilemma. Those statesmen that do not recognise the security dilemma are likely to conclude that to continue the arms race is the correct option, when in actual fact it is not.

66. Herz, *Political Realism*, p. 3.

Chapter Two

Uncertainty and Malign Intent

> International relations literature distinguishes between deterrence and
> spiral models of conflict . . . According to Snyder, this dichotomy ignores
> a third generic kind of conflict, what he calls a 'security dilemma'. This
> occurs when each adversary believes that its security requires the
> other's insecurity. When this happens, neither unyielding deterrent
> policies nor concessions will succeed in moderating, let alone resolving,
> conflict.[1]

This chapter is concerned with the deterrence and spiral models of conflict
and the relationship that exists between them and the security dilemma.
In exploring this relationship, it will be revealed that Jack Snyder's definition of the security dilemma is different from that expounded in the
previous chapter. The result of this subtle difference is that the security
dilemma is applied to situations in which it is inappropriate and, contrary
to the claims for it, does not explain the actions taken by the states. The
three characteristics highlighted in the previous chapter, together with
Herbert Butterfield and John Herz's tragedy element, are used to examine
this new development for the security dilemma.

The security dilemma expounded in the previous chapter is the traditional security dilemma and it operates in Robert Jervis's spiral model.
The difference between this model and the deterrence variant is the issue
of the adversary's intentions. In the deterrence model, the adversary's
intentions are hostile; it is only by deterring the adversary that decision-
makers can protect their state. This model is therefore marked by the
perception that resolve is necessary in dealing with the adversary, since
any sign of weakness will be exploited. During the Cold War, some
observers believed that this model captured the relationship between the
superpowers. Only by appearing resolute, even on minor matters, could
the USA thwart Soviet expansion and maintain the freedom of the capitalist
West. According to this view, the USA had to embark upon competitive
policies *vis-à-vis* the USSR; to show a lack of resolve was to signal weakness
which would encourage the USSR to believe it could expand safely. War
in this model was prevented by the willingness of the USA to match Soviet
power and so deter the communist aggressor from expanding westwards.
In contrast, the spiral model emphasises the setting in which statesmen
conduct state relations. In this model, the anarchic nature of international
relations compels statesmen to provide for their state's own security. In
so doing, a problem arises:

When states seek the ability to defend themselves, they get too much and too little – too much because they gain the ability to carry out aggression; too little because others, being menaced, will increase their own arms and so reduce the first state's security.[2]

This fear that the other intends harm can lead both states to acquire more and more arms, which in turn creates an arms race. Thus, in the spiral model, the pursuit of competitive policies compounds the problem by inadvertently worsening the relationship between the states. Hence Charles Glaser writes:

The spiral model holds that cognitive biases cause the adversary to exaggerate the defender's hostility, thereby provoking an unduly hostile response to competitive policies. The deterrence model holds that cooperation encourages the adversary to underestimate unjustly the defender's resolve and therefore to dismiss threats made in earnest, which can lead to war.[3]

The deterrence and spiral models are clearly applicable to the hypothetical scenario described in the previous chapter, where states A and B pursued competitive policies. A and B were in a spiral model, but the decision-makers acted on the basis of the deterrence model and thereby exacerbated the security dilemma. This is very important; it was because the states were in a spiral model that the security dilemma was able to operate. However, the security dilemma became exacerbated because the statesmen acted on the premise of the deterrence model. The relationship between these two models, and how they drive the security dilemma, is illustrated in the following example.

In January 1948 Ernest Bevin, British Foreign Secretary, sought to resurrect Churchill's call in his famous Fulton speech for a fraternal association of the West and began to explore the possibility of doing so with France and the USA. On 13 January Bevin sent a telegram to Georges Bidault, French Foreign Minister, and to George Marshall, US Secretary of State. What is of interest from the security dilemma perspective is that Bevin tried to explain what the Soviet reaction might be to his proposal.

I am aware that the Soviet Government would react against this policy as savagely as they have done against the Marshall Plan. It would be described as an offensive alliance directed against the Soviet Union. On this point I can only say that in the situation in which we have been placed by Russian policy half measures are useless. If we are to preserve peace and our own safety at the same time, we can only do so by the mobilisation of such a moral and material force as will create confidence and energy on the one side and respect and caution on the other. The alternative is to acquiesce in continued Russian infiltration and helplessly to witness the piecemeal collapse of one Western bastion after another.[4]

If the relationship between the western democracies and the Soviet Union was one of deterrence, then the action Bevin sought was the only option. However, if Soviet intentions were benign, then the relationship was a spiral one and the measures which were designed to boost western security at the expense of the Soviet Union were only going to create insecurity in the USSR. Thus Bevin was right to recognise that the Soviet Union would describe his proposals as offensive, but he reasoned that peace could best be achieved by a show of resolve – without, it would seem, considering that this perpetuated rather than solved their worsening relations. He failed to appreciate that 'half measures' would appear less threatening and thus more useful than useless. In a spiral model, to act on the premise of the deterrence model can only exacerbate the security dilemma.

It is thus contended that the security dilemma operates in a spiral model, but is exacerbated when decision-makers act on the basis of the deterrence model. Therefore, spiral theorists hold the key to mitigation, or even escape from, the security dilemma. However, this assumption has been challenged in some recent writings, where it is claimed that the operation of the security dilemma has occurred because of state design, not the anarchic international system. Nicholas Wheeler and Ken Booth distinguish this type of security dilemma from the traditional variety outlined in the previous chapter (which they refer to as 'system-induced') by referring to it as 'state-induced'. It is now necessary to look at this new security dilemma to determine whether the situation it describes is a security dilemma and what its relationship is with the deterrence and spiral models. The consequences of Snyder's assertion that 'neither deterrent nor spiral axioms can resolve this kind of security dilemma' will also be noted.[5] The focus of attention will fall on Nicholas Wheeler and Ken Booth's assertion that it is unresolvable uncertainty which is the defining characteristic of the security dilemma.

Insecurity and State-Induced Security Dilemmas

The appearance of the new security dilemma stems from a criticism that John Herz and Robert Jervis levy at Herbert Butterfield. Butterfield captures the scenario outlined in Chapter 1 for states A and B when he writes: 'both sides anxious to avoid war, but each desperately unsure about the intentions of the other party; each beset by the devils of fear and suspicion, therefore; and each side locked in its own system of self-righteousness'.[6] For Butterfield, this scenario represents a tragedy; neither side has sought war, yet this becomes the most likely outcome because of the policies they are pursuing. It is this tragedy that leads him to comment that 'the greatest war in history could be produced without the intervention of any great criminals who might be out to do deliberate harm in the world'.[7] Butterfield's tragedy centres on the security dilemma (although he does not use this term) because both sides are unable correctly to identify the benign intentions of the other (unresolvable uncertainty) and, as a result, they pursue paradoxical policies. For Butterfield, this scenario represents an absolute predicament/irreducible dilemma which lies 'in the very geometry of human conflict. It is at the basis of the structure of any given episode in that conflict. It is at the basis of all the tensions of the present day.' [8]

Butterfield's exposition of the security dilemma is criticised by Herz and Jervis for his assertion that the dilemma played a role in all conflicts. In response to Butterfield's claim that 'so far as the historian is concerned here is the basic pattern for all narratives of human conflict',[9] Herz responds by asserting that if this is true, 'history must consist of one continual race for power and armaments, an unadulterated rush into unending wars, indeed, a chain of "preventive wars". This obviously has not been the case.' [10] Herz refutes Butterfield's exposition on two counts.

The first is historical, with Herz arguing that the security dilemma was attenuated in the seventeenth and eighteenth centuries. According to Herz, the European states could satisfy 'certain minimum requirements of security without creating insecurity in their neighbours'.[11] It was only in the nineteenth century, when the European states found they were competing with one another as their empires expanded, that they faced the security dilemma. An action by one was now seen to impose upon the interests – and this invariably included security interests – of another. Herz's second reason for disagreeing with Butterfield is that war can occur from state design. Herz writes that the Second World War was 'provoked by Hitler's policy of world domination. It can hardly be maintained that it was a German security dilemma which lay at the heart of that conflict, but rather one man's, or one regime's, ambition to master the world.' [12] In other words, it is not an example of a security dilemma, according to Herz, because of the role of political ambition on the part of Germany. In Butterfield's terms, Hitler was a great criminal who was deliberately seeking to do harm.

Jervis's critique of Butterfield's point also centres on the role of political ambition. Jervis concurs with Herz by making the same observation that the anarchical system is not the only cause of war; war can also occur from state design.[13] According to Wheeler and Booth, 'Jervis echoes Herz's criticism of Butterfield: it would be a mistake to assume that the security dilemma lies at the root of all interstate conflict. Sheer political ambition can also play a part.' [14] However, Jervis implies elsewhere in his writings that he views political ambition not as refuting the existence of a security dilemma, but rather as indicating the existence of what Wheeler and Booth classify as a deliberate or state-induced security dilemma. They write: 'Jervis talks about the security dilemma "not as the unintended consequence of policy but rather as its object". Here he is referring to the deliberate security dilemma, where one state believes it can only be secure if others are insecure.'[15] By a 'deliberate' or state-induced security dilemma, Wheeler and Booth mean that the situation has occurred because the actions of one state have created, in the minds of another's decision-makers, a security dilemma. Wheeler and Booth have therefore identified a new reference to the security dilemma which was first given prominence by Jack Snyder. Snyder defines a security dilemma as 'a situation in which each state believed that its security *required* the insecurity of others' (emphasis added).[16] In order to determine if this new definition of a security dilemma is accurate it is necessary to consider it in the light of the three characteristics noted in Chapter 1: benign intent, unresolvable uncertainty, and self-defeating or paradoxical policies. Wheeler and Booth have identified two types of state-induced security dilemmas: revisionist/revolutionary; militaristic status quo.[17]

Revisionist/revolutionary states

Wheeler and Booth argue that a state-induced security dilemma occurs when a state 'adopts a posture designed to lull the target state into a false sense of security'.[18] Returning to the hypothetical example posited in Chapter 1, but this time assuming that state B did intend to attack state A, a very different scenario is produced. B is now seeking to create a security dilemma because its political ambition is the defeat of the target state. Unlike the spiral model, where it is the anarchic system that induces conflict, conflict is now a result of B's desire to expand. This scenario represents Jervis's deterrence model; the conflict between the states is not over an illusory issue – this is real.

In order to make victory more likely, B, while increasing its military capability, will be attempting to reassure A that it means no harm. According to Wheeler and Booth, A will be uncertain of B's intentions due to the apparent contradiction between its capability and declared policy. A is therefore unsure of how to respond and, in this time of hesitancy, is vulnerable to attack. A has fallen victim to a deliberately created security dilemma because it is uncertain of B's intentions. To know if this is true, it is necessary to refer back to the three characteristics: benign intent, unresolvable uncertainty, and self-defeating or paradoxical policies.

Although state A is uncertain as to state B's intentions, the determining factor of whether A is faced with a dilemma depends upon the options available to it. Is it possible for A to adopt a satisfactory solution and not engage in self-defeating actions which indicate that a paradoxical policy is being pursued? It is likely that A will assume that B is acting in a hostile manner, for the same reasons that pertained in the spiral model in Chapter 1. Therefore, A is likely to raise its own military capabilities. Whether A is in a dilemma will depend upon the effect this has on B. Will it prove to be a satisfactory policy and thwart B's political ambitions? If it does, A was not in a dilemma. In this case, A's actions would not have been paradoxical despite A's uncertainty of B's intentions. Interestingly, if A's actions were in vain and B still attacked and won, then A *was* in a dilemma; no matter what it did, it could not prevent its defeat. However, being uncertain of B's intention is immaterial; it is not uncertainty that creates the dilemma, but the lack of desirable options. This then raises serious implications for the usefulness of uncertainty as the determining characteristic of a security dilemma.

The reaction of state A in this example not only highlights the misuse of uncertainty as a determining factor, but also raises doubts about this type of security dilemma. By pursuing an aggressive policy, B clearly does not have benign intentions towards A. The existence of B's malign intent becomes problematic for the existence of a security dilemma. By pursuing an aggressive policy, B would need to be creating insecurity for itself, as well as for A, for it to 'fit' the security dilemma concept – decreasing the security for all. Yet if A does thwart B's ambition and both states increase their military power, they are both pursuing appropriate policy options since they are not self-defeating. Since malign intent exists, A is correct to try to raise its military profile in order to deter B. Likewise, B is correct to raise its military capabilities if it wishes to realise its political goal. Is this second example really a security dilemma, or is B just posing A with a security problem?

Assuming that state A is able to deter state B, but the latter is prepared to raise its military capability again to gain its political ambition, are the states in a security dilemma? This situation is an example of Jervis's deterrence model and, because it was suggested earlier that security dilemmas only operated in spiral models, this is an important question to raise. Jervis writes:

> The aggressor [B], of course, is hostile because its expansion is blocked, but this does not develop the unfounded fear that the status quo power [A] is menacing its existence. It may increase its arms because it sees that its foreign policy aims have outrun its military strength, and the increase of arms and tensions can continue for several cycles as each side matches the other's belligerence. But this process resembles that explained by the spiral model only superficially. It is completely rational. Each side is willing to pay a high price to gain its objectives and, [B] having failed in its initial attempt to win a cheap victory, is merely acting on its unchanged beliefs about the value of the issue at stake. The heightening of the conflict does not represent, as it does in the spiral theory, the creation of illusory incompatibility, but only the real incompatibility that was there from the beginning.[19]

In other words, although A and B are acting in exactly the same manner as they were in the spiral model, this time they are not in a security dilemma, because they are in conflict over a real issue; one of the participants harbours malign intent. Since the issue is real, at least one state is pursuing a desirable policy. A security dilemma is not at work in this deterrence model. However, Barry Buzan suggests that although the states may start in the deterrence model, they can transfer over to the spiral model or the two models can overlap. He is therefore contradicting Jervis, who claims that B will not feel threatened by A's reciprocal increase in military power – once in a deterrence model, states cannot transfer into a spiral model.

Buzan acknowledges these two models, but he refers to them as the 'power struggle' (deterrence model) and the 'security struggle' (spiral model). He claims:

> that the international system as a whole can seldom be characterized purely in terms of one or the other. Some relations within it will fit the power model, others the security model ... To confuse matters, there is no reason why both struggles cannot be operating simultaneously within a single case. A relatively mild power rivalry could easily generate an acute and overriding security struggle.[20]

For this transfer to occur, state B would no longer see a benefit in attacking state A, but would continue to arm because it felt its own security was in danger from a heavily armed A. The two would then be in conflict over an illusory issue; as long as B continued to have no desire to attack A, they would have transferred from a deterrence model to a spiral model. In order for this transference to occur, B's political ambition must change and become benign. That is, it must stop seeking to lull A into a false sense of security. The security dilemma that is now in operation is not a result of state action, but of the anarchic nature of international society. It is a system-, not a state-induced, security dilemma.

The relationship between an aggressive state and the security dilemma has also been noted by Jack Snyder. He refers to the relationship as the 'imperialist dilemma'. He suggests that, from the outset, the aggressor state seeks a goal that would require the target state to forfeit a valuable asset (e.g., territory, sovereignty), much like the scenario posited by Jervis earlier. However, unlike Jervis, Snyder asserts that the imperialist state would become fearful of the status quo power. Snyder does this by using a similar scenario to that used by Jervis. Snyder writes:

> In order to achieve its expansive ... goals, the aspiring imperialist state (B) develops offensive military forces for the purpose of conquest or intimidation. When resistance is met, a testing of will and capabilities ensues. An arms race occurs as the imperialist and its opponent (A)

both try to prove that they have the capability to achieve their ... aims. Crises are staged as the states test each other's willingness to risk war rather than retreat.[21]

Snyder suggests that if either state believes that it might be taken advantage of during a period of temporary weakness (a window of opportunity), it may initiate a preventive or pre-emptive war. That is, B does believe that A intends to do it harm and therefore B arms not only to acquire its original goal, but also to protect itself.

However, this situation cannot be a security dilemma, since it is clear that the imperialist state harbours malign intent and it appears as though the target state also sees aggression as the only means of achieving security. The malign intent behind B's original requirement remains, according to Snyder, because it mitigates a compromise that is mutually beneficial: 'mutual security guarantees [are] difficult to devise because they may rule out the kinds of capabilities that the imperialist needs for its campaign of limited expansion'.[22] The incompatibility between the states remains real. The scenario began as a deterrence model/power struggle and remained as such. Is Snyder right to consider this a security dilemma? Snyder writes:

> In sum, the *imperialist dilemma is a security dilemma* that is a by-product of the competition over nonsecurity interests. It is a dilemma in the sense that both competitors may prefer some compromise to a major war, but they are unable to reach it because the dynamics of the arms race and brinkmanship make their security interests incompatible [emphasis added].[23]

However, the existence of incompatibility is not enough for the situation to be regarded as a security dilemma; the incompatibility must be illusory. If one state, or both, actually intend to harm the other and they are being foiled by the other state's policies, then those policies are not paradoxical. Jervis is therefore right to claim that while this type of arms race may resemble a spiral model, it is actually the workings of the deterrence model. The states in Snyder's imperialist dilemma may be in a dilemma, but it is not a security dilemma.

It is not a security dilemma, because one of the states, or even both, actually intend harm to the other. This situation is not what Butterfield or Herz were referring to when they saw a tragedy at the heart of the security dilemma whereby war occurred although neither state had sought war. Thus the crucial ingredients of benign intent and the inadvertent pursuit of self-defeating policies are not met in this example. The situation in which one state tries to lull the other into a false sense of security is a deterrent model/power struggle and, while the state may face a serious problem, it does not face a security dilemma. A security dilemma can only occur in a spiral model/security struggle, because it is only in these scenarios that the incompatibility is illusory and the element of tragedy exists.

Militaristic status quo powers

A state-induced security dilemma occurs here when a state pursuing an aggressive policy designed to create insecurity in the target state inadvertently creates a security dilemma for itself and the target state. The difference between the two state-induced versions is that, in this example, the aggressive policy is only meant to intimidate; it is not a precursor to war. The difference between this type of security dilemma and the traditional system-induced security dilemma is that, in the latter, the first state is not adopting aggressive policies at all; the target state just perceives it this way.

The popular example for this type of deliberate security dilemma is the relationship between France and Germany between the wars. Jervis is the first to use the Franco-German relationship, but he comes to an erroneous conclusion. Commenting on French security concerns after the First World War, Jervis claims: 'French security ... depended on having clear military superiority. Thus France could only be secure if Germany was insecure. The security dilemma here operated not as the unintended consequence of policy but rather as its object.'[24] This is extremely important; Jervis is claiming that, rather than an unintended consequence of policy, the security dilemma operated as a French objective. However, the likelihood of a security dilemma being the object of state policy appears incongruous. Given that the paradoxical element within a security dilemma affects both parties to their detriment, to suggest that the security dilemma is an objective of state policy implies that the state is consciously pursuing an unsatisfactory policy. This is an extremely unlikely scenario and there is no evidence to suggest that France was consciously pursuing such a policy. Even using Wheeler and Booth's uncertainty principle alone, there is strong evidence against Jervis's claim.

According to Wheeler and Booth, a dilemma arises only when the target state is uncertain as to the other state's intentions. After the First World War, France wanted to make sure Germany could not attack it again. Hence the French insisted upon restrictions being placed on the quality and quantity of Germany's armed forces. This would provide the French with a credible superiority over the Germans. However, the French did not want the Germans to be unsure or uncertain as to why they had a greater military capability; in fact, quite the opposite. The French wanted the Germans to be absolutely certain that if they broke the Versailles Treaty, then the French would use their superior force to punish the Germans and redress the status quo. The French did not want Germany to be uncertain as to their intention and, therefore, Jervis is wrong to claim that the security *dilemma* was the objective of French policy. Rather, they wanted Germany to be confronted with a security *problem*.[25]

While Wheeler and Booth acknowledge that the French objective was not to create a security dilemma for Germany, they imply that a security dilemma did occur as a result of the policies France pursued. Since the French felt that they could only be secure if Germany was insecure, the policies they embarked upon sought to make Germany feel insecure. What effect would these French policies be expected to have had upon Germany? According to Wheeler and Booth, 'the other state (what we will call the target state [Germany]) may be thrown into a dilemma as a result of the apparent contradictions between the other's [France] declared defensive intentions and its (threatening) military capabilities'.[26] That is, Germany might be thrown into a dilemma because the apparent contradiction between France's declared policy and military capabilities left Germany uncertain as to their intention. This uncertainty led the Germans to feel insecure. Wheeler and Booth would claim that Germany was faced with a dilemma of interpretation. This might be true, but, according to them, Germany would also need to be faced with a dilemma of response for a security dilemma to arise. I will suggest that this was not the case. Gustav Stresemann, the German Foreign Minister, was painfully aware of the limitations that the Versailles settlement placed upon German foreign policy. In 1924 he wrote: 'how narrow the path of active German foreign policy is bound to be, how necessary it will be to manoeuvre the ship of state whenever the grand gesture would only be ridiculous because it would lack the grand deed'.[27] There were to be no 'grand gestures' or 'sabre-rattling' in Stresemann's foreign policy. Stresemann wanted to liberate Germany from the constraints of the Versailles Treaty, but 'he knew ... that a diplomatic war of attrition against the Treaty of Versailles was more likely to be effective than impulsive attacks which would win applause at home but alarm public opinion abroad and so prove self-defeating'.[28] As Henry Bretton has written:

> Stresemann himself was convinced of the need for a revision of the Treaty of Versailles, but this revision would have to be a peaceful one, and would have to be based on a policy of reconciliation with at least some of the former enemy states. Painfully aware of the lack of a strong military and economic backing for such a policy, Stresemann developed the concept of fulfilment of Allied demands in return for piecemeal concessions ... his [was an] over-all strategy of an inoffensive foreign policy designed to realise greater objectives.[29]

Hence he sought a reconciliatory policy which would make France more amenable to German breaches of the Versailles Treaty's constraints. It was the cultivation of this relationship with the West, and primarily with France, that was the key to his success. Stresemann was able to do this because, unlike his successors, he was able to convince the French that Germany's policies were not revanchistic and, therefore, not a threat to French security.[30]

Stresemann was not faced with a dilemma of response. Germany's weakened position left him little room for manoeuvre; he had to seek a reconciliatory policy with France because there was no other way he could pursue his policy objectives. The very fact that he could 'play it craftily' and realise his aims vis-à-vis the French is strong evidence that he was pursuing a satisfactory policy.[31] Ultimately, with Stresemann's death, the depression and the rise of Nazism, relations between Germany and France deteriorated. However, this deterioration did not occur because there existed a security dilemma between Germany and France in the 1920s.

Although this throws doubt upon this type of state-induced security dilemma, it does not refute its existence. The reason why Germany and France were not in a state-induced security dilemma during the 1920s is because Stresemann was able to revive German power without creating insecurity in France. Indeed, their relationship improved. However, just because this example is a poor one, it does not refute the existence of this type of security dilemma.

What is perhaps most notable about this type of state-induced security dilemma is that it shares two important characteristics with the traditional system-induced variety. The first is that the incompatibility between states is illusory. Even though one state believes it *requires* the other to be insecure for it to be secure, it does not actually intend to use this advantage to threaten the existence of the other state. It does not harbour any malign intent towards the other state. Not surprisingly, the other state is unlikely to be able to distinguish such a policy from a revisionist power that does have malign intent. In other words, as in the hypothetical example, uncertainty causes one state to misperceive the intent of another and thus to assume it to be hostile.

The second characteristic is that the policies pursued create insecurity although they are perceived as having the opposite effect. The state that believes security can be achieved at the expense of others will continue to pursue this policy even if its increases in absolute power do not translate into increases in relative power. Indeed, far from gaining security, this policy is likely to fuel insecurity, as the state witnesses the other state foiling its goal by enhancing its own military potential. The other state's actions are likely be regarded as aggressive, since the state knows it does not actually intend them harm and thus continues to seek security by increasing its relative power – an action that causes concern in the other state, which continues to reciprocate and so the polices prove self-defeating.

If the relationship between France and Germany between the wars is a poor example of this type of state-induced security dilemma, then perhaps the relationship between the Soviet Union and the NATO Alliance during the 1970s/early 1980s is a better example. The combination of Marxist-Leninist ideology and the historical experiences of the Soviet Union led to the belief that the western powers harboured malign intent. The belief that the western 'imperialists' were an inherent danger to the socialist cause because they might seek to 'reverse the course of history' seemed very real to the Soviet leadership. Brezhnev often claimed: 'history teaches that while imperialism exists, the dangers of new aggressive war remains'.[32] Indeed, the possibility of conflict occurring was heightened by the enemy image that the West held of the USSR, and this was seen as providing the incentive for the imperialists to destroy the Soviet Union. The involvement of western powers during the Russian Civil War and Hitler's invasion in 1941 seemed to provide evidence of this. These factors combined with the Soviet sense of isolation and encirclement to heighten their feelings of insecurity and vulnerability. This belief that war was inevitable led the Soviet Union to seek security by maintaining a force of sufficient strength to defeat NATO's armed forces should the West attack. Denis Ross interprets this show of strength as part of a Soviet deterrence by denial strategy. He claims: 'Soviet fears of vulnerability, together with their perception of Western hostility and persistent threat, have produced a natural tendency to conceive of deterrence in denial terms.'[33] Thus, for the Soviet Union, security was achieved by making the West fully aware that, should a war begin, NATO could not achieve victory. Indeed, it was not uncommon for Soviet military writers to emphasise the inability of the West to achieve victory by referring to the Soviet Union as winning. Hence Ross's statement that 'the Soviet view appears to be that the better their armed forces are prepared to fight and win a nuclear war, and the more any adversary knows this to be the case, the more successful is Soviet deterrence'.[34] Therefore, if the Soviet force posture caused consternation in western thinking, this reduced the likelihood of the West launching an attack and thus enhanced Soviet security. In this sense, western insecurity would be viewed as a positive development by the Soviet Union, since an insecure opponent would be deemed unlikely to attack.

Of course, the danger is that, far from interpreting the Soviet force posture as an effective defence, the West could construe it as having a more sinister objective. This was exactly how the West reacted, since, as Barry Buzan states: 'the Soviet commitment to the traditional strategic objective of military victory sat uneasily beside the idea that the basic Soviet commitment was to deterrence by denial'.[35] The growing unease felt by the Atlantic Alliance concerning the Soviet build-up was expressed in various NATO communiqués. The Defence Planning Committee's communiqué in May 1975 noted:

It remains a fact that the Warsaw Pact continues to maintain a military capability much greater than that needed for self-defence. In the strategic nuclear field the Soviet Union, having already attained rough parity with the United States, now seems to be seeking to attain a strategic advantage through the development of more sophisticated and powerful missiles. Improvements are also being made in the offensive capabilities of aircraft, tanks, artillery and missiles. At sea the expansion of Soviet maritime forces over the past decade and their world-wide deployment have added a new dimension to their capabilities which are now such that, independently of a land/air attack on NATO territory, Soviet maritime forces could be used against NATO forces at sea or against our maritime lines of communication in order to interfere with the economies and vital supplies of NATO nations.[36]

In the aftermath of the Soviet invasion of Afghanistan, the North Atlantic Council noted:

The enormous growth over a number of years of Warsaw Pact and in particular Soviet military power gives rise to legitimate concern in Europe and throughout the world. This build-up contradicts the frequent assurances by the Warsaw Pact countries that their aim is not military superiority.[37]

Therefore, Soviet efforts to acquire security by procuring the weapons necessary to defeat an attack from the NATO Alliance actually made matters worse by creating the perception that they harboured malign intent. As Buzan asserts:

preparations for warfighting, even if justified in deterrence terms, make each actor look aggressive in the eyes of those trying to deter it. Appearances of aggressiveness in the form of broad spectrum offensive military capability are easily interpreted by opponents as evidence of high basic motivation to resort to force.[38]

By creating western concern, the Soviet approach to achieving security could only exacerbate the security dilemma which lay at the heart of the Cold War. Hence Jervis's claim that a Soviet approach 'designed to deter war by developing counterforce capabilities [can only] exacerbate the security dilemma'.[39] In 1978 and 1979 party apparatchiks Boris Ponomarev and Andrey Kirilenko both 'publicly and explicitly defend[ed] the Soviet Union's right to have forces superior to any one of its adversaries, because of a proclaimed need to match the collective capabilities of all of them'.[40] If the Soviet build-up was designed to achieve security at the expense of the Western Alliance – that is, generating insecurity in NATO – then it was a state-induced security dilemma that lay at the heart of the deterioration in East–West relations which was to trigger the second Cold

War. It is thus contended that where a state requires another to be insecure but does not harbour any malign or aggressive intent towards it, a security dilemma can inadvertently occur.

This new type of security dilemma, although only slightly different from the original, does create problems for mitigation. In the hypothetical system-induced security dilemma posited in Chapter 1, both states could have mitigated the dilemma by seeking to reassure each other about their benign intent. In the state-induced security dilemma, where one state requires the other to be insecure, it is unlikely that the other state, even if it assumed that its adversary had benign intent, would accept such vulnerability. It is this problem that led Snyder to assert that: 'if threats could not resolve the security dilemma, neither could concessions', because 'appeasing the security fears of one's neighbour would have entailed accepting one's own insecurity'.[41] Mitigating this security dilemma would require the other state to change the circumstances or the adversary's understanding of the circumstances. This creates a more complex approach to mitigation than is required in the system-induced security dilemma, and this will be analysed in the following chapter.

Conclusion

The claim that a security dilemma can occur where one state requires the insecurity of its neighbour in order for it to feel secure has expounded and developed the concept. From Jervis's assertion that political ambition does not necessarily refute the existence of a security dilemma, through to Snyder's definition that the security dilemma could require another state's insecurity, the security dilemma has evolved. In addition to the security dilemma of Herbert Butterfield and John Herz which Wheeler and Booth categorise as system-induced or inadvertent, there is now another security dilemma, one which Wheeler and Booth term state-induced or deliberate.

The appearance of this state-induced security dilemma has had the effect of creating some confusion over what constitutes a security dilemma. With Wheeler and Booth concentrating solely on the uncertainty principle as their defining characteristic, they produce an erroneous example of a security dilemma. Their first example, where one state seeks to lull another into a false sense of security, is too detached from the tragedy of Butterfield and Herz's dilemma for it to be an accurate extension of the concept. The existence of malign intent creates a real incompatibility between the states. The target state is correct in thinking that it is in a deterrence model; far from exacerbating tensions by procuring arms and making war more likely, its procurement of arms might deter its opponent and make war less likely. A security dilemma does not occur where malign intent exists since the adoption of the most prudent policies are likely to be the most appropriate. Thus Snyder is inaccurate when he writes: 'in a security dilemma, the adversary's malign intentions ... ', because the adversary's malign intentions negate the existence of a security dilemma.[42] It is only the second example of a state-induced security dilemma, therefore, that can really be considered to be a security dilemma.

The reason why the second example is an accurate evolution of the security dilemma is because it shares the three characteristics of the system-induced dilemma. The requirement of insecurity does not indicate a desire to attack the other state; it merely indicates that the first state perceives it can acquire security when the other is fearful of it. The state requiring the insecurity therefore has benign intentions towards the other state, though of course the latter is unlikely to perceive this to be the case. The other state's inability to comprehend that its insecurity is all that the first state requires – as opposed to territory or subjugation – while not unsurprising, does indicate the existence of uncertainty. Finally, even if statesmen in the target state did consider the possibility that the other state did not harbour malign intent, could they take the risk of not procuring arms when their neighbour did seek superiority? What is perhaps most notable about this type of state-induced security dilemma is that the processes involved are the same as the system-induced security dilemma. This is not surprising, since they are both examples of the spiral model. The crucial difference between them arises over the issue of mitigation or escape. Hence Snyder's assertion, when referring to a security dilemma in which insecurity is required, that 'although the security dilemma was in some sense a spiral process, it was not a spiral that could be unwound by the concessionary policies that spiral theorists usually advocate'.[43] This is examined further in Chapter 3, where the issue of escaping the security dilemma is analysed. In concluding this chapter it is sufficient to note that, in addition to the anarchical system creating the security dilemma, a security dilemma can also arise from state action.

Notes

1. Richard Ned Lebow, 'Conclusions', in Robert Jervis, Richard Ned Lebow and Janice Gross Stein (eds), *Psychology and Deterrence* (Baltimore: 1985), p. 223.
2. Robert Jervis, *Perception and Misperception in International Politics* (New Jersey: 1976), p. 64.
3. Charles L. Glaser, 'Political Consequences of Military Strategy', *World Politics*, 44/4 (1992), p. 499.
4. Summary of a memorandum representing Mr Bevin's views on the formation of a western union, in *Foreign Relations of the United States*, Western Europe, vol. III, 1948, p. 6.
5. Jack L. Snyder, 'Perceptions of the Security Dilemma in 1914', in Robert Jervis, Richard Ned Lebow and Janice Gross Stein (eds), *Psychology and Deterrence* (Baltimore: 1985), p. 154.
6. Herbert Butterfield, *History and Human Relations* (London: 1951), p. 19.

7. Ibid.

8. Ibid., p. 20.

9. Ibid.

10. John Herz, *International Politics in the Atomic Age* (New York: 1966), p. 235.

11. Ibid., p. 239.

12. Ibid., p. 234 n5.

13. Jervis, *Perception*, p. 75.

14. Nicholas Wheeler and Ken Booth, 'The Security Dilemma', in John Baylis and N. J. Rengger (eds), *Dilemmas of World Politics: international issues in a changing world* (Oxford: 1992), p. 41.

15. Ibid., p. 39.

16. Snyder, 'Perceptions of the Security Dilemma', p. 153.

17. Wheeler and Booth, 'The Security Dilemma', p. 31.

18. Ibid.

19. Jervis, Perception, p. 80.

20. Barry Buzan, *People, States and Fear: an agenda for international security studies in the post-Cold War era* (Hemel Hempstead: 2nd edn, 1991), p. 298.

21. Snyder, 'Perceptions of the Security Dilemma', p. 165.

22. Ibid., p. 166.

23. Ibid.

24. Robert Jervis, 'Security Regimes', International Organization, 36/2 (1982), p. 361.

25. For more on French concerns regarding Germany, see Paul Kennedy, *The Rise and Fall of the Great Powers: economic change and military conflict from 1500 to 2000* (London: 1988), pp. 372–3.

26. Wheeler and Booth, 'The Security Dilemma', p. 31.

27. Henry L. Bretton, *Stresemann and the Revision of Versailles* (California: 1953), p. 39.

28. A. J. Ryder, *Twentieth-Century Germany: Bismarck to Brandt* (New York: 1973), p. 259.

29. Bretton, *Stresemann*, p. 38.

30. Franco-German relations had improved sufficiently for France to sign the Locarno Pacts, support German membership of the League of Nations, ignore Germany's surreptitious rise in military capability and withdraw her forces from the Rhineland. For more details, see William Carr, *A History of Germany* (London: 1979), pp. 296–303, and A. J. Ryder, *Twentieth-Century Germany*, pp. 254–60. According to Rochus, Baron von Rheinbaben, Stresemann 'was able to pursue his policy, because while freeing Germany it was capable at the same time of satisfying France; because he had convinced the French people that a new course would be steered, and that he believed himself in a policy of Franco-German reconciliation': Rochus, Baron von Rheinbaben, *Stresemann the Man and the Statesman* (New York: 1929), pp. 259–60.

31. Ryder, *Twentieth-Century Germany*, p. 259.

32. Quotation in Denis Ross, 'Rethinking Soviet Strategic Policy: Inputs and Implications', *Journal of Strategic Studies*, 1/2 (1975), pp. 10, 27 n26. After returning from the USA in July 1973, Brezhnev claimed: 'The aggressive forces of imperialism will probably not lay down their arms for a long time yet; and there are still adventurists who ... are capable of kindling a new military conflagration.' Quoted from Leon Goure, Foy D. Kohler, Mose L. Harvey, *The Role of Nuclear Forces in Current Soviet Strategy* (Florida: 1974), p. 1.

33. Ross, 'Rethinking Soviet Strategic Policy', pp. 10–11.

34. Ibid., p. 6.

35. Barry Buzan, *Introduction to Strategic Studies: military technology and international relations* (London: 1987), p. 156.

36. Defence Planning Communiqué, *NATO Review*, 23/3 (1975), p. 29.

37. North Atlantic Council Communiqué, *NATO Review*, 29/1 (1981), pp. 25–6.

38. Buzan, *Introduction to Strategic Studies*, p. 196.

39. Robert Jervis, 'Realism, Game Theory, and Cooperation', *World Politics*, 40/3 (1988), p. 333.
40. Harry Gelman, 'Gorbachev and the Future of the Soviet Military Institution', *Adelphi Paper 258* (Spring 1991), p. 6.
41. Snyder, 'Perceptions of the Security Dilemma', pp. 154–5.
42. Ibid., p. 155.
43. Ibid.

Chapter Three

Mitigation?

It was noted in the introduction that the issue of escaping the security dilemma is a controversial one. It is not the intention to revisit those arguments here; rather, it is to concentrate upon two different methods that mitigate and promise an escape from the security dilemma's detrimental effects. The previous chapters have highlighted that the dynamics of the security dilemma drive an ever-increasing spiral of insecurity. These dynamics can be placed in two broad categories. The first is the anarchic nature of the international system and the resulting belief amongst statesmen that they must provide for their own security; it is a self-help system and there is no guarantor to provide protection. The second is the perception amongst statesmen that others may intend their state harm. Such perceptions are generated from many sources, with historic rivalry and enemy imaging being two notable examples. Since the security dilemma is premised on the basis of misunderstanding (a tragedy amongst benign powers), it may seem that the solution to this tragedy lies in removing the cloud of suspicion via cooperative undertakings. The second part of this chapter will pursue this argument by focusing on the value of common security and security regime theory to the security dilemma. While such an approach may provide a means for mitigating and possibly escaping the security dilemma, achieving cooperation amongst egoists is fraught with difficulties. Such an approach is not impossible, but an approach that could mitigate/escape the security dilemma without the need for cooperation is very intriguing. It is precisely this prospect that Robert Jervis raises when he claims: 'it would ... be possible for states to escape from the security dilemma without developing the sorts of cooperative understandings that help ameliorate political conflicts across a broad range of issues'.[1] The means to do this were outlined in his seminal work, *Cooperation under the Security Dilemma*, and it is this that will be analysed in the first part of this chapter.[2]

Altering Force Postures

In the previous chapters, a hypothetical model was postulated in which two states fell victim to a security dilemma as they adopted understandable but paradoxical policies. The first part of this chapter is concerned with one aspect of that model: the inferences that each state made about the other from the military postures they adopted. The purpose behind analysing a state's military posture is to determine to what extent its posture exacerbates the security dilemma, and whether, by adopting different postures, it is possible to mitigate or even escape the security dilemma without the need for cooperation. It is the ability of states to negate the security dilemma unilaterally that lies at the heart of Jervis's argument.

The need for examining military strategies is encapsulated within the adage 'actions speak louder than words': the real intentions of states can best be determined not by the pronouncement of statesmen, but from the actions of states. In the security field, this means the actions of the state's military forces. Defence specialists refer to this by claiming that it is the military forces under the control of the state that should determine how threatening a state appears, not policy pronouncements, which can be short-term and subject to change. For example, Raymond Garthoff claims that utmost in 'Soviet calculations [of western intent were] the hard results of American military policy – force allocations, budgetary allotments, deployment of forces, and the development and procurement of weapons'.[3]

This part of the chapter is divided into two sections, with the first concentrating on the interaction between two variables: the offensive/ defensive characteristics of weapons and postures; and whether offence or defence is perceived as holding the advantage as a method of waging war. The analysis from this first part suggests that, in certain circumstances, mitigation of the security dilemma may be possible. The second part is concerned with the impact of nuclear weapons on the interaction of the two variables. The analysis suggests that a minimum deterrence approach may enable the security dilemma to be mitigated at the nuclear level. It is suggested that in order for this mitigation to provide an escape from the security dilemma, an improvement in state relations is necessary.

The central point of the security dilemma is that an increase in one state's security decreases the security of others. The dynamics of the security dilemma could immediately be nullified if a state could increase its security without having this detrimental effect on the security of other states. For Jervis, it is the type of military forces procured and the prevailing belief on how to wage war that will determine if a state can acquire security without causing its neighbours to fear its intentions. He highlights two crucial variables: first, 'whether defensive weapons and policies can be distinguished from offensive ones, and [second] whether the defence or offence has the advantage'.[4]

Distinguishing between defensive and offensive weapons/postures

According to Jervis, the security dilemma will operate where offensive weapons are believed to hold the advantage. In this instance, status quo powers will procure and deploy weapons for defence that have the capability for attack, because they are seen as the most effective means of defending the state. Of course, because they are capable of offensive action, their deployment will appear threatening to other states and thus cause the security dilemma to operate. Indeed, where a weapon system possesses offensive and defensive characteristics, thus making it ambiguous and difficult to characterise, a security dilemma will still occur. In this instance, although the weapon may be deployed in such a manner as to highlight its defensive characteristics, the very fact that it has an offensive potential will give rise to insecurity in neighbouring states. After all, if deployment is possible to emphasise its defensive characteristics, the opposite must also be true. By the same token, if the weapon can be clearly characterised as a defensive weapon, then the security dilemma need not operate. In this instance, status quo powers will be able to procure and deploy systems for defence that are incapable of offensive action and will thus not appear threatening. A status quo power will be able to increase its security without this having a detrimental effect on another state's security, because this state need not be uncertain as to its intentions. Hence Jervis writes: 'when offensive and defensive postures are different, much of the uncertainty about the other's intentions that contribute to the security dilemma is removed'.[5]

However, at least two problems exist that suggest that mitigating the security dilemma might not be so easy. The first concerns status quo powers deploying offensive forces even if offence and defence are distinguishable; the second concerns the practical difficulties of categorising weapons in this manner.

Offensive forces in the armoury of a status quo power

Jervis makes an important admission when he notes: 'if the offence's advantage is great enough, status quo powers may find it too expensive to protect themselves by defensive forces and decide to procure offensive weapons even though this will menace others'.[6] In other words, even though the status quo power intends no harm to others, it will deliberately forgo procuring weapons that unambiguously support such intent, because they may not provide adequate security. In certain circumstances, therefore, even if weapons could be categorised as either offensive or defensive, the security dilemma could still arise, because both status quo and revisionist states would procure the same weapons.

Jervis claims that, in those circumstances in which 'the defence is at least as potent as the offence', status quo powers will procure defensive weapons; hence, mitigation of the security dilemma is possible.[7] In this case, status quo powers will not threaten one another, but revisionist powers will reveal their identity and malign intent by the weapons they procure. However, although it may be possible to mitigate the security dilemma, a further complication arises over what constitutes a defensive posture. A truly defensive posture is one where the state's armed forces are incapable of launching an attack. The state will provide for its safety by withstanding an attack and maintaining its territory. Thus Carl von Clausewitz claims:

> What is the concept of defence? The parrying of a blow. What is its characteristic feature? Awaiting the blow. It is this feature that turns any action into a defensive one; it is the only test by which defence can be distinguished from attack in war.[8]

However, for a state completely to forgo the capability of offensive action would require that state to harbour no ambition of recapturing lost territory. If the attacker achieved some initial success (a distinct possibility if the attack achieved surprise), the defender would have no option but to accept the new status quo – a circumstance that may encourage the aggressor to seek more territorial aggrandizement. It is this lack of counter-attacking options that led Clausewitz to assert: 'pure defence, however, would be completely contrary to the idea of war, since it would mean that only one side was waging it'.[9]

Clausewitz advocates that a defensive operation requires counter-attacks – 'the defensive form of war is not a simple shield, but a shield made up of well-directed blows'[10] – thus, even in a defensive approach to waging war, there will exist offensive operations. Gideon Akavia distinguishes these offensive operations from the general defensive nature of the operation by referring to defensive *aims* and offensive *means*. He concurs with Clausewitz that such means are necessary when he asserts: 'it is essentially impossible to achieve defensive aims by defensive means only. Some offensive, or potentially offensive, means and actions are always required.'[11] Therefore, so long as the offensive means support the state's defensive aims – recapture of lost territory – then the operation can be categorised as defensive. However, should the offensive means contain the capability to invade the adversary's territory, then the aim is not so easily distinguishable as defensive; the capability could support an offensive aim.

Charles Glaser distinguishes the offensive capabilities required for defensive aims as *necessary* offence and those required for offensive aims as *optional* offence.[12] The difficulty facing status quo powers is ascertaining how much offensive capability is required to achieve necessary offence. The security dilemma once again becomes a distinct possibility. The status quo power must procure enough offensive forces to make its defensive approach credible, yet it must not procure so many that its offensive capability can be perceived by others as optional offence. If the offensive potential is perceived by the adversary as containing more than is required for necessary offence, then even though the aim may be defensive, it will be perceived as offensive. In such a circumstance, the adversary will perceive the state as adopting an offensive strategy; while this does not necessarily infer malign intent, it is still likely to cause insecurity. In this instance, adopting a defensive means of waging war is not distinct from an offensive means. The security dilemma will be much in evidence in this outcome. Hence Akavia's warning that 'if those with defensive aims develop offensive capabilities it may look as if they are developing offensive aims, and others may have to react accordingly. This is one aspect of the "Security Dilemma".'[13] Glaser makes the same point when he notes: 'the defender should avoid offensive policies, because they can increase the adversary's insecurity in two mutually reinforcing ways: first, by threatening military capabilities that the adversary believed are necessary for deterrence and/or defence; and second, by suggesting the defender harbours malign intent.'[14]

Adopting a means of waging war that is clearly defensive while maintaining an offensive potential is the puzzle that non-offensive defence (NOD) architects confronted in Europe during the Cold War. It is because NOD ideas seek to do this that their advocates propose NOD as a means of mitigating the security dilemma. Hence Ken Booth's assertion that strategies 'of non-provocative defence ... seek to deal with the military problem which lies at the heart of the security dilemma'.[15] Although there were many NOD plans towards the end of the Cold War, they shared the characteristic of not projecting forces into another state's territory, and the mobile forces that did exist in some NOD plans were limited in their range.[16] Thus it was that the 'spiders' (mobile forces) in the spider and web proposal and its hybrids had limits placed on their mobility. Hence David Gates comment that 'the "spider" elements would lack a capacity for offensive operations and would thus not be seen as provocative or threatening by neighbouring states'.[17] The danger of just seeking necessary offence, however, is that the force posture may not appear credible as a means of defence. This is the criticism that is often levelled at NOD plans and explains the following comment by Colin McInnes: 'The non-offensive defence schemes which have been developed to date vary in their military credibility. Though some have been developed over a number of years and display considerable sophistication, none are totally convincing, and most share a number of major problems.'[18]

It would appear that it is too simplistic to assume that where offensive and defensive weapons can be distinguished, status quo powers will only procure defensive weapons; they will also procure offensive weapons. Determining intent therefore requires ascertaining whether the offensive weapons provide just a necessary capability or an optional capability.

Distinguishing between offensive and defensive characteristics

In order to refer to states procuring defensive weapons or adopting defensive postures, it must be possible to distinguish these from their offensive counterparts. If it is not, then, at best, status quo powers can only adopt ambiguous policies that will do little to mitigate the security dilemma because they fail clearly to signal benign intent. Barry Buzan writes: 'the ambiguity of military means often makes it difficult to distinguish between defensive and offensive intentions'.[19] There is, of course, no simple criteria for categorising weapons in this manner, a limitation that Jervis acknowledges. Although not perfect, he implies that mobility is a useful criterion: 'The essence of defence is keeping the other side out of your territory. A purely defensive weapon is one that can do this without being able to penetrate the enemy's land.'[20]

The use of mobility as a criterion clearly has the advantage of distinguishing those weapon systems that are fixed as defensive. Thus George Quester, in referring to minefields, fixed artillery positions and fixed aircraft guns, claims:

> Since it cannot be decided that these weapons will be brought to the enemy, the enemy must decide to come to the weapon. The weapons become supremely defensive, whenever a foreign decision to violate frontiers is indispensable to providing them with a target.[21]

It should be noted that the existence of such defensive weapons does not mean that defence is the method of waging war that is to be adopted. Akavia is correct to warn: 'While it is true that the immediate local function of fortifications is obviously defensive, fortifying some area may support an offensive move elsewhere. A perfect shield may protect the perfect base for offensive operations.'[22] In addition to this concern, the mobility criterion also becomes problematic when a mobile weapon system is capable of performing a defensive operation. Thus, while the tank spearheaded the German blitzkrieg attack against the Allies in 1940, Bernard Brodie contends: 'if the French had disposed of a properly armoured reserve, it would have provided the best means for their cutting off the penetration and turning into a disaster for the Germans what became instead an overwhelming victory'.[23] Thus, although the complete lack of mobility can be useful in distinguishing a defensive weapon system – if not a defensive posture – mobility can produce ambiguous results. This point is clearly understood by Jervis, since he writes: 'if total immobility clearly defines a system that is defensive only, limited mobility is unfortunately ambiguous'.[24] This seemingly intractable difficulty of categorising many weapon systems is neatly captured in a statement made by Salvador de Madariaga, the Spanish statesman at the disarmament negotiations conducted in the interwar years: 'A weapon system is either offensive or defensive according to which end of it you are looking at.'[25] This intractability is given further substantiation by Bjorn Moller, an ardent proponent of NOD. Implicitly recognising the difficulties of distinguishing between offensive and defensive weapons, he asserts that NOD rests on the assumption 'that a meaningful distinction can be made between offensive and defensive postures, strategies and tactics. Not (as often alleged by critics) a distinction between offensive and defensive weapons.'[26] Given that NOD proponents would have much to gain from such a distinction, this would support the assumption that such a distinction is problematic.

This suggests that to refer to conventional weapon systems as offensive/defensive can be misleading, since it is rare that one type of system can be so categorised. However, Moller's assertion that a distinction can be made between an offensive and defensive posture suggests the security dilemma can be mitigated and possibly even escaped if status quo powers can distinguish between such postures.

Does offence or defence hold the advantage in times of war?

Jervis defines the difference between offence and defence thus:

> When we say that the offence has the advantage, we simply mean that it is easier to destroy the other's army and take its territory than it is to defend one's own. When the defence has the advantage, it is easier to protect and to hold then it is to move forward, destroy, and take.[27]

Where it is believed that offence has the advantage in times of war, the incentive to pre-empt the other state will be great. This has serious implications for the security dilemma. Here even status quo powers regard the only means of achieving security to be found in organising their forces for the offensive. Their force postures are therefore designed to attack; as such, they simply cannot help but appear menacing. With the pressures of pre-empting or even waging a preventive war, it is quite possible that two status quo powers will attack each other even though they do not want war. The pressure to pre-empt will be great because whoever strikes first is likely to gain a decisive advantage.[28] Given this, statesmen are likely to view the most ambiguous of incidents as aggression and act accordingly; the security dilemma here is operating at its highest pitch. If the defence has the advantage, the security dilemma is much less in evidence; any war is likely to be long and costly, so the incentive to start one is reduced. The build-up of armaments by one state does not appear so threatening therefore.

The suggestion that offence exacerbates the security dilemma has been challenged by Jack Snyder, who asserts that because:

> offence is virtually never easier than defence ... the question should be not whether offence or defence has the advantage but whether the defender's advantage is small or large. If this view is correct, one of the alleged engines of the structural security dilemma runs in reverse!

The exigencies of military operations tend to mitigate the security dilemma, not exacerbate it.[29]

Snyder's contention is unhelpful, however, because he artificially separates decision-maker's perceptions from these considerations. When considering perceptions, he later argues that the bias of the military is towards the offensive, thus implying that although defence may be easier, offence is preferred. So long as states perceive that an offensive approach towards waging war is the best method of acquiring security, then they will act on this premise. In other words, even if Snyder is right that defending is nearly always easier than attacking, if the states perceive the opposite to be true, then offence will be regarded as holding the advantage.

In summary, the case for mitigating – and thereby creating the conditions for escaping – the security dilemma by altering states' military postures is based upon the interaction of two variables: offensive/defensive weapon and posture characteristics; and whether offence or defence holds the advantage in time of war. Jervis's argument is that if offence is prevalent in both variables, then the security dilemma will be operating at its highest pitch. He states quite categorically that 'the security dilemma is at its most vicious when commitments, strategy, or technology dictate that the only route to security lies through expansion'.[30] He is supported in this by Glaser, who writes: 'the security dilemma is most severe when offence dominates defence, and the two are indistinguishable; it is least severe when defence dominates, and offence and defence are distinguishable'.[31] Thus, where defence is prevalent, there exists an opportunity to mitigate the security dilemma. Jervis proposes four possible worlds based upon the interaction of these two variables.[32]

	OFFENCE HAS THE ADVANTAGE	DEFENCE HAS THE ADVANTAGE
OFFENSIVE POSTURE NOT DISTINGUISHABLE FROM DEFENSIVE ONE	I Doubly dangerous	2 Security dilemma, but security requirements may be compatible
OFFENSIVE POSTURE DISTINGUISHABLE FROM DEFENSIVE ONE	3 No security dilemma, but aggression possible. Status quo states can follow different policy than aggressors. Warning given	4 Doubly stable

In Jervis's first two worlds, offensive and defensive postures cannot be distinguished and the security dilemma occurs in both worlds – status quo powers are unable to determine intent from the weapons that other states procure. In the first world, offence is perceived to hold the advantage in time of war, and there is therefore pressure to pre-empt another state during a crisis. In this world, the security dilemma is operating at its highest pitch. In the second world, defence holds the advantage, thus dampening the immediate fear of attack. The security dilemma still exists, since determining intent is still difficult, but status quo powers are able to react more slowly to a state they perceive as menacing, thus providing a greater opportunity to try and avert the dynamics of the security dilemma causing a war.

According to Jervis, the security dilemma is mitigated, and even escaped, in the third and fourth worlds. This occurs because these worlds share the characteristic that offensive and defensive weapons can be distinguished. Of the two variables, therefore, Jervis highlights the first as the more important for escaping the security dilemma. Hence he asserts: 'The advantage of the defence can only ameliorate the security dilemma. A differentiation between the offensive and defensive stances comes close to abolishing it.'[33] The third and fourth worlds differ as to which method of waging war is perceived to hold the advantage. In the third world, offence is perceived to hold the advantage, whereas defence holds the advantage in the fourth world.

In the third world, it is possible for a status quo power, to identify a revisionist power, since the latter requires offensive weapons in order to achieve its objectives. The status quo power, by identifying its adversary as a revisionist, is faced with a real incompatibility and thus Jervis notes that the security dilemma will not be in operation. However, this analysis is questionable; with offence perceived to hold the advantage, status quo powers may procure offensive weapons because they are perceived to be more effective in achieving security. In this situation, where all states prefer offensive weapons, a security dilemma may form because a status quo power may incorrectly identify another status quo power as a revisionist power. Jervis refers to this possibility as a security problem, but not a security dilemma. Yet a security dilemma could arise: neither intends the other harm, but because both procure offensive weapons, they send a contradictory signal. Indeed, because the option exists to procure defensive weapons, the status quo powers are more likely to assume hostility. Surely, if the other state is a status quo power, it will not procure offensive weapons.[34] The dangers of a security dilemma forming in this world are quite marked. Glaser alludes to this when he writes: 'given the opportunity to forgo offence and project a relatively unthreatening image, US pursuit of offence is especially likely to appear provocative'.[35] However, he supports Jervis's contention that this situation is a problem and not a dilemma. He continues:

In certain ways, buying offence when there is no security dilemma is worse than buying offence when it is more severe. When the United States faces a security dilemma there is at least some possibility that the Soviets will recognise the dilemma and moderate their conclusions about US offence. However, when there is no security dilemma, even Soviet leaders who would be sensitive to a US security dilemma have little choice but to impute aggressive intentions to US offence.[36]

Glaser's argument that there is no security dilemma, however, appears to make little sense. If it assumed that the USA is a status quo power, then, by 'imputing aggressive intentions', Soviet leaders are perceiving malign intent where none exist. If the Soviets respond as Glaser infers, a security dilemma will be in existence.

In Jervis's fourth world, defence is perceived to hold the advantage as a means of waging war; Jervis refers to it as 'doubly safe'. He asserts:

> The differentiation between offensive and defensive systems permits a way out of the security dilemma ... There is no reason for a status quo power to be tempted to procure offensive forces, and aggressors give notice of their intentions by the posture they adopt.[37]

According to Jervis, the security dilemma does not occur in this world for two reasons. First, status quo powers will *only* procure defensive weapons and thus they cannot threaten one another; benign intent is clearly signalled. Second, revisionist powers will easily be identified, because they will be the only states that require offensive weapons. However, as previously argued, defence cannot be accomplished via defensive means alone; even in this world, status quo powers will seek some offensive capabilities. While the amount remains within Glaser's necessary levels, the dangers of a security dilemma occurring are quite small. However, should a status quo power be perceived as acquiring too many offensive weapons (optional offence), then a security dilemma can occur, as other status quo powers misinterpret the intent behind these forces. A security dilemma can therefore occur even in Jervis's fourth world, but, unlike the third world, the likelihood is rather small.

It is clear from the analysis so far that while an opportunity to mitigate the security dilemma via unilateral changes to force postures is possible, it is fraught with difficulties. Whether nuclear weapons exacerbate these difficulties, lessen them, or leave them untouched is the next concern. What impact have nuclear weapons had on these two variables?

Nuclear weapons and the primacy of defence

According to Jervis, when the concepts of offence and defence are applied to nuclear weapons, 'common-sense definitions have to be turned on their heads'.[38] Jervis claims:

> Concerning nuclear weapons, it is generally agreed that defence is impossible – a triumph not of the offence, but of deterrence. Attack makes no sense, not because it can be beaten off, but because the attacker will be destroyed in turn. In terms of the [security dilemma] the result is the equivalent of the primacy of the defence.[39]

At the core of Jervis's argument is the impact of nuclear weapons upon deterrence by punishment. Jervis makes the obvious yet important point that nuclear weapons have 'greatly enhanced the role of punishment'.[40] For the first time, states possess the capability utterly to destroy one another. So long as states possess a secure second-strike capability, they can threaten one another with punishment that could not possibly be outweighed by any benefits. In such a situation, where both sides hold the other's society as hostage, there exists mutual assured destruction (MAD). So long as neither side lacks the capability to wreak devastation upon the other, even after it has suffered a nuclear attack, neither side can benefit from starting a war. The result is that neither side can gain from beginning hostilities, but both have everything to lose if such hostilities begin. Both have strong incentives, therefore, to avoid war. Because of MAD, Jervis claims, attack makes no sense and so deterrence by punishment has the effect of raising the primacy of the defence. Anything that seeks to weaken MAD, and therefore make attack a viable option, is viewed as offensive. Accordingly, the offence/defence definitions are turned on their heads:

> That is, offence is the ability to take one's cities out of hostage; conversely, the ability to destroy the other side's population and the other values, previously associated with the offence, is now considered defensive because such an act could be credibly threatened only as retaliation for the other's attack.[41]

The impact of nuclear weapons, according to Jervis, is to make previously associated means of defence, offensive and offence policies appear defensive. It was this reasoning that led Herbert York, the Director of Defence Research and Engineering during Eisenhower and Kennedy's presidency, and Jerome Wiesner, who had been Kennedy's science adviser, to claim:

> Paradoxically, one of the potential destabilizing elements in the present nuclear standoff is the possibility that one of the rival powers might develop a successful antimissile defence. Such a system, would effectively nullify the deterrent force of the other, exposing the latter to a first attack against which in could not retaliate.[42]

Jervis's reasoning at this point is concentrated solely on how nuclear weapons can raise the primacy of the defence. For the security dilemma to be mitigated/escaped, it is essential for defence to be perceived as holding the advantage; if it is not, then, as explained earlier, the dynamics of the security dilemma will operate even if offensive and defensive weapons are distinguishable. However, the security dilemma can still operate even if defence is perceived as holding the advantage but the weapon systems are indistinguishable. Nuclear weapons must therefore also have an effect upon the first variable – distinguishing between offensive and defensive weapons/postures.

Assuming the reverse logic, that protecting cities and taking them out of hostage is offensive because it undermines MAD, determining whether a weapon system is offensive also needs to follow this logic. Hence Jervis's comment that 'in the context of deterrence, offensive weapons are those that provide defence',[43] and Glaser's statement that:

> when countries depend on deterrence to maintain their security, forces that threaten the adversary's deterrent forces are offensive, while forces that enhance one's deterrent forces are defensive. Thus, in MAD, US counterforce and area-wide strategic defences, because they threaten Soviet retaliatory capabilities, are offensive. By the same logic, US countervalue capabilities are defensive.[44]

Is it possible, though, to divide nuclear weapons into those that support and those that undermine MAD – and, hence, those that are defensive and those that are offensive?

Glaser suggests that strategic defences and counter-force weapons can be considered offensive, since any weapon that seeks to defend cities (passive defence), or possesses the capability to destroy the adversary's armoury (active defence) undermines MAD. Bradley Klein makes this point when he writes:

> In the deracinated logic of the nuclear strategists, vulnerability was thus a virtue insofar as it assured all countries that no one of them might achieve impunity should it choose to seize the initiative and attack. A country that sought – or found – invulnerability would have abandoned its ability to be humbled through the threat of retaliation. With nothing to stop it, its leaders would have no reason to fear retaliation. Thus no country would feel safe from it.[45]

Thus, an anti-ballistic missile (ABM) site designed to protect a city is offensive, since it is designed to take the city's population out of hostage. However, ABM sites are not always offensive. For instance, ABMs designed to protect an inter-continental ballistic missile (ICBM) site are defensive, because they increase the chances of a secure second strike and, hence, strengthen MAD. ABM sites therefore exhibit both offensive and defensive capabilities depending upon where they are deployed. Hence Glaser's caveat that the strategic defences have to be area-wide in order to be considered offensive.

The ambiguity in weapon categorisation is more acute with ICBMs, as Jervis acknowledges when he writes: 'land-based ICBMs are both offensive and defensive'.[46] They are offensive, because they can be used as counter-force weapons, and defensive, because they can be used as counter-value weapons. Since ICBMs are ambiguous in this situation, a state that detects a rise in another state's ICBM capabilities will be unable accurately to infer the state's intentions. Is the state merely strengthening MAD by ensuring it can destroy all, or at least most of, an opponent's metropolitan centres, or is it seeking to gain superiority and adopt war-fighting capabilities? The latter, because these forces threaten the other state's deterrent capability, is likely to communicate malign intent. The former, since it does nothing to enhance the state's ability to launch a decapitating strike, is less likely to raise doubts about the first state's intent. The state cannot be sure which is the correct interpretation, so it is likely to play safe and increase its own ICBM capabilities. If an arms race results from this, then the security dilemma that is in operation has occurred because, although both states accept MAD as a strategic reality, their weapon systems signal to their adversaries that they hold the opposite view.

According to Jervis, however, when both sides use submarine-launched ballistic missiles (SLBMs), a distinction between offensive and defensive weapon systems does occur and thus a security dilemma need not arise. The reasons for SLBMs being defensive, Jervis argues, are twofold: 'first, they are probably not accurate enough to destroy many military targets. Second, and more important, SLBMs are not the main instrument of attack against other SLBMs.'[47] Even when Jervis postulated this argument in the late 1970s, the first reason was under threat from changing SLBM technology. Today SLBMs are extremely accurate and, as such, do possess counter-force capabilities; the first reason is therefore no longer valid.[48] Jervis considers the second reason to be more important anyway, so it is this reason which requires careful scrutiny.

The second reason is indeed of great importance: if SLBMs are not 'the main instrument of attack' against one another, and assuming both sides use SLBMs as their secure second-strike capability, then neither will possess a first-strike option. If one side chose to increase its arsenal of SLBMs, this does not provide it with any greater capacity for launching a decapitating first strike. Unlike the rise in ICBM capability mentioned earlier, the other state need not fear that MAD is being undermined and thus does not need to respond to this rise by increasing its own SLBM strength. As Jervis comments: 'because one side's SLBM's do not menace the other's, each side can build as many as it wants and the other need not respond'.[49] Since the increase in one state's military capabilities is not giving rise to insecurity in the other, they do not need to increase their military capabilities and the security dilemma does not occur.

The issue at the core of this second reason is that SLBMs are not a threat to each other. It is certainly true that anti-submarine warfare (ASW) capabilities have not yet been successful in making submarines vulnerable launching platforms for nuclear weapons. While this remains the case, SLBMs are invulnerable; they cannot be targeted by other SLBMs, or indeed by any weapon. It would seem, therefore, that it is their invulnerability that assures a secure second strike and thereby strengthens MAD. The fact that Jervis's first reason is no longer valid is irrelevant because, even with counter-force capabilities, SLBMs are still incapable of locating one another. So long as they remain invulnerable, they provide a secure second strike and are thus defensive weapons. To undermine this invulnerability would be offensive, and so Jervis concludes that a 'status quo state that wanted to forgo offensive capability could simply forgo ASW research and procurement'.[50]

It would appear that so long as the states adopt strategic postures which support MAD, defence holds the advantage in times of war. This is because, in MAD, there is little incentive for either side to take the offensive, thus dampening the pressures of pre-emption. Indeed, there are great incentives to avoid offensive action. Jervis claims:

> Mutual Assured Destruction escapes from the security dilemma as each side gains security not from its ability to protect itself, but from its ability to retaliate and so to deter the other from launching an attack. If both sides followed this doctrine neither would need to expand its nuclear arsenal beyond the point where it could absorb the other's strike and still destroy the other's cities; neither would need to react if the other were to purchase excessive forces.[51]

However, Jervis's claim is only valid as long as both sides are following this doctrine. This is where the importance of distinguishing weapons and postures becomes apparent. A MAD-type strategy can only be pursued by both sides if they recognise the weapons the other is procuring as defensive. If the weapons are ambiguous, then even though both states may be status quo powers, they might fear the other is seeking to undermine MAD. In such circumstances, a security dilemma may arise. Jervis suggests that SLBMs may overcome this problem, but another solution may lie in what is known as minimum deterrence.

MAD-type strategy: minimum deterrence

The main criterion of minimum deterrence is that it requires a large enough force to inflict unacceptable damage on an opponent should that opponent initiate hostilities. Hence Barry Buzan states that minimum deterrence requires 'a secure second-strike force of sufficient size to make threats of [assured destruction] credible'.[52] Minimum deterrence therefore meets Jervis's criteria for mitigating the security dilemma by only requiring those forces necessary for maintaining a credible retaliatory capability; neither side will have the capability to launch a decapitating first strike, which is the equivalent of defence holding the advantage.

Since minimum deterrence is concerned with defence, there is no role for counter-force nuclear weapons; war-fighting is not a requirement.[53] Instead, minimum deterrence emphasises the need to ensure that the assured destruction capability remains credible. Thus the concerns of minimum deterrence advocates relate to the concerns that Jervis and Glaser raise about the type of system that undermines MAD. Those who advocate a minimum deterrence posture are manifestly aware of the need for states to procure discernibly 'defensive' nuclear weapons. Hence minimum deterrence proponents advocate the need for invulnerable counter-value weapons and, if ABM sites are necessary, limited point defences. This latter requirement is made explicit in the following minimum deterrence proposal: 'We are not ... suggesting any deployment of defences meant to protect populations. Instead, our advocacy of reconsidering the role of defences stems from one concern – the survivability of strategic nuclear arsenals.'[54] The need for invulnerable counter-value systems often means that minimum deterrence proposals favour inaccurate single-warhead ICBMs or SLBMs. It is then usual to find minimum deterrence advocates proposing plans that minimise reliance on multiple independently targetable re-entry vehicles (MIRVs).[55] However, would the adoption of a minimum deterrence strategy mitigate or even escape the security dilemma?

There are two main obstacles that might preclude against minimum deterrence having this effect. The first is the concern that a unilateral adoption of minimum deterrence would be incredible where the relationship between the parties is marked by hostility. In such a scenario, decision-makers may perceive there to be something woefully inadequate about a deterrence stance which explicitly places its faith in the adversary refraining (albeit enforced) from launching an attack. For instance, a revisionist state that seeks to overturn the current status quo might seek to undermine MAD and thus no longer be deterred by a MAD-type doctrine. If the perceived adversary is seen to be undermining MAD via new technology (improved defences/more accurate warheads) or seeking limited goals (a local incursion), then minimum deterrence might seem incredible. If unilateral adoption is problematic, then this raises problems for minimum deterrence as a sole mitigator of the security dilemma. The need to combine minimum deterrence with an improvement in relations is examined in the second part of this chapter.

The second obstacle concerns the impact of minimum deterrence on a conventional security dilemma. Jervis is rather ambiguous on this point. He writes that:

> if our analysis is correct and even if the policies and postures of both sides were to move in this direction [MAD doctrine], the problem of violence below the nuclear threshold would remain. On issues other than defence of the homeland, there would still be security dilemmas and security problems.[56]

The ambiguity arises because it is difficult to determine whether Jervis is acknowledging that MAD only escapes the security dilemma at the strategic nuclear level and conventional security dilemmas can therefore still occur, or that MAD escapes the security dilemma between the super-powers both at the conventional and the nuclear level, but does not escape the conventional security dilemma for other commitments like extended deterrence (ED). The second interpretation is based upon 'violence below the nuclear threshold' occurring for 'issues other than defence of the homeland'. In other words, MAD might have escaped the US/Soviet security dilemma entirely and was only thwarted from doing so because of extended deterrence commitments. This seems to gain tacit support from Glaser, who comments that 'in MAD nuclear weapons essentially eliminate the security dilemma'.[57] This interpretation may, however, be wrong. It is equally plausible that Jervis considered that a conventional security dilemma would still remain. If this is correct, then conventional security dilemmas can still occur; it is just unlikely they will do so concerning defence of the homeland, because it is an unrealistic scenario. Since our interest is in whether conventional security dilemmas can still occur if minimum deterrence is adopted, the important fact is that, in both interpretations, a conventional security dilemma can still occur, in part due to ED commitments.

Jervis's argument that, with a nuclear stalemate, security dilemmas can occur below the nuclear threshold is a controversial one. Waltz argues that conventional arms racing is unlikely between two nuclear states and that American policy 'teaches lessons that mislead'.[58] He claims that, as nuclear deterrence works, so 'conventional arms races will wither'.[59] The difficulty with this argument is that relying upon national suicide to protect the state is extraordinarily risky, since it assumes that the other nuclear states are all status quo powers. Faced by a revisionist state that seems prepared to use nuclear weapons to acquire part of the target state's territory, the target state may find surrender of that territory preferable to national suicide.[60] In such circumstances, deterrence would have failed. Given the perception that other states might be revisionist, the availability of conventional forces to prevent such 'salami' tactics may appear prudent. Even if all the states are status quo powers, the perception that some might not be could easily generate a desire for conventional forces which, in turn, may lead to conventional security dilemmas.

On its own, therefore, minimum deterrence strategy might not be enough to mitigate the security dilemma. Such a strategy may need to be complemented by an attempt to reduce the threat-inducing qualities of conventional forces. Chapter 7 examines the Soviet interest during the Gorbachev era in 'reasonable sufficiency' and 'defensive defence' from this standpoint. The problem of complementarity is that NOD ideas of reducing the threatening aspects of force postures are often anti-nuclear. How minimum deterrence and the broader NOD concept of common security can complement one another is examined later in this chapter.

Summary

The analysis suggests that certain military postures can mitigate the security dilemma, at least in theory, if certain conditions are met. The first is that defence must be perceived as holding the advantage in times of war. If offence is perceived as being advantageous, then even if offensive and defensive weapons are distinguishable, status quo powers may well procure offensive weapons. A second condition is that an offensive posture (as opposed to weapon) must be distinguishable from a defensive one, otherwise status quo powers will be unable to distinguish another status quo power from a revisionist power. So long as defence holds the primacy in time of war and defensive postures are distinct from offensive ones, mitigation may occur. Both variables are of equal importance; the first is not more important, as Jervis states with his matrix of four possible worlds. However, even when both variables are favourable, a security dilemma could still arise if a status quo power acquires too many offensive forces.

It is suggested that nuclear weapons do not aid mitigation of the security dilemma below the nuclear threshold, but if placed in a minimum deterrence strategy, they can mitigate the security dilemma at the nuclear level. Adopting the reversal of common-sense definitions, certain weapon systems and targeting policies, by supporting MAD, are defensive. Since minimum deterrence supports MAD, strategies that fall within this concept provide the means necessary to mitigate the strategic security dilemma. However, mitigation requires two obstacles to be overcome. First, the concern that minimum deterrence strategies are largely incredible as a viable deterrent; second, that minimum deterrence needs to be married to a conventional strategy that is similar in outlook to NOD proposals. Thus mitigation may be possible via changes to military postures, but there are many difficulties and obstacles to be overcome. In the second part of this chapter these changes will be seen as part of a broader move towards improving the relationship between states. This improvement in relations may go some way to overcoming these obstacles and enable the process of mitigation also to escape the security dilemma.

Common Security

In the hypothetical model of the security dilemma discussed in Chapter 1, both states mistakenly perceived each other as harbouring aggressive malign intent. They perceived their struggle over security as a real incompatibility, even though neither intended the other harm. Therefore, if it is possible via common security to convince states that their incompatibility is illusory, the security dilemma might be attenuated. Given that the dynamics of the security dilemma work to deepen and compound misperceptions, and hence exaggerate the belief that the other does harbour malign intent, such self-enlightenment is difficult to achieve. Yet this is the challenge that common security needs to address and overcome in order to mitigate the security dilemma.

What is common security?

Before our examination can begin, it is necessary to add a caveat that, as with the security dilemma, writing on common security has produced a diverse range of definitions. Thus Bjorn Moller claims:

> The actual status of common security remains unclear ... [T]o seek to assemble the entire literature on common security in order to reconstruct inductively a coherent theory of common security would probably be futile because of the abundant ambiguities and inconsistencies in and between various authors.[61]

The various definitions of common security have produced an umbrella concept in which there exist many alternative ideas about security. The immediate consequence of this is that drawing specific conclusions from common security proponents can lead to assertions that are contentious within the common security community. While the phrase may be relatively new – it was first coined by the Palme Commission[62] in 1982 – many of the ideas that fall within its parameters have been in existence for a long time.[63] Thus, under the common security banner, it is possible to find such diverse and age-old debates as defensive defence, a holistic approach to security, and the value of international organisations. Common security is therefore seen to relate to NOD ideas, a belief that security amounts to more than military defence,[64] and an interest in cooperative undertakings of states.[65] While there exists much disagreement amongst common security advocates, they do agree that the essence of the concept is that lasting security can only be achieved when all states feel secure; common security is mutual security. Since our interest is in how common security can mitigate the dynamics of the security dilemma (distrust, suspicion), we have an interest in the cooperative aspects of common security.

Common security and cooperation

Common security advocates tend to differ over the levels of cooperation that can be attained and the ultimate goal that such cooperation should seek. These two issues are linked: the greater the intensity and diversity of cooperation attained, the greater the goal that such cooperation can produce. Regardless of the level or goal of cooperation, all common security writers begin from the same assumption: cooperation is needed and is possible because states share a common interest. This common interest is security and, with the advent of nuclear weapons, survival. The Palme Commission expounded on this by noting that the destructive power of a nuclear war was so great that all nations would be affected: 'All nations would be united in destruction if nuclear war were to occur. Recognition of this interdependence means that nations must begin to organise their security policies in cooperation with one another.'[66] The emphasis placed on cooperation by common security proponents, therefore, is not based upon idealistic or altruistic notions of state behaviour. Rather, cooperation occurs through the enlightened self-interest of states in their search for security and survival. This is where common security can mitigate the security dilemma. The willingness of states to initiate common security manifests a recognition that previous policies have not provided the degree of security sought and that an alternative approach is available. By engaging in cooperative ventures, states may create codes of behaviour that lessen their uncertainty and, by benefiting from cooperation, they might question their perception that the other harbours malign intent. Two questions thus present themselves: first, how does cooperation mitigate the security dilemma? Second, how do states in an adversarial relationship engage in cooperation?

Levels of cooperation

In its most limited form, according to Richard Smoke, 'a mutual security policy is simply a policy that aims to improve the security of both sides, under conditions of some mutual insecurity'.[67] However, common security has been regarded in much more far-reaching terms. The Palme Commission set the pace by claiming that:

> Acceptance of common security as the organising principle for efforts to reduce the risk of war, limit arms, and move towards disarmament means, in principle, that cooperation will replace confrontation in resolving conflicts of interest ... nations must come to understand that the maintenance of world peace must be given a higher priority than the assertion of their own ideological and political position.[68]

The Palme Commission's assertion that the goal of common security is to reform the international system gains support from a number of its advocates.[69] Clearly, the level of cooperation required for such an outcome is greater than that needed for Smoke's more limited definition. Cooperation that seeks limited goals may help to ameliorate the security dilemma, while cooperation that seeks to change the international order may escape the security dilemma.

The types of limited cooperation that have a bearing on the security dilemma are those designed to generate confidence that neither side harbours malign intent. Such confidence-building can be generated through measures that create transparency, such as, at its most simplistic, the hot line, through to more complex confidence- and security-building measures (CSBMs) and institutionalised crisis management centres. Since the crucial dynamic of the security dilemma is the uncertainty of each state regarding the other's intention, measures which create transparency between states make accurate threat perception easier. Such measures are limited in scope, of course, because they do not reduce the military forces that create concern. Nevertheless, by addressing the sources of mistrust, the implementation of CSBMs can lessen the suspicions each has of the other and act as a precursor to greater cooperation in the future.

Cooperation at a higher or greater level means the pursuit of policies, whether jointly or unilaterally, that reduce the threats that each state has been making to the other. This receives much coverage in common security writings, since it is concerned with the greatest obstacle to common security implementation – those weapons that, in a spiral model, are fuelling insecurity rather than achieving security. This type of cooperation is extremely important, since it might reveal an awareness amongst policy-makers that previous policies were paradoxical; a reduction, not an expansion, in weaponry enhances security. Stan Windass refers to this higher level of cooperation as a 'cooperative security strategy', in which the parties embark upon confidence-building and arms reduction measures.[70] Combined with his 'defence strategy', which is synonymous with NOD, he implies their value to mitigating the security dilemma by writing:

> The primary objective of a Normal Times regime is to elaborate a code of conduct whereby antagonists can credibly reassure one another both that no attack is intended and that no attack would succeed. The second is the objective of defence policy, the first of cooperative security policy.[71]

The term 'Normal Times regime' is rather clumsy, but if it refers to a security struggle, and Windass's definition of such a regime does infer this, then joint pursuit of the two strategies could mitigate the security dilemma.

The levels of cooperation that require the greatest degree and diversity of cooperation are the ones that can escape the security dilemma. Whereas the previous levels were primarily concerned with political-military relations, the type of cooperation sought here advocates a broader approach to security. It is in this conception of common security that non-military approaches to security are advocated. This envisages not just the reduction of threats *vis-à-vis* one another, but also threats from a third source such as internal dangers. Smoke writes:

> thus if the other side were to be threatened by, for instance, severe economic collapse, large-scale continuing terrorism, or societal breakdown, such dangers could not help but diminish the first side's security. To protect its own security, the first side has an interest in taking action to forestall such threats to the other side. This idea represents one version of mutual security because the extent the first side helps forestall the emergence of such dangers the security of both is enhanced.[72]

The greater the ties between the states, the broader their dependence upon one another becomes. As their interdependence widens to encompass areas other than security, so it is likely that their political relations will improve and they will become more confident about the benign intentions of each other. The development of such a relationship could occur in what Karl Deutsch terms a 'security community', in which there exists 'mutual consultation, communication and cooperation' and whose existence signifies that the security dilemma has been escaped.[73] A security community 'is one in which there is a real assurance that the members of that community will not fight each other physically, but will settle their disputes in some other way. If the entire world ... [was] a security community, wars would be automatically eliminated.'[74] Deutsch suggests two types of security communities: amalgamated, where two independent units merge; and pluralistic, where they remain independent. The existence of either would end the destabilising effects of the security dilemma for those member states.

While there are differences between these conceptions of common security, it is conceivable that the more limited form of cooperation is a precursor to the greater form of cooperation. For example, once states appreciate the benefits of greater confidence about another state's intentions, they might be more willing to negotiate over the issues that caused the concern at the outset. With greater confidence about the benign intentions of the other, it may then become possible for states to extend their cooperative undertakings into other areas. However, this clearly requires cooperation to generate trust and for both states to gain from further cooperation. While cooperation between states is clearly a valuable instrument for mitigating the security dilemma, the ascertainment of its true value depends upon whether the adversarial states are able to engage in such cooperation.

Engaging in cooperation

One means of cooperation that attracts the attention of security dilemma writers is the establishment of security regimes. Robert Jervis provides the accepted definition of a security regime: 'I mean those principles, rules, and norms that permit nations to be restrained in their behaviour in the belief that others will reciprocate.'[75] Jervis is explicit in stating that the form of cooperation that this reciprocation entails is more than the following of short-run self-interest. That is, statesmen are prepared to accept short-term losses on the understanding that, in moments of relative weakness, they will not be taken advantage of (i.e., other states will be restrained), that other states will also endure moments of relative weakness (i.e., the roles will be reversed and reciprocation will occur), and that ultimately their security will improve. Clearly, the importance of this to the security dilemma is immense. If states can exist in a security regime, then an increase in the military potential of one state, thus producing a relative weakening for others, will not lead other states to reciprocate the increase. Instead, states tolerate their weakened position in the knowledge that the accepted norms of behaviour will restrain the relatively stronger state from taking advantage of its temporary position of power. If such a regime exists, then the security dilemma will not be in operation.

However, as well as providing the incentive for security regime formation, the security dilemma also provides the obstacle. Jervis writes: 'the fear that the other is violating or will violate the common understanding is a potent incentive for each state to strike out on its own even if it would prefer the regime to prosper'.[76] Thus the main obstacle to security regime formation is the fear that the other does indeed harbour malign intent and will defect. This fear of defection is manifest in two of the four criteria that Jervis identifies for regime formation.[77] He notes that states must perceive that they share the same ideas on mutual security and cooperation, otherwise their fear of defection, even if neither state does harbour aggressive intent, makes regime formation problematic. He also asserts that if one state believes security to lie in expansion, then an existing regime will collapse. The other two criteria are that states must prefer an environment in which their actions are more regulated – this implies that they must be content with the status quo – and, finally, states must consider the use of force in their relationship to be costly and ultimately incompatible with their enlightened self-interest. Since the fear of defection provides such a key obstacle, a means of overcoming it must be found in order for mitigation of the security dilemma to occur. These means must both lessen the fear of defection and maintain the incentives for regime formation.

Two complementary approaches may be able to provide a solution to the problem of defection: sub-issue security regimes and institutionalised security regimes. The first approach is to consider not a comprehensive security regime that would be applicable to all aspects of the relationship, but, rather, a number of regimes covering different aspects. Thinking of security regimes in this respect explains the following comment by Joseph Nye:

> the existence of regimes is a matter of degree ... Rather than focusing on whether the overall US–Soviet relationship can be categorized as a security regime, we should more fruitfully consider it as a patchwork quilt or a mosaic of subissues in the security area, some characterized by rules and institutions we would call a regime and others not.[78]

The establishment of security regimes over sub-issues of secondary import-ance reduces the fear of defection in two ways. First, if defection does occur, then the 'sucker' will only suffer in relation to the issue over which the states are cooperating. The fear of defection is therefore lessened because defection does not irrevocably damage the state's security. Second, if these regimes establish a pattern and principle of restraint, then they might generate confidence about the benign intent of the perceived advers-ary. In this instance, defection is lessened as the states lessen their uncertainty of the adversary's intentions.

The establishment of successful security regimes on sub-issues of secondary importance may provide the states with the incentive to do so on issues that give rise to their greatest concerns. Of course, the estab-lishment of security regimes at this threat-reduction level may take a considerable amount of time, because it will require the adversaries to be confident that the other state will not use such restraint to its advantage. Such confidence in restraint will be crucial at this level, given the signifi-cance of the issues at stake. The first advantage of security regimes on sub-issues that was noted above will no longer apply and, as a result, the paradox that Jervis noted earlier reappears. At the threat-reduction level, where the security dilemma can be greatly mitigated, the incentives for defection – even if both states want the security regime – are also great. How, then, if the incentives and obstacles for security regime formation operate at the same intensity, can security regimes – even on sub-issues – constitute viable means of mitigating the security dilemma?

It was noted above that institutionalised security regimes could com-plement sub-issue security regimes and provide a solution to the fear of defection. With regard to the former, Kupchan and Kupchan claim:

> institutions promote cooperation by clarifying and operationalizing a set of norms, rules, principles and procedures that guide state behaviour and allow for increased coordination of policy. Rules and procedures create a road-map; they define a range of behaviour associated with the notion of cooperation and provide states with a set of instructions for preserving a cooperative setting. Institutions also alter a state's

expectation about how other states will behave in the future and about how its own behaviour will affect the future behaviour of other states. States become more willing to cooperate because they assume others will do the same.[79]

Thus, institutions seek to reduce the fear of defection by reducing the level of uncertainty that states have about one another's intentions. This confidence-building occurs because institutionalised security regimes create greater transparency. Greater transparency not only enables an increase in accurate information about other states, which in turn reduces the chances of misinterpreting their intentions, but it also makes it easier to detect attempts to defect from the regime's restraining norms. Transparency therefore helps to mitigate the security dilemma by reducing the uncertainty dynamic.

Kupchan and Kupchan's argument goes further than this, because they contend that institutions are capable of encouraging a shift from the lesser to the greater degree of cooperation. They write:

> We contend that the ability of institutions to promote cooperation increases substantially as consensual beliefs [agreement on sub-issues] among the major powers dampen the rivalries and incentives of a Hobbesian setting. When inter-state cooperation has already begun to emerge because of shifts in elite beliefs [gaining in confidence and engineering trust], and the Realist assumptions of a competitive, self-help world are thus relaxed, a fertile ground exists for institutions to play a much more prominent role in shaping state behaviour [movement to a greater degree of cooperation].[80]

Their contention that such cooperation can alter state behaviour is clearly a movement towards greater cooperation. Thus they note that, via institutionalism, states may come to share similar views on the conduct of international relations: 'Institutions hold the potential to promote inter-state socialization, to transform a 'minimum of political solidarity' into an international community in which states share similar values and normative orientations.'[81] They also note that the role of resolve, such an important factor in exacerbating the security dilemma, becomes increasingly less important as 'reassurance and mutual assistance [become] the key instruments that foster cohesion'.[82] With resolve playing a reduced role, they argue that states will no longer need to deploy large numbers of offensive forces to deter adversaries.

In summary, common security is advocated as a mitigator of the security dilemma because it highlights the fact that true and lasting security is only possible when all states feel secure. It therefore recognises the limitations of the traditional unilateral attempts to achieve security. Hence Moller's comment:

If states in their quest for security through power become less, rather than more secure, does this not point to the need for a revision of the entire theory of power and security? To resolve these puzzling dilemmas is exactly what the theory of common security ... is all about.[83]

In order to remove the distrust and suspicion that characterise a spiral model/security dilemma, common security proposes cooperation as an instrument for reducing the uncertainty that causes the distrust. Such cooperation may be possible via the establishment of institutionalised security regimes, since these encourage the maintenance of cooperation by constraining state activity. This reduces fears of defection and makes behaviour more predictable. Common security appears to be relevant to mitigating the security dilemma, because its implementation provides a solution to the condition of unresolvable uncertainty.

Unfortunately, prior to the arrival of Mikhail Gorbachev, common security had not been implemented by the participants of the Cold War. There is therefore a question mark over the concept's viability. The second part of this section will examine why common security might appear appropriate to policy-makers; in so doing, the relationship between nuclear weapons and common security will be introduced. The final part of this chapter will examine the relationship between common security and minimum deterrence and how, pursued in conjunction, they can mitigate and even escape the security dilemma.

Interdependence: the link between common security and the security dilemma

Richard Rosecrance uses the relationship between Conan Doyle's famous detective Sherlock Holmes and his adversary Professor Moriarty to good effect in describing interdependence. Rosecrance quotes the following extract from 'The Final Problem':

> 'You crossed my path on the fourth of January,' said Professor Moriarty. 'On the 23rd you incommoded me; by the middle of February I was seriously inconvenienced by you; at the end of March I was absolutely hampered in my plans; and now, at the close of April, I find myself placed in such a position through your continual persecution that I am in positive danger of losing my liberty.'[84]

Their fates had become interdependent: whatever aided Holmes had a detrimental result for Moriarty and vice versa; the two characters were faced with a zero-sum game. As Rosecrance comments: 'If Holmes triumphed, Moriarty would be destroyed. If Moriarty were to succeed, Holmes had to be eliminated.'[85] This description of the relationship between Holmes and Moriarty is not too dissimilar to the hypothetical model of the security dilemma expounded in Chapter 1 – although in the hypothetical model, unlike Doyle's characters, the incompatibility is illusory. The result of this misperception is that the states' relationship deteriorates to such an extent that, like Holmes and Moriarty, they see it in zero-sum terms. Their attempts to gain security are thus dependent upon the actions of each other – their security is interdependent. However, unlike Moriarty, neither state realises that its fate has become dependent upon the actions of the other; although interdependence marks the states' relationship in the spiral model/security dilemma, they are unaware of this crucial factor. This explains why state A reaches the false conclusion that it has thwarted state B's goal when B fails to launch an attack against A. Thus A, although realising that the source of its insecurity is B, believes that the solution to this problem is to deter/dissuade B from launching an attack by showing military strength. In other words, when facing a threatening neighbour, A belives it can gain security via a unilateral approach to security.

By developing the model and assuming that, over a period of time, both states acquire nuclear weapons, a subtle but important change occurs. They still believe that the other means harm and that the best way to achieve security is through the unilateral method of showing that the other cannot hope to gain anything from initiating hostilities, but, as both states acquire secure second strikes and MAD becomes a strategic reality, their perception of their security relationship alters.[86] The cause of this change is the different manner in which nuclear weapons are used to achieve security. Whereas conventional weapons defend the state, nuclear weapons are deployed to annihilate the other's territory. Since there is no defence against a nuclear attack, both states realise that they are utterly reliant upon the goodwill (albeit enforced by the prospect of assured destruction) of the other for their security. Thus, although their security has been interdependent all along, it is only now that they appreciate this dependency.

States could react to this new situation in two entirely different ways. They may conclude that since they are reliant upon each other for their security, traditional unilateral attempts to achieve security are no longer viable. A new approach is needed, and this is where the concept of common security becomes important. However, states may conclude that relying for their security on the restraint, albeit enforced, of their perceived foe is far from satisfactory. Rather than concluding that interdependence requires a common security approach, they may try to escape their dependence via unilateral means. While they cannot escape the reality of interdependence – after all, their fates are ultimately dependent on one another – these attempts may provide a feeling of security. The Strategic Defense Initiative (SDI) is perhaps the most spectacular attempt to escape dependence, but such ideas as the US countervailing strategy can also be seen in this light (this receives greater attention in Chapter 5).

The arrival of nuclear weapons therefore makes states' interdependence explicit; while this does not necessarily mean that they will adopt a different approach to achieving security, they might. If they do seek an alternative policy, then they may implement common security. The importance of nuclear weapons in this regard is noted by the Palme Commission:

> *there are no effective defences against missiles armed with nuclear warheads; none exist now and none are likely to be deployed in the foreseeable future ...* Thus, one central irony that must be faced is that no matter what unilateral choices a nation makes in pursuit of security, it will remain vulnerable to nuclear attack and thus ultimately insecure [emphasis in original].[87]

The key to appreciating that security is interdependent is therefore the existence of nuclear weapons. Other common security proponents have also acknowledged the primary role of nuclear weapons in this regard. Hence Mikhail Beznikov and Andrei Kortunov comment that: 'the events of the second half of the twentieth century have ... *demonstrated* the imperfections of this instrument [unilateral approach] for ensuring security in a divided world' (emphasis added).[88] Wiseman writes that common security 'is founded on the assumption that nuclear weapons have produced a situation of strategic interdependence where states cannot achieve security at each other's expense'.[89] Those proponents who do not explicitly tie nuclear weapons to common security often seem to imply this by referring to interdependence as something new. For example, Buzan writes that the 'core insight [of common security is] that the security of states in the *contemporary* international system is fundamentally interdependent' (emphasis added), and Booth and Wheeler also note that common security is a 'rational response to the *new* condition of security interdependence' (emphasis added).[90]

Herein lies the answer to the question of why statesmen might consider common security to be an appropriate option for mitigating the security dilemma. It is because nuclear weapons make states' interdependence explicit in a fashion that cannot be equalled by conventional forces that statesmen might come to reconsider the value of pursuing unilateral methods of acquiring security.[91] However, just because common security may appear viable does not mean that it will necessarily be chosen. Common security is based on the premise that none of the participants is a revisionist power; thus, even if this is the case, but the perception is that one or more may be, then common security may appear to be too dangerous a policy to implement. Common security may only appear appropriate if statesman appreciate they are victims of a security dilemma and that their adversary does not intend them harm. It might indeed provide a means of mitigating a security dilemma, but it may seem a risky policy and, although statesmen recognise their interdependence, they may seek to 'play safe' by trying to minimise their reliance upon one another via unilateral methods.

It would be misleading, however, to consider common security an appropriate means of mitigating all security dilemmas. It was noted in Chapter 2 that, in addition to the traditional system-induced security dilemma, there is the relatively new idea of a state-induced security dilemma. The latter differed from the former in that it arose in those circumstances where one state required others to be insecure for it to be secure. It is clear that the dynamics of the state-induced security dilemma ensure that it is incompatible with a common security approach. Quite simply, if the state's strategic assumption is that security can only be acquired if others are insecure, then mutual security will appear inappropriate. In addition, since the state has no interest in mutual security, common security is also inappropriate for the other states. Hence Jack Snyder's assertion that, prior to the First World War, the European states could not mitigate the security dilemma via concessionary policies:

> On major issues meaningful concessions were impossible because a stable, mutually acceptable bargain could not exist, given the prevailing strategic assumptions. Appeasing the security fears of one's neighbour would have entailed accepting one's own insecurity.[92]

In this scenario, mitigation only becomes possible if the state that requires others to be insecure alters its strategic assumptions. Charles Kupchan argues that the 'end of the Cold War represents', by the Soviet Union, 'a remarkable instance of successful and peaceful strategic adjustment'.[93] In Chapter 1 it was argued that Stresemann was able to prevent the emergence of a state-induced security dilemma by altering the French perception that it required German insecurity. Thus, common security is only useful as a mitigator of a system-induced security dilemma.

If it is true that, in certain circumstances, common security can be seen as an appropriate policy option for mitigating the security dilemma, then its relationship to force postures and, in particular, nuclear weapons becomes important. If common security and nuclear weapons are incompatible, and neither state is prepared to surrender its nuclear weapons, then the implementation of common security becomes problematic. The final part of this chapter, therefore, is concerned with the compatibility of nuclear weapons and common security.

Combining Common Security and Minimum Deterrence

This final section is concerned with two separate but related questions. First, are nuclear weapons and common security compatible? If they are mutually exclusive and neither power in a security dilemma is prepared to disarm its nuclear arsenals, then implementation of common security becomes problematic. Second, do the ideas expounded earlier concerning minimum deterrence complement common security? If they do complement each other, then common security may provide the answer to the obstacle of malign intent noted earlier in relation to minimum deterrence.

It is perhaps worth reiterating that there does exist a relationship between common security and nuclear weapons. The relationship is *not* that nuclear weapons make the security of states interdependent, but, rather, that they manifest interdependence in a manner that cannot be equalled by conventional forces. If nuclear weapons are taken out of the equation, then security remains interdependent, but the concern is that decision-makers will no longer perceive this to be the case. In such a scenario, states may pursue unilateral methods of achieving security, and thereby exacerbate the security dilemma, because common security no longer appears appropriate. This is what Bjorn Moller was referring to when he wrote:

> If the mutual deterrence stalemate were to disappear, the premise of the common security argumentation would fall apart, and many often-heard common security propositions would become blatantly untrue: wars might, once again, become winnable and security might well become obtainable through national policies pursued in complete disregard of one's opponents.[94]

The literature on common security and nuclear weapons can be divided into two groups: one group considers the two as antithetical and the other views them as compatible. Both groups begin from the shared assumption that a nuclear war would be so devastating that neither side could win and that MAD is therefore a strategic reality.[95] This realisation not only leads to the futility of trying to achieve security at the expense of others, but also provides the states with a common interest in survival. However, while the two groups may agree that nuclear weapons make the mutuality of security explicit, they disagree over the future role of nuclear weapons. Thus, although the Palme Commission concludes: 'security in the nuclear age means common security', it proposes a programme to eliminate them: '*A doctrine of common security must replace the present expedient of deterrence through armaments*' (emphasis in original).[96] In contrast, Bjorn Moller concludes that, rather than replacing nuclear weapons, 'common security is quite compatible with, *perhaps indeed preconditioned on*, mutual deterrence as a framework condition for security policy' (emphasis added).[97] In order to determine the compatibility of common security and nuclear weapons, it is thus necessary to examine the reasons given for these different conclusions.

The case for incompatibility

The Palme Commission was aware of the security dilemma and considered that one of the factors that exacerbated it was the build-up of weapons.[98] Thus the commission considered arms – and in particular nuclear arms – to be part of the problem that common security should solve. Hence the commission notes that: *'International Peace must rest on a commitment to joint survival rather than a threat of mutual destruction'* (emphasis in original).[99] The solution, at least in theory, was simple: states should cooperate for their security and they should begin by reducing and ultimately eliminating their arsenals.[100]

> Unless they show mutual restraint and proper appreciation of the realities of the nuclear age ... the pursuit of security can cause intensified competition and more tense political relations and, at the end of the day, a reduction in security for all concerned ... There must be partnership in the struggle against war itself ... *The Commission strongly supports the goal of general and complete disarmament* [emphasis in original].[101]

The commission's line of argument receives support in a SIPRI study. Raimo Vayrynen and Allan Krass argue that nuclear deterrence cannot provide a stable basis for security and, as such, is incompatible with common security. The argument is slightly different from that of the Palme Commission's because Vayrynen and Krass both place great importance on the consistent dynamism of technology to undermine existing deterrence postures. Vayrynen comments:

> The theory and policy of nuclear deterrence underestimate the dynamism of science and technology in fostering arms competition: advances and breakthroughs in military technology constantly upset the military balance and give rise to new threat perceptions. Stable nuclear deterrence presupposes a stable technological environment, whereas in fact military technology is changing very rapidly indeed.[102]

According to this argument, consistent technological innovations in the military field, or at least the perception that such innovations can occur, prevent states from being confident that their military capabilities will remain credible for a long period of time. The fear that an adversary may achieve a devastating technological breakthrough and undermine their deterrence credibility will ensure that technological advances are sought in order to prevent such an outcome. Thus, as Krass writes: 'if ... an improvement can be obtained by technological advances, it is extremely difficult to refrain from making such advances'.[103] The technological advancement in weapon procurement thus undermines a stable nuclear stalemate because there is always the possibility that a breakthrough will be found which gives one side a decisive advantage.

This technological dynamism is referred to by Buzan as the 'techno-logical imperative'.[104] He acknowledges that states continually improve their weapon capabilities and provides two reasons for this.[105] First, a state may well be seeking to gain a decisive advantage and alter the military balance. If a new weapon system is deployed for this reason, then the state must perceive the current balance of military power to be unfavour-able. Weapons procured to alter the military balance are likely to be seen as detrimental by other states; as a result, they are likely to try and regain the advantage. This is clearly not stable and – because an arms race is in operation – it is not compatible with a common security approach.

The second reason concerns the need to replace old systems as they become obsolete. When states replace ageing weapons, they invariably introduce replacements that have a greater potency. The decision to modernise is thus not designed to change the military balance; the inten-tion is to maintain the balance.[106] Although this might be the intention, however, the fact that the replacement has a greater potency will ensure that it will be perceived as altering the military balance by other adversarial states.[107] Thus it makes little difference whether the weapon is intended to alter the balance or not; the perception of others is likely to be that the new, more powerful weapon system alters the balance and undermines the credibility of their deterrents. If states want to maintain parity, the only option seems to be to play safe and match/supersede the new weapon system.

Buzan's claim regarding the technological imperative is slightly different from that of Vayrynen and Krass. He recognises that 'outside observers may have difficulty distinguishing between changes designed to maintain military strength, and those designed to increase it'.[108] Indeed, since it is so difficult to determine accurately which reason lies behind the new weapon system, Buzan acknowledges that 'prudence dictates caution about benign assumptions'.[109] In other words, it is wiser to play safe and match the new weapon system. However, the implication of Buzan's case is that if states can distinguish the reasons for the new weapon system, then they need not respond to a system that is procured in order to maintain the military balance. By not responding, the destabilising effects of the tech-nological imperative are overcome. Unfortunately, this is not necessarily true; even if the other states know the intention is not to alter the equilibrium, they need – unless they are prepared to accept an unfavourable balance – to reciprocate in order to maintain parity.

The technological imperative therefore has the effect of driving an arms race between states and can be an important force behind the security dilemma. Even if neither state is interested in gaining a decisive advantage over the other, it still seems that, despite states' mutual vulnerability, Vayrynen and Krass are right to be sceptical about the compatibility of nuclear deterrence and common security – a conclusion that appears to be supported by Buzan.

> New technologies will continue to open up new military possibilities regardless of whether military applications are intended or not. Since states will remain responsible for their defence for the foreseeable future, they cannot escape from the pressure that these options create. There is therefore no question about whether the power-security dilemma will continue to exist: it will.[110]

Given that these 'options' are to continue the arms race, it is not surprising that Vayrynen states: 'even if efforts are made to make nuclear deterrence more stable, it cannot provide a sound basis for common security'.[111]

According to this argument, the technological imperative driving the development of ever more potent weapon systems creates the possibility that one state may achieve a decisive breakthrough. Even if neither state is seeking a decisive breakthrough to enable them to escape their vulnerability, the perception that an adversary might achieve this is sufficient to ensure that they will continue to improve their systems in order to maintain their deterrence credibility. The technological imperative therefore stimulates an arms race, enhances the image of malign intent and exacerbates the security dilemma. The result is that weapons – and in particular nuclear weapons – are seen as the problem that common security needs to overcome. Far from being compatible, 'common security was intended to render superfluous ... nuclear deterrence'.[112]

If the successful implementation of common security requires the removal of nuclear weapons, then it is unlikely to be taken seriously as a policy option by two nuclear powers in an adversarial relationship – especially if those powers consider their nuclear arsenals to be of the utmost importance in deterring one another. Thus the case against the compatibility of common security and nuclear weapons raises serious implications for the implementation of common security and, hence, its value as a mitigator of the security dilemma. However, it is the contention of this chapter that common security and nuclear weapons are compatible and that it is only when they are considered together that long-term mitigation, leading to escape, can occur.

The case for compatibility

The case against nuclear deterrence is invariably, and understandably, based upon the deterrence policies that the superpowers have pursued. While it is not the intention to examine these strategies now (they are examined in Chapter 5), it is necessary to note that these policies resembled maximum deterrence strategies.[113] Maximum deterrence strategies that emphasise the need to deter the aggressor at any level of hostility require a whole gamut of nuclear weapons to ensure that, even at a low level of violence, their use is credible. Strategies that focus on the ability to fight limited nuclear wars fall within this category. These strategies are the antithesis of the minimum deterrence approach outlined earlier in the chapter. Richard Smoke provides a clear distinction between the two when he refers to minimum deterrence as:

> a posture in which each side's strategic nuclear arsenal is designed by the single criterion of achieving its fundamental goal – deterring the other side from any rational use of strategic nuclear weapons. No other goals are added, explicitly or implicitly, that might complicate or compete with the arsenal's capacity to accomplish its fundamental goal.[114]

It is because the case against nuclear weapons is often based upon the history of the Cold War that Moller suggests: 'What common security advocates seem to have in mind may not in fact be the situation of deterrence, but, rather, particular national policies of deterrence.'[115] The case for compatibility between common security and nuclear deterrence is thus based on the adoption of a minimum deterrence strategy. This, however, raises the question of how minimum deterrence – characterised by counter-value weapons holding an opponent's population as hostage – can be compatible with common security? After all, the former is based upon the threat to do something dreadful, while the latter seeks cooperation. Are these really compatible?

Buzan provides one answer by noting three areas of common interest between minimum deterrence and common security; he refers to these as 'parallel commitments'. The first is that 'both are based on the desire to reduce, and preferably eliminate, the resort to war in relations between states'.[116] While this is certainly true, the same similarity can be noted between common security and maximum deterrence strategies. Deterrence strategies – maximum or minimum – seek to 'reduce and preferably eliminate the resort to war'. They differ on how they seek to achieve this objective, not over the objective itself. Thus this first similarity is just too general in helping to promote the compatibility of minimum deterrence and common security. It implies that maximum deterrence and common security could be compatible – which is implausible, since maximum deterrence strategies emphasise unilateral means of achieving security.

The second common interest is that minimum deterrence 'is built on the common security assumption that the military securities of states are intimately interdependent'.[117] Buzan notes that minimum deterrence, with its reliance on both states' populations being held hostage, is in accordance with the strategic reality of MAD. The adoption of minimum deterrence by both states will therefore be an explicit acknowledgement of their security interdependence, which stems from mutual vulnerability. By highlighting mutual vulnerability, minimum deterrence is compatible with common security. This link is very important and deserves repetition. If nuclear weapons are initially required to make security appear inter-dependent to states, then the adoption of minimum deterrence can be seen to be in accordance with common security.

Buzan's second common interest raises an interesting problem from the perspective of the security dilemma. The argument being advanced is that minimum deterrence and common security provide a joint means of mitigating the security dilemma. However, it was noted earlier how Jervis considers that nuclear weapons configured to support a MAD-type strategy can provide an escape from the security dilemma without the need for cooperation. Glaser supports Jervis's assertion that common security is unnecessary when he writes that 'nuclear weapons are a revolution for the defence and thus eliminate the security dilemma'.[118] However, there are reasons to be cautious about the claim that adopting MAD without cooperative undertakings will escape the security dilemma. The most important is that the real distrust and hostility that the states have for one another remains. The concern that the other harbours malign intent still plays upon the minds of decision-makers. Does the adversary's adop-tion of a MAD-type strategy conceal a surreptitious attempt to undermine the state's security? For example, if the superpowers had adopted a MAD-type strategy during the Cold War, it seems that a conventional security dilemma would have existed. Western distrust of Soviet intentions might have led them to believe that the Soviet acceptance of MAD was a ruse to decouple the United States from western Europe and thus nullify US nuclear threats. As a result – probably in response to the concerns of the European members of NATO – additional US conventional forces might have been deployed to deter Soviet adventurism. The arrival of more American forces on the European continent could have fuelled Soviet distrust of western intentions. The insecurity spiral/security dilemma thus continues at the conventional level. Even if the West did not believe that the Soviets were using MAD to decouple the Atlantic partners, the sus-picious nature of their relationship would have continued to produce worst-case analysis about future developments. Given the ambiguity in conventional weapons' defensive/offensive characteristics, and in particular the offensive force posture of the Warsaw Pact's conventional forces, the pressure to 'play safe' (assume the worst) by the West and deploy more conventional forces would have been considerable.

Buzan's third common interest between common security and nuclear deterrence is that 'common security and minimum deterrence are motiv-ated by a commitment to dampen down the arms race, and to minimize the disruptive impact of technological innovation on military relations between states'.[119] It is certainly the case that minimum deterrence could nullify the dynamics of an arms race. The fact that minimum deterrence only requires a force of sufficient size to be able to inflict assured destruction after a nuclear attack places a limit on the weapons needed. Whilesoever the nuclear weapons remain secure from a decapitating first strike and are capable of hitting their targets, the state need not respond to an increase in weapon capabilities by another state. It is this effect that Jervis is referring to when he comments that, with a MAD doctrine:

> each side's decision on the size of its force depends on technical questions, its judgement about how much destruction is enough to deter, and the amount of insurance it is willing to pay for – and these considerations are independent of the size of the other's strategic force. Thus the crucial nexus in the arms race is severed.[120]

This is in direct contrast to maximum deterrence strategies, where the adequacy of force is determined by comparison with the opponent's force capabilities. The required force level is measured against that of the opponent and, as such, there is no upper limit. While it is agreed that minimum deterrence can reduce the likelihood of an arms race, and is thus compatible with common security, it can only mitigate the nuclear security dilemma. Full mitigation and even escape of the security dilemma requires the reduction of the perception of malign intent.

Buzan's claim that minimum deterrence can minimise the effect of technological innovation on military relations is extremely important. The main argument against the compatibility of common security and nuclear deterrence is that, because of technological breakthroughs, nuclear deterrence is not a stable basis from which common security can evolve. The argument is simply that if states cannot be certain that their strategies will remain credible in the face of new technology, then they need to engage in the necessary research to prevent a potential adversary achieving a unilateral breakthrough that will undermine this credibility. At the centre of minimum deterrence is the accepted belief that the nuclear force is both capable of striking its targets and itself invulnerable to a decapitating first strike. A technological breakthrough in either strategic defences or counter-force accuracy/potency could undermine the state's ability to threaten assured destruction. A strategy of minimum deterrence is thus highly sensitive to technological breakthroughs. If minimum deterrence is to be regarded as complementing common security, then technological innovations are a challenge that need to be solved.

Buzan's claim that minimum deterrence can minimise this 'disruptive impact' on military relations between states appears dubious. So long as both states seek to alter the reality of mutual vulnerability, then minimum deterrence is extremely difficult to pursue. As Wheeler states:

> The principal motivation behind the search for self-reliance in the security field has been the desire of both sides to escape the fact their security has depended upon the restraint of the 'other'. This has been

extremely difficult for both Moscow and Washington to live with, for it has meant dependence upon an enemy perceived to be the antithesis of its values and beliefs ... [Yet if minimum deterrence is to be viable] both sides will have to give up the search for unilateral advantage through the exploitation of new military technologies.[121]

There are a number of reasons why it is difficult to believe that states will forgo research and development (R&D) of new weapon technologies. Two of these reasons are pertinent to this discussion.

The first is that not all new technologies undermine the minimum deterrence doctrine. Using Jervis's reversal of common-sense definitions, any improvements to defence (e.g., making nuclear weapons harder to target) strengthens the weapon's ability to threaten assured destruction and thus strengthens minimum deterrence. It is unlikely, therefore, that states will relinquish the opportunity to improve their deterrence cred- ibility. Such R&D, of course, would strengthen minimum deterrence rather than undermine it. Unfortunately, the development of some systems that enhance minimum deterrence (e.g., ABM sites defending C^3I facilities) might be perceived by an adversary as undermining minimum deterrence by protecting counter-value targets. Thus, non-disruptive R&D may still be perceived in this manner.

The second reason is that, according to Buzan, there exists a 'techno- logical imperative [which] drives a relentless and continuous improvement in the performance of weapons'. The result of this imperative, Buzan states, is 'that the military sector possesses an independent dynamic that functions regardless of ups and downs in political relations'.[122] The implic- ation of this is that, at least in the short-term, the modernisation of weaponry is divorced from political control. Buzan notes that the con- sequence of this is that a state embarking on conciliatory policies can easily send confusing signals if it is also improving its military capabilities. Whether weapon modernisation is actually divorced from political control appears dubious, since weapon modernisation requires the authorisation of the political leadership – the Ministry of Defence, for instance. The explanation for the 'separate' dynamic is probably the enormous influence of the military-industrial complex on political decision-makers. The pri- mary objective of this influential body is its own well-being (e.g., enhancing profits, securing jobs, etc.), with the result that there exists a process of arms accumulation that appears to have a logic of its own. According to Buzan, this 'logic did not always serve the national interest, and it was both strong enough and independent enough to be an important part of the problem defined as arms racing'.[123] The influence of the military- industrial complex in the USA is enormous, as it was in the former Soviet Union. While this remains the case, limitations on technological innov- ations appear unlikely. However, with the end of the Cold War and the subsequent decline in threat perception, the influence of the military-industrial complex may also decline as resources are diverted into other areas. This is especially true for the former Soviet Union, where resources have diminished drastically. Nevertheless, writing immediately after the Cold War, Hugh Miall warns: 'In the Soviet Union, the military industrial sector still takes priority, in access to skilled people, materials and funds, over civilian sectors. In the United States the military industrial complex retains a stranglehold on the political system.' [124]

Buzan's claim that minimum deterrence can minimise technology's disruptive impact appears dubious, therefore, because minimum deterrence is highly susceptible to R&D breakthroughs, thus ensuring that states will embark upon R&D if only to prevent the perceived opponent achieving a breakthrough. It is suggested that, although minimum deterrence does not exacerbate the factors that drive technological innovation in the same fashion as maximum deterrence strategies do, it alone does not overcome the destabilising influences of the technological imperative; more is needed than minimum deterrence.

The perception of malign intent is crucial, therefore, in making minimum deterrence a problematic doctrine to adopt. This is where common security can complement minimum deterrence. If minimum deterrence is part of a broader approach to achieving security, such as common security, then the gradual improvement in the relations between states will help to minimise the disruptive impact of technological changes. For instance, an agreement on restricting the deployment of strategic defences (an institutionalised security regime) will help support a minimum deterrence strategy. The implementation of a common security approach helps to reduce the perception of malign intent and makes the adoption of minimum deterrence more favourable. Minimum deterrence and common security are not only compatible, therefore, but also complement one another when it comes to mitigating the security dilemma. By reducing the perception of malign intent, common security reduces the concern that minimum deterrence lacks credibility in the face of a determined opponent. Likewise, the adoption of minimum deterrence signifies an acknowledgement by the participants that their security is interdependent, thus making common security a viable option for them to pursue.

Conclusion

The purpose of the chapter has been to determine whether the security dilemma can be mitigated, or even escaped, through the implementation of common security policies and the adoption of defensive force postures. It is noted that because common security highlights security as a mutual concept, it is of value as a mitigator of the security dilemma. That is, if states conceive of security as mutual, they will have little incentive to seek it at others' expense; this lessens the dynamics of the security dilemma. The adoption of a discernibly defensive conventional force posture and a minimum nuclear deterrence strategy were also seen as removing the perception that a neighbouring state harboured malign intent. However, this adoption was made problematic by the existence of the perception of malign intent, and thus it is argued that a combined common security/force posture approach is required.

The key to implementing common security is for states to cooperate. Cooperation amongst adversaries is difficult to achieve, but in a security dilemma, where the incompatibility is illusory, it might be achievable if the uncertainty between the states could be overcome. It is suggested that, in order to achieve cooperation, it is necessary to reduce the fear of defection. States may be able to accomplish this by entering into agreements that create transparency and thus lessen their mutual mistrust. If they become more confident about each other's intent, then it may be possible for them to form institutionalised security regimes, an action that would mitigate the security dilemma.

Common security is therefore considered to be a good means of mitigating the security dilemma. However, its value can only be ascertained if common security appears appropriate or attractive to decision-makers. It is suggested that states are always dependent upon the actions of others for their security and, as a result, their security is interdependent. It is proposed that nuclear weapons, while not making security interdependent, do make it explicit in a manner that has not been equalled by conventional forces. While this does not necessarily make common security appear attractive, it does make its implementation possible by highlighting that its core assumption is in place: state security is interdependent and, therefore, cannot be achieved unilaterally. The relationship between common security and minimum deterrence is thus very important.

The implication of this relationship has split common security advocates into those who see common security as replacing nuclear deterrence and those who view the two not only as compatible, but also complementary. This latter view is extremely useful, since the perception of malign intent was noted as an obstacle to the implementation of minimum deterrence. If common security is compatible and complements minimum deterrence, then together they may overcome this and mitigate the security dilemma. In order to reach this conclusion, however it was necessary to examine the anti-nuclear arguments of common security proponents. The major concern of this group is that technological change ensures that nuclear deterrence is unstable and that states are encouraged to seek unilateral means of achieving security. It is suggested that a minimum deterrence strategy combined with a common security approach will help to dampen the effects of technological change. The main reason for this is that common security reduces the perception of malign intent (via greater transparency), thus minimising the concern that others will seek a decisive breakthrough. Indeed, it is suggested that not only does common security support minimum deterrence, but minimum deterrence also supports common security by manifesting the state's security as interdependent.

The implementation of common security will therefore be possible in a world in which the nuclear powers are determined to maintain their nuclear arsenals. The implementation of both will mitigate the security dilemma: common security by improving relations; and minimum deterrence by making defence hold the advantage in times of war. This conclusion stands in marked contrast to Jervis's position that minimum deterrence does not require common security to escape the security dilemma. However, Jervis's position does not adequately explain the possibility of conventional security dilemmas, and his conclusion contradicts his claim elsewhere that the security dilemma cannot be escaped.[125] The attempted implementation of common security and minimum deterrence – and their success in mitigating the security dilemma – is the subject of discussion in Chapter 7. However, before examining the Gorbachev era to see if the ideas elucidated in this chapter played a role in mitigating the Cold War security dilemma, it is necessary to provide evidence of the security dilemma during the Cold War. The Cold War is examined in the following two chapters to highlight the ways in which state relations and defence postures exacerbate the security dilemma.

Notes

1. Robert Jervis, 'Security Regimes', *International Organization*, 36/2 (1982), p. 374.
2. Robert Jervis, 'Cooperation under the Security Dilemma', *World Politics*, 30/1 (1978), pp. 167–214.
3. Raymond L. Garthoff, *Soviet Strategy in the Nuclear Age* (London: 1958), p. 118.
4. Jervis, 'Cooperation under the Security Dilemma', pp. 186–7. Glaser also notes the importance of these variables when he writes: 'the severity of the security dilemma depends upon two factors: the degree to which offence dominates defence; and the degree to which offence and defence are ambiguous': Charles L. Glaser, *Analyzing Strategic Nuclear Policy* (Princeton: 1990), p. 94.
5. Jervis, 'Cooperation under the Security Dilemma', p. 201.
6. Ibid., p. 199.
7. Ibid.
8. Carl von Clausewitz, *On War*, translated and edited by Michael Howard and Peter Paret (Princeton: 1984), p. 357.
9. Ibid.
10. Ibid.
11. Gideon Y. Akavia, 'Defensive Defence and the Nature of Armed Conflict', *The Journal of Strategic Studies*, 14/1 (1991), p. 31.
12. Charles L. Glaser, 'Political Consequences of Military Strategy', *World Politics*, 44/4 (1992), p. 509.
13. Akavia, 'Defensive Defence', p. 34.
14. Glaser, 'Political Consequences', p. 509.

15. Ken Booth, 'The Interregnum: world politics in transition', in Ken Booth (ed.), *New Thinking about Strategy and International Security* (London: 1991), p. 20.
16. For an excellent and succinct history of NOD, see Hans Gunter Brauch, 'Debate on Alternative Conventional Military Force Structure Designs for the Defence of Central Europe in the Federal Republic of Germany', in Hans Gunter Brauch and Robert Kennedy (eds), *Alternative Conventional Defence Postures in the European Theatre: Volume 3* (Washington: 1993), pp. 6–22. For the continuities in NOD thinking, see Bjorn Moller, *Resolving the Security Dilemma in Europe: the German debate on non-offensive defence* (London: 1991), pp. 2–14.
17. David Gates, *Non-offensive Defence: an alternative strategy for NATO?* (London: 1991), p. 67.
18. Colin McInnes, 'Alternative Defence', in Colin McInnes (ed.), *Security and Strategy in the New Europe* (London: 1992), p. 139. For more detailed criticism, see Colin McInnes, *NATO's Changing Strategic Agenda: the conventional defence of Central Europe* (London: 1990), pp. 177–83; Gates, *Non-offensive Defence*, chapter 4.
19. Barry Buzan, *People, States and Fear: an agenda for international security studies in the post-Cold War era* (Hemel Hempstead: 2nd edn, 1991), p. 297.
20. Jervis, 'Cooperation under the Security Dilemma', p. 203.
21. George Quester, *Offense and Defense in the International System* (Toronto: 1977), p. 3.
22. Akavia, 'Defensive Defence', p. 45 n12.
23. Bernard Brodie, *War and Politics* (New York: 1973), p. 325.
24. Jervis, 'Cooperation under the Security Dilemma', p. 203.
25. Quoted ibid., p. 201.
26. Bjorn Moller and Hakan Wiberg, 'Introduction', in Bjorn Moller and Hakan Wiberg (eds), *Non-offensive Defence for the Twenty-First Century* (Boulder: 1994), p. 1.
27. Jervis, 'Cooperation under the Security Dilemma', p. 187.
28. An excellent example of this was the war in 1967 between Israel and her Arab neighbours. Threatened by the build-up of Egyptian, Jordanian and Syrian forces, Israel launched a pre-emptive attack so decisive that, within six days, Israel had destroyed the military capabilities of these countries.
29. Jack Snyder, 'Perceptions of the Security Dilemma in 1914', in Robert Jervis, Richard Ned Lebow and Janice Gross Stein (eds), *Psychology and Deterrence* (Balitmore: 1985), pp. 158–60.
30. Jervis, 'Cooperation under the Security Dilemma', p. 187.
31. Glaser, *Analyzing Strategic Nuclear Policy*, p. 95.
32. Jervis, 'Cooperation under the Security Dilemma', p. 211.
33. Ibid., p. 199.
34. This is hypocritical, of course, since both status quo powers are procuring offensive weapons. However, this is where Jervis's remark that statesmen rarely consider their own actions as threatening is of import. Although both states are procuring offensive weapons, the first state knows it does not intend the other harm, so it sees no reason why that state should feel threatened. Jervis writes: 'because the state believes that its adversary understands that the state is arming because it sees the adversary as aggressive, the state does not think that strengthening its arms can be harmful': Robert Jervis, *Perception and Misperception in International Politics* (New Jersey: 1976), p. 69.
35. Glaser, *Analyzing Strategic Nuclear Policy*, p. 96.
36. Ibid.
37. Jervis, 'Cooperation under the Security Dilemma', p. 214.
38. Robert Jervis, 'Realism, Game Theory, and Cooperation', *World Politics*, 40/3 (1988), p. 332.
39. Jervis, 'Cooperation under the Security Dilemma', p. 198.
40. Robert Jervis, *The Meaning of the Nuclear Revolution: statecraft and the prospect of Armageddon* (Ithaca and London: 1989), p. 10.

41. Jervis, 'Realism', pp. 332–3.
42. Quoted from Lawrence Freedman, *The Evolution of Nuclear Strategy* (London: 2nd edn, 1989), p. 252.
43. Jervis, 'Cooperation under the Security Dilemma', p. 206.
44. Glaser, *Analyzing Strategic Nuclear Policy*, p. 74.
45. Bradley Klein, *Strategic Studies and World Order* (Cambridge: 1994), p. 61.
46. Jervis, 'Cooperation under the Security Dilemma', p. 207.
47. Ibid.
48. See Owen Cote, 'The Trident and the Triad: collecting the D-5 dividend', *International Security*, 16/2 (1991), pp. 117–45.
49. Jervis, 'Cooperation under the Security Dilemma', p. 208.
50. Ibid.
51. Jervis, 'Realism', p. 374.
52. Barry Buzan, *An Introduction to Strategic Studies: military technology and international relations* (London: 1987), p. 193.
53. Some strategies that are labelled as minimum deterrence strategies do in fact contain limited counter-force options in order to avoid the morally repugnant city-targeting, spasm-like attack option. See Lawrence Martin, 'Minimum Deterrence', in Faraday Discussion Paper No. 8, Council for Arms Control (January 1987); David Lewis, 'Finite Counterforce', in Henry Shue (ed.), *Nuclear Deterrence and Moral Restraint: critical choices for American strategy* (New York: 1989), pp. 51–44.
54. Jan Kalicki, Fred Chernoff, Eric Mlyn, Sergei Fedorenko, Andrei Kortunov and Aleksandr Pisarev, 'Fundamental Deterrence and Mutual Security beyond START', in Richard Smoke and Andrei Kortunov (eds), *Mutual Security: a new approach to Soviet–American relations* (London: 1991), p. 260.
55. For example, Graham Barral's proposal for 800 strategic-warheads on a combination of single-warhead ICBMs and SLBMs. See Graham Barral, 'The Lost Tablets: an analysis of the concept of minimum deterrence', *Arms Control*, 13/1 (1992), pp. 58–84.
56. Jervis, 'Cooperation under the Security Dilemma', p. 214.
57. Glaser, *Analyzing Strategic Nuclear Policy*, p. 364.
58. Kenneth N. Waltz, 'The Spread of Nuclear Weapons: more may be better', *Adelphi Paper 171* (Autumn 1981), p. 22.
59. Ibid., p. 23.
60. Being faced by a state that seems prepared to use nuclear weapons is where the disagreement is likely to occur. Waltz claims that the archetypal revisionist state, Hitler's Germany, 'would almost surely have been deterred' (ibid., p. 20), the argument being that Hitler's Germany, in a nuclear world, would have been deterred because it would have been irrational to assume that the target state would not use its nuclear weapons. The fact that deterrence is assured of working because nuclear weapons exist was coined as 'existential deterrence' by McGeorge Bundy. The intention here is not to enter the existential debate. Instead it is to note that, with regard to MAD and conventional security dilemmas, Bundy does support the argument that MAD is not an escaper of the security dilemma. He writes: 'A defence based on nuclear weapons alone would not sustain the self-confidence of Western Europe; it would not persuade those nearest to the Soviet Union that no Kremlin leader would be tempted to try for easy pickings. Conventional forces are indispensable.' For the Bundy quotation, see McGeorge Bundy, *Danger and Survival* (New York: 1990), p. 599. For existential deterrence, see McGeorge Bundy, 'The Bishops and the Bomb', *The New York Review of Books*, 16 June 1983. See also Lawrence Freedman, 'I Exist; Therefore I Deter', *International Security*, 13/1 (1988), pp. 184–90.
61. Bjorn Moller, *Common Security and Nonoffensive Defence: a neorealist perspective* (London: 1992), p. 28.
62. The Report of the Independent Commission on Disarmament and Security Issues

under the chairmanship of Olof Palme produced a book entitled *Common Security: a programme for disarmament* (London: 1982), hereafter known as the Palme Report.

63. See Geoffrey Wiseman, *Common Security and Non-provocative Defence: alternative approaches to the security dilemma* (Canberra: 1989), chapters 2–3, esp. pp. 40–1.

64. For a brief examination of common security that emphasises the holistic approach and defensive defence, see Colin McInnes, 'NATO Strategy and Conventional Defence', in Ken Booth (ed.), *New Thinking about Strategy and International Security* (London: 1991), pp. 171–2.

65. For more emphasis on the cooperation ideas, see John Baylis and Ken Booth, *Britain, NATO and Nuclear Weapons: alternative defence versus alliance reform* (London: 1989), pp. 355–9.

66. Ibid., p. 6.

67. Richard Smoke, 'A Theory of Mutual Security', in Richard Smoke and Andrei Kortunov (eds), *Mutual Security: a new approach to Soviet–American relations* (London: 1991), p. 61.

68. Palme Report, pp. 7–8.

69. For instance, see Moller, *Common Security*, pp. 31–2; Raimo Vayrynen, 'Introduction: towards a strategy of common security', in Stockholm International Peace Research Institute (SIPRI), *Policies for Common Security* (London: 1985), p. 1; Stan Windass, 'What is Common Security?', in Stan Windass and Eric Grove (eds), *The Crucible of Peace: common security in Europe* (London: 1988), p. 4.

70. See Windass, 'What is Common Security?', pp. 10–11. Specific examples of such measures receive attention in Chapter 7, below.

71. Ibid., p. 11.

72. Smoke, 'Mutual Security', p. 82.

73. Karl Deutsch, *Political Community and the North Atlantic Area: international organization in the light of historic experience* (New Jersey: 1957), p. 200.

74. Ibid., p. 5.

75. Jervis, 'Security Regimes', p. 357.

76. Ibid., p. 358.

77. Ibid., pp. 360–2.

78. Joseph S. Nye, Jr., 'Nuclear Learning and US–Soviet Security Regimes', *International Organization*, 41/3 (1987), pp. 375–6. Nye's view gains support from Alexander George, Philip Farley and Alexander Dallin: see George, Farley and Dallin, 'Research Objectives and Methods', in George, Farley and Dallin (eds), *US–Soviet Security Cooperation: achievements, failures, lessons* (New York: 1988), p. 14.

79. Charles A. Kupchan and Clifford A. Kupchan, 'Concerts, Collective Security, and the Future of Europe', *International Security*, 16/1 (1991), p. 131. Robert Keohane makes the same point when he writes: 'International regimes, and the institutions and procedures that develop in conjunction with them, perform the function of reducing uncertainty and risk by linking discrete issues to one another and by improving the quantity and quality of information available to participants. Linking issues is important as a way to deal with potential deception': Robert O. Keohane, 'The Demand for International Regimes', *International Organization*, 36/2 (1982), pp. 345–6.

80. Kupchan and Kupchan, 'Concerts, Collective Security, and the Future of Europe', p. 131.

81. Ibid., p. 132.

82. Ibid., p. 135.

83. Moller, *Common Security*, p. 18.

84. Quoted from Richard Rosecrance, 'International Interdependence', in Geoffrey L. Goodwin and Andrew Linklater (eds), *New Dimensions of World Politics* (London: 1975), p. 20.

85. Ibid.

86. Indeed, the belief that the other intends harm might be exacerbated by the arrival of

nuclear weapons: state B is in danger of confirming state A's image of it as an aggressor by targeting A with its nuclear forces.

87. Palme Report, p. 5.

88. Mikhail Beznikov and Andrei Kortunov, 'Interdependence: A Perspective on Mutual Security', in Smoke and Kortunov, *Mutual Security*, p. 11.

89. Wiseman, *Common Security and Non-provocative Defence*, p. 7.

90. Barry Buzan, 'Common Security, Non-provocative Defence, and the Future of Western Europe', in *Review of International Studies*, 13/4 (1987), p. 265. Nicholas Wheeler and Ken Booth, 'The Security Dilemma', in John Baylis and N. J. Rengger (eds), *Dilemmas of World Politics: international issues in a changing world* (Oxford: 1992), p. 46.

91. This does not imply that conventional forces are not highly destructive. Rather, while states believe they can defend themselves against conventional munitions, these weapons are not likely to persuade states that security cannot be achieved unilaterally.

92. Snyder, 'Perceptions of the Security Dilemma', pp. 154–5.

93. Charles A. Kupchan, *The Vulnerability of Empire* (Ithaca: 1994), p. 495.

94. Moller, *Common Security*, p. 31. Moller's argument is a little different, since he is suggesting that interdependence would disappear. This is probably wrong; the suggestion proposed is that the perception of interdependence might disappear, but the relationship would still be interdependent.

95. The Palme Commission makes numerous references to this. For example: 'In the event of a major world war, which would escalate inexorably to the use of nuclear weapons, all nations would suffer devastation to a degree that would make "victory" a meaningless word': Palme Report, p. 12; see also p. 141.

96. Ibid., p. 139.

97. Moller, *Common Security*, p. 31.

98. The commission notes: 'military strength is seen as a symbol of resolve, but the continuing expansion of national arsenals is in turn interpreted by the other nations as evidence of hostile intent, a cycle which undermines the security of the international community as a whole': Palme Report, p. 3.

99. Ibid., p. 139.

100. It is necessary to note that while the emphasis was placed on nuclear weapons, the concern regarding arms accumulation and the need to reduce such high levels was also directed towards other weapons of mass destruction and conventional weapons.

101. Palme Report, pp. 138–9.

102. Vayrynen, 'Introduction', p. 4.

103. Allan Krass, 'The Death of Deterrence', in SIPRI, *Policies for Common Security*, p. 125.

104. Buzan, *Introduction to Strategic Studies*, pp 108–10.

105. There are, of course, more than two reasons to explain the improvements made in weapon capabilities. There are such diverse issues as prestige, inter-service rivalry, the dynamics of the military-industrial complex, the need to preserve an industrial base, the complex decision-making process (G. T. Allison's bureaucratic politics) and even corruption. The tenacity with which the British government fought to keep the Germans involved in the European Fighter project (EFA) is better explained by the reasons above than by Buzan's two reasons. However, the purpose is not to suggest that Buzan's reasons are invalid, but, rather, to note that there are domestic reasons that influence weapon procurements.

106. The British decision in 1979 to replace the Polaris nuclear deterrent with the Trident system can be seen as an example of this reason. Concern regarding the deployment of a BMD around Moscow led the British to believe that Polaris lacked the necessary credibility to act as a deterrent. Thus, to maintain the British deterrent it was regarded as necessary to procure a more potent system, capable of overcoming the Soviet defence system. For details see C. J. McInnes, *Trident: the only option?* (London: 1986), esp. pp. 44 and 97.

107. The Soviet reaction to the British decision to modernise Polaris was to regard the move as 'taking new steps forward in the arms race'; it would 'only continue to poison the political climate in Europe and lead to a further increase in tension': Vasily Maslov, 'Militaristic Furor', *Current Digest of the Soviet Press*, 32/29 (20 August 1980), p. 17.
108. Buzan, *People, States and Fear*, p. 313.
109. Ibid.
110. Ibid., p. 320.
111. Vayrynen, 'Introduction', p. 5.
112. Author unknown, *NOD and Conversion*, 28 (January 1994), p. 43.
113. Buzan suggests that, when referring to different deterrece strategies, it is best to think of a spectrum where a pure maximum deterrence strategy lies at one end and a pure minimum deterrence strategy lies at the other end. In between these two extremes, various strategies exist that exhibit more characteristics of one type than the other, depending upon where they are on the spectrum. See Buzan, *Introduction to Strategic Studies*, pp. 193–6.
114. Smoke, 'Mutual Security', pp. 91–2.
115. Moller, *Common Security*, p. 31.
116. Buzan, 'Common Security', p. 269.
117. Ibid.
118. Glaser, *Analyzing Strategic Nuclear Policy*, p. 192 n56.
119. Buzan, 'Common Security', p. 269.
120. Jervis, 'Cooperation under the Security Dilemma', p. 208.
121. Nicholas J. Wheeler, 'Minimum Deterrence and Nuclear Abolition', in Regina Cowen Karp (ed.), *Security without Nuclear Weapons?: different perspectives on non-nuclear security* (Oxford: 1992), p. 258.
122. Buzan, *People, States and Fear*, p. 312.
123. Buzan, *Introduction to Strategic Studies*, p. 101.
124. Hugh Miall, 'New Visions, New Voices, Old Power Structures', in Ken Booth (ed.), *New Thinking about Strategy and International Security* (London: 1991), p. 308.
125. Jervis writes: 'Mutual Assured Destruction *escapes from the security dilemma* as each side gains security not from the ability to protect itself, but from its ability to retaliate and so deter the other from launching an attack' (emphasis added). In contrast he also asserts: 'the security dilemma cannot be abolished, it can only be ameliorated'. The first quotation is from 'Security Regimes', p. 374, and the second from *Perception*, p. 82.

II

The Cold War

Chapter Four

Creation

The purpose of the next two chapters is to examine the Cold War to determine whether a security dilemma was in operation.[1] This chapter will focus upon the period between 1945 and 1946 when the Grand Alliance was replaced by mutual suspicion and the prevailing belief that post-war security could not be pursued through cooperation with the Soviet Union. The chapter is specifically concerned with how uncertainty about one another's foreign policy objectives created a security dilemma. The role of military forces and the security dilemma is examined in Chapter 5.

It was noted in Chapter 1 that there are three characteristics which need to be evident for a security dilemma to be in operation: benign intent, uncertainty of intention, and the inadvertent pursuit of paradoxical policies. If a security dilemma was operating during this period, then these characteristics would have to be in existence. This chapter begins by examining the proposition that, during the immediate post-war period, the Soviet Union did not intend to launch an attack against the West; its intentions were benign towards its wartime allies. The chapter then examines Roosevelt's plans for peace and how they related to the common security ideas noted in the previous chapter. It is suggested that unilateral attempts to achieve security and suspicion about each other's true intent undermined Roosevelt's plans and the Grand Alliance. It is then shown how various factors exacerbated the belief of the wartime allies (the Big Three – the United States, Great Britain, Soviet Union) that resolve was required between the USA/Great Britain and the USSR to acquire security. It is argued that because they were victims of a spiral model, rather than a deterrence model, their resolve only fuelled their insecurity. Before examining this period, however, two caveats need to be noted.

The first is the sparsity of Soviet archival documents. With the end of the Cold War, documents are becoming available,[2] but those pertaining to the period immediately after the Second World War are still classified.[3] The lack of documentary evidence ensures that analysis of Soviet capabilities and intentions is controversial. It is important to note this, since one of the characteristics of the security dilemma is that the perceived incompatibility between states is illusory. It is therefore necessary to determine if Soviet intentions towards the USA and western Europe during this period were benign.[4] However, until Soviet archives release the necessary documents, it is impossible to assess Soviet intentions accurately. Indeed, even this will not guarantee success, because it is likely, as is the case with western documents, that they will produce conflicting analysis. Thus the caveat is that evidence of the security dilemma can only be inferred from what is presently known.

The second caveat concerns the conflicting analysis of western actions during this period. The controversy centres not on whether the intent towards the USSR was benign, but, rather, who was to blame for the Cold War. Three schools of thought emerged during the Cold War on this subject: orthodox, revisionist and post-revisionist.[5] The purpose of examining this period is not to attribute blame for the Cold War, nor is it to claim that the security dilemma was the sole cause of the Cold War. Howard Jones and Randall Woods are probably correct when they write: 'it seems safe to argue that not only did both the Soviet Union and the United States contribute to the beginnings of the Cold War but that other nations and other considerations played a role as well'.[6] The purpose in studying this period is to ascertain if the security dilemma was in operation.

The Three Characteristics

The USSR's intentions before 1949

Four broad arguments are raised to suggest that the Soviet Union did not intend to attack its wartime allies. The first is that the USSR was exhausted at the end of the Second World War and that the immediate concerns of the Kremlin were to rebuild the devastated Soviet economy. Estimates have suggested that 25% of fixed capital had been destroyed, national income had been reduced by 25–30%, and income from agriculture had fallen by 35–40%. The Soviet authorities were confronted with the destruction of six million buildings and twenty-five million homeless people (1,710 towns and 70,000 villages had been destroyed). Sixty-five thousand kilometres of railway track had been ruined in addition to the destruction of 15,800 locomotives and 428,000 freight cars.[7] According to Michael Cox, 'it was palpably clear that the Soviet's overriding postwar objective was not further expansion westwards, but the reconstruction of its devastated economy, a task likely to take at least a decade according to reliable Western sources'.[8]

Isaac Deutscher supports this by asserting:

> if one thing was or should have been clear, it was this: Russia, with 20 million of her people killed and uncounted millions crippled, for many years to come would not be able to wage any major war. She might perhaps fight for her survival if forced, but she was certainly in no physical or moral condition to undertake any large-scale invasion of foreign countries.[9]

The second argument is linked to the need for reconstruction. The Soviet Union was relying upon reparations from Germany and the 'fruits of victory' from the territories it now occupied in eastern Europe to finance the reconstruction of its economy. Concerned that the peoples of eastern and central Europe would show the Soviet people how poor their living standards were in comparison to the West, and fearful that the West would learn of the desperate state of the Soviet economy, the Red Army imposed strict control.[10] Far from being a springboard for a westward attack, these new territories required rigorous control in case they became rebellious. Indeed, as late as 1951 Harry Truman, US President 1945–53, thought 'Stalin was having [too much] trouble with the satellites to launch any military offensive'.[11]

A third argument is that in 1945 the United States possessed considerable military power. At the time it was estimated that the Red Army had some 175 divisions and another 75 east European divisions at its disposal; facing this force was less than 20 western divisions. However, Michael Evangelista has suggested that this is rather misleading. Of the 175 divisions, apparently only 60 were at full strength and only 30 were deployed in eastern Europe. He suggests that when troop figures are compared, the forces on both sides were roughly equal.[12] Indeed, Raymond Garthoff claims that in 1945 US armed forces outnumbered the Soviet Union by 12,123,000 to 11,365,000. By 1948 *both* sides had demobilised, with the Soviet forces numbering 2,874,000 to the United States 1,446,000.[13] It also needs to be taken into account that the Soviet Union had a woefully inadequate navy and long-range bomber fleet. In addition, they lacked an atomic capability – a circumstance that was not overcome until some years after 1954, when nuclear weapons first became available to the Soviet armed forces.[14]

The fourth argument lies with the Soviet premier. Joseph Stalin, 1927–53, was not an adventurer or a Marxist revolutionary, but a pragmatic Russian nationalist. He sought to transform the territories that the Red Army occupied, not risk the war gains of the Soviet Union by recklessly challenging the West. According to Robert Tucker, Stalin, while espousing the world communist revolution, was more concerned with maintaining control of an area already occupied: 'The operative aim, implicit in all that Stalin did, was to get control of territory and people and to absolutize that control by every available means, the principal one being police terror.'[15] The primacy of building socialism in one country was so profound that, according to Deutscher, 'no one contained communism more effectively ... than Stalin himself did'.[16] It is certainly true that Stalin did little to aid the Greek communists,[17] and he showed little enthusiasm for Mao and his Chinese communists.[18]

The proposition here is that, in the immediate post-war period, the USSR did not intend to attack the West. Any fear that the West may have had that the USSR was a threat to them, and they may have had very good reasons, were therefore illusory. Gar Alperovitz, in his classic revisionist work, writes:

> If the Russians were secretly harbouring plans for an ultimate takeover, they certainly were preparing trouble for themselves by sponsoring free politics, pulling out the Red Army (it is not particularly shrewd to have to reintroduce foreign troops), and ripping up the Red Army's main rail connections across Poland – as they did in the fall of 1945.[19]

The Grand Alliance's policies

With the arrival of the United States in the Second World War, President Franklin D. Roosevelt introduced a plan for peace that he hoped would avoid the errors of the interwar years: 'We have profited by our mistakes. This time we shall know how to make full use of victory. This time the achievements of our fighting force will not be thrown away by political cynicism and timidity and incompetence.'[20] Roosevelt sought a 'grand design' which would provide a long-lasting peaceful postwar era built upon the continuing collaboration of the Big Three after the war. The key goal of his grand design was that no Great Power should feel isolated and insecure. Instead they should form an association in which they all enjoyed security; the grand design was a mutual or common security policy. John Lewis Gaddis writes:

> FDR sought to ensure a stable postwar order by offering Moscow a prominent place in it; by making it, so to speak, a member of the club. The assumption here – and it is a critical one for understanding Roosevelt's policy – was that Soviet hostility stemmed from insecurity, but that the sources of that insecurity were external.[21]

Roosevelt therefore sought to reduce Soviet concerns by encouraging the socialist state to cooperate with its 'external' sources of insecurity – the western capitalist world. Roosevelt's awareness that Soviet insecurity might be the result of western actions signifies that the US President was sensitive to the security dilemma. By seeking to overcome these Soviet concerns via cooperation, Roosevelt's grand design may have avoided a security dilemma between the two superpowers. Gaddis confirms the importance of the USSR when he notes: 'Roosevelt's main emphasis was on trying to make the Grand Alliance survive Hitler's defeat by creating relationships of mutual trust among its leaders. The focus of his concerns ... was Stalin.'[22]

Roosevelt's grand design, based upon cooperation and mutual trust, was to be accomplished by the realisation of four objectives.[23] The first objective was to remove the regimes in the Axis powers, since these were considered incompatible with the conditions needed for long-lasting peace. Thus the unconditional surrender of the Axis powers was the first objective. The second and the third were closely linked; the requirements for long-lasting peace were political and economic. Hence Woods and Jones's comment that, 'assured of economic and strategic security, the Soviet Union could assume its place among the Great Powers'.[24] The political objective was that the peoples of the world should have the right to govern themselves, the right to self-determination: 'We believe that any nationality no matter how small, has the inherent right to its own nationhood.'[25] The economic objective was the reconstruction of the world economy. By encouraging world trade, it was hoped that the economies of the major powers would become interdependent and thus expand; this would also reduce the likelihood of war. The fourth objective was the establishment of an international organisation through which the wartime allies and China (the Big Four/Four Policemen) could preserve and maintain international peace and security. These objectives became the principles of the Atlantic Charter; if they had been successfully implemented, they might have created a peaceful world in which the major participants enjoyed mutual security.

If Roosevelt's grand design had been implemented, it might have nullified the dynamics that gave rise to the security dilemma. However, for Roosevelt to be successful in implementing his grand design, he needed the Big Three to share a common perception of what 'being secure' involved. Thus he did not ignore 'almost entirely the fundamental problem of *security*, the foundation on which peace has always rested' (emphasis in original), as Don Cook claims.[26] Rather, he sought to accommodate the divergent security interests of the two allies into his grand design.[27] Ultimately, it was the incompatibility of these security interests that would undermine his blueprint for world peace. The unilateral approaches to security pursued by the two European powers created concern in one another that their attempts to acquire security were being undermined. That is, instead of creating a greater feeling of security, these policies led both to consider the other as hostile; the polices were paradoxical, ultimately unsatisfactory and thus inappropriate.

The Yalta Conference in February 1945 highlights the difficulty that Roosevelt was to face in implementing a mutual security approach to the new era. Yalta was to be Roosevelt's last Grand Alliance conference. In his last public speech to Congress on 1 March 1945 Roosevelt said:

> Never before have the major allies been more closely united – not only in their war aims but also their peace aims. And they are determined to continue to be united with each other ... so that the ideal of lasting peace will become a reality.[28]

He went on to claim:

> The Crimea Conference ... spells – and it ought to spell – the end of the system of unilateral action, the exclusive alliances, the spheres of influence, the balance of power and all the other expedients which have been tried for centuries and have always failed.[29]

Harry Hopkins, Roosevelt's special assistant at Yalta, also considered the conference to be a success. His only concern was the survival of Stalin, whom he saw as vital to the success of Roosevelt's grand design. Hopkins commented:

> We really believed in our hearts that this was the dawn of the new day we had all been praying for and talking about for so many years. We were absolutely certain that we had won the first great victory of the peace – and, by 'we' I mean *all* of us, the whole civilised human race. The Russians had proved that they could be reasonable and far seeing and there wasn't any doubt in the mind of the President or any of us that we could live with them and get along with them peacefully for as far into the future as any of us could imagine. But I have to make an amendment to that – I think we all had in our minds the reservation that we could not foretell what the results would be if anything should happen to Stalin. We felt sure that we could count on him to be reasonable and sensible and understanding [emphasis in original].[30]

For the Americans, there had been a meeting of minds at Yalta; mutual security was possible.

For the Soviet Union, the post-war world was going to provide security, but not in the way that Roosevelt or Hopkins sought. Security for Stalin meant an extension of Soviet influence and control in central and eastern Europe. A key provision for the Soviet Union at Yalta was therefore the Polish issue: 'It was a question of strategic security not only because Poland was a bordering country but because throughout history Poland had been the corridor for attack on Russia.'[31] The Polish elections were therefore rigged to ensure a communist victory – an outcome orchestrated by the Soviet Union throughout central and eastern Europe. To Stalin, such actions were not a betrayal of agreements with his wartime allies, of which he was accused; they were a necessary requirement for Soviet security. In an interview with a *Pravda* correspondent in March 1946 Stalin stated:

> The following circumstances should not be forgotten. The Germans made their invasion of the USSR through Finland, Poland, Romania, Bulgaria and Hungary. The Germans were able to make their invasion through these countries because, at the time, governments hostile to the Soviet Union existed in these countries. As a result of the German invasion, the Soviet Union has lost irretrievably in the fighting against the Germans, and also through the German occupation and the

deportation of Soviet citizens to German servitude, a total of about seven million people [subsequently estimated at twenty million]. In other words the Soviet Union's loss of life has been several times greater than that of Britain and the USA put together. Possibly in some quarters an inclination is felt to forget about these colossal sacrifices of the Soviet people which secured the liberation of Europe from the Hitlerite yoke. But the Soviet Union cannot forget about them. And so what can there be surprising about the fact that the Soviet Union, anxious for its future safety, is trying to see to it that governments loyal in their attitude to the Soviet Union should exist in these countries? How can anyone who has not taken leave of his senses, describe these peaceful aspirations of the Soviet Union as expansionist tendencies on the part of our state.[32]

Apparently, after Yalta Britain took leave of its senses.

Prior to February 1945 the British were becoming concerned about the rise in Soviet power and about the weight of the communist state *vis-à-vis* Britain, France and Germany after the war. For the British, security meant balancing the power of the communist state and this could best be achieved by a revitalised France, a rehabilitating peace treaty with Germany, and keeping the Americans interested in European affairs. As Churchill commented to Eden prior to the Yalta Conference: 'we should not be left alone to share the cage with the bear'.[33] At Yalta the British had *realpolitik* on their minds.

The Big Three had seen Yalta as an opportunity to create a long-lasting peace; however, 'each had a different perception of how that peace could best be achieved'.[34] The British saw the balance of Soviet power as the key; the Soviet Union saw domination of eastern Europe as the key; and the Americans were wedded to the ideals of Roosevelt's grand design. Within a couple of years the western democracies and the Soviet Union viewed the actions of each other as incompatible with their own goals. It did not take long for this incompatibility to be regarded as an attempt to undermine security. Gaddis acknowledges this when he writes:

> Both Washington and Moscow wanted peace, but strong internal influences caused each to conceive of it in contradictory ways. These clashing perceptions of a common goal wrecked the Grand Alliance at the moment of victory, creating an ironic situation in which simultaneous searches for peace led to the Cold War.[35]

The emphasis on how both states sought peace, but their efforts 'ironically' had the opposite effect and led to a deteriorating relationship, supports the case that the security dilemma was in operation; the Cold War was a tragedy, as the states adopted understandable but paradoxical policies.

After Yalta, Roosevelt was unable to convince either Britain or the USSR that long-term security, through the implementation of his grand design, could only be achieved if they were all able to feel secure.[36] The reasons behind their reluctance to adopt a mutual approach to security had much to do with their history and decision-making apparatus, but an equally important factor was the lack of the mutual trust required by Roosevelt's grand design. The Grand Alliance's ability to avoid the security dilemma was further hampered by the fact that the Soviet Union and the western democracies had not enjoyed good relations prior to 1939; underlying their wartime cooperation was a degree of suspicion.

The Big Three's intentions

It is perhaps pertinent to note that the relationship amongst the members of the Grand Alliance was different to that of the humans and aliens noted in Chapter 1. With no knowledge of what either side (humans/aliens) wanted, Alexander Wendt suggested that their relationship did not begin as a security dilemma. Instead he argues that it depends upon the actions that each undertakes; it is from these actions that the humans and aliens infer the intent of one another. Wendt's claim is that the security dilemma is avoidable. By cooperating against a common foe, the Grand Alliance was not an obvious example of a security dilemma at the end of the Second World War. However, unlike Wendt's example, the Big Three did have knowledge of one another – knowledge that caused the western democracies and the Soviet Union to be suspicious of each other's intentions. Such a mind-set decreases accurate threat perception, since ambiguous incidents are interpreted as evidence of malign intent. Thus, although their relationship did not begin as a security dilemma, the chances of avoiding a security dilemma were further reduced by their perception of one another.

The attitude of the western democracies towards Stalinist Russia is encapsulated in both Churchill and Roosevelt's use of the Devil as a metaphor for their wartime ally. When Germany invaded the USSR, Churchill's private secretary, J. R. Colville, remarked on the irony of Churchill's favourable comments about communist Russia. In his famous retort, Churchill replied: 'If Hitler invaded Hell I would make at least a favourable reference to the Devil in the House of Commons.'[37] Less well known was Roosevelt's paraphrase of an old Balkan proverb to his friend Joseph Davies: 'I can't take communism nor can you, but to cross this bridge I would hold hands with the Devil.'[38] If the western democracies' opinion of their ally was understandable given Stalin's 'reign of terror', then the Soviet leader's concern about the western allies also appears understandable. After all, both had sent forces to support the anti-Bolshevik army (Whites) during the Russian Civil War and had ostracised the communist state from international relations (the USSR was barred from joining the League of Nations in 1919 and was not invited to join until 1934; it was excluded from the Washington Naval Conference and did not receive US recognition until 1933). Yet Roosevelt's grand design was reliant upon the cooperation and support of the Great Powers for its success. Given the poor relations before the war between the USA and the Soviet Union, it was going to be his ability to create mutual trust and understanding between them that would determine his success.

As the war neared its end, it was becoming obvious that the USA and the USSR would emerge as the two strongest nations. If a postwar peace was to be accomplished, it would rely upon cooperation between them. Roosevelt acknowledged this when he said: 'we either work with the other great Nations or we might some day have to fight them. And I am against that.'[39] He was keenly aware of the differences between the USA and USSR, but believed that Russia's hostility towards the West was due to a lack of knowledge:

> I think the Russians are perfectly friendly; they aren't trying to gobble up all the rest of Europe or the world. They didn't know us, that's the really fundamental difference. They are friendly people. They haven't got any crazy ideas of conquest ... and now that they have got to know us, they are much more willing to accept us.[40]

In order to bring this vision into reality, Roosevelt sought to manipulate the Soviet Union. He seemed to believe that he could 'baby Uncle Joe along' into his vision of a better world. However, Roosevelt's greatest obstacle to establishing cooperative relations with the USSR was beyond his control. This obstacle was Stalin's paranoiac attitude towards his wartime allies. According to Oleg Gordievsky, the People's Commissariat for Internal Affairs (NKVD) and State Security (NKGB) were able to provide Stalin with information about American and British interests at Yalta.[41] Yet his suspicious nature and preoccupation with conspiracy theories 'limited his ability to derive maximum benefit from the intelligence he received'.[42] In other words, despite having access to the thinking behind western motives, Stalin's paranoia prevented him from accurately determining their intent. Stalin was even convinced that the Vatican was orchestrating plots against him.[43] Stalin's paranoia became manifest just two weeks after the Yalta Conference.

In early March General Karl Wolff, a high-ranking SS officer, arrived in Berne to discuss surrender terms for the German troops in Italy. Although the Americans informed the Soviet Union of this meeting, they rejected the Soviet request to have officers present. The Americans regarded it as a purely military matter, and the presence of Soviet officers may have affected the Germans' willingness to surrender. The Soviet response was hostile, with their Foreign Affairs Commissar, Molotov, accusing the western allies of collusion with Nazi Germany.[44] When Roosevelt wrote directly to Stalin to ensure him that this was not the case,

Stalin responded by claiming his military colleagues knew 'the negotiations ... [had] ended in an agreement with the Germans, on the basis of which the German commander on the Western front – Marshal Kesselring, [had] agreed to open the front and permit the Anglo-American troops to advance to the East, and the Anglo-Americans [had] promised in return to ease for the Germans the peace terms'.[45]

The responses of Churchill and Roosevelt to this accusation reveal their different attitudes to pre-war security. Roosevelt's response to Stalin's accusation was indicative of his attempts to keep trying to cooperate with the Russians. He replied:

> it would be one of the great tragedies of history if at the very moment of the victory, now within our grasp, such distrust, such lack of faith should prejudice the entire undertaking ... Frankly I cannot avoid a feeling of bitter resentment toward your informers, whoever they are, for such vile misrepresentations of my actions or those of my subordinates.[46]

In other words, Stalin's distrust would lead to a tragic failure on the part of the wartime allies to achieve a durable peace. In Roosevelt's eyes, the spiral model or security struggle loomed large. Churchill's response, indicative of the British position, highlights not the tragedy of Stalin's distrust, but rather its ominous undertones. For Churchill, it was the deterrence model or the power struggle that loomed on the horizon. On 5 April 1945 he wrote to Roosevelt:

> We must always be anxious lest the brutality of the Russian messages does not foreshadow some deep change of policy for which they are preparing ... If they are ever convinced that we are afraid of them and can be bullied into submission, then indeed I should despair of our future relations with them and much else ... All this makes it the more important that we should join hands with the Russian armies as far to the east as possible and if circumstances allow, enter Berlin.[47]

As Soviet distrust bred British distrust, only Roosevelt held on to the hope of preventing a security dilemma.

When the Berne issue died down, Roosevelt wrote to Churchill and Stalin in order to defuse the recent exchanges between the three of them. To Churchill he wrote: 'I would minimise the general Soviet problem as much as possible because these problems, in one form or another, seem to arise every day and most of them straighten out.'[48] In correspondence with Stalin, on the day he died, he wrote: 'the Berne incident [which he described as minor despite Harriman's protests] ... now appears to have faded into the past without having accomplished any useful purpose. Mutual distrust of this character should not [be allowed to] happen in the future.'[49]

The Berne incident was just one example of Stalin's suspicions. With Berlin the next Soviet target, Stalin became even more anxious lest the democracies side with the Germans. In Austria during the second half of April the Soviet Union built defensive installations which included anti-aircraft facilities – despite the lack of any German air activity. They also used loudspeakers to announce to enemy forces that 'the greatest treason of world history is under way. If you don't want to fight on against us on the side of the capitalist powers, come over to us.'[50] According to Mastny, this 'imaginary danger continued to obsess Moscow despite compelling evidence of Western loyalty to the alliance'.[51]

The death of Roosevelt was a bitter blow in avoiding the security dilemma, but it would be erroneous to consider this one event as the crucial turning-point in Soviet–American relations. Roosevelt's policy of seeking trust and cooperation was floundering. The success of his grand design relied upon the willingness of the other two wartime allies to share his vision of security. Such cooperation was illusory, however, with both powers growing ever more suspicious of each other. It is only possible to speculate whether Roosevelt would have persevered with his grand design. According to John Lewis Gaddis, 'events such as Berne make it seem unlikely that Roosevelt, had he lived, would have continued it much longer'.[52] What is certain is that his successor altered the direction of US foreign policy dramatically. Not only did he overturn Roosevelt's policy, but he also overturned two of America's three traditional foreign policy pillars – isolationism and neutrality.

At the beginning of his presidency, Harry Truman had high hopes of continuing Roosevelt's grand design. He wrote in his diary: 'to have a reasonably lasting peace, the three great powers must be able to trust each other ... I want peace and I am willing to work hard for it'.[53] In an attempt to arrest the slide in relations between the Americans and the Russians, Truman sent Hopkins to Moscow in late May. The choice of Hopkins was a clear sign that Truman sought a continuation of Roosevelt's desire to foster peace through cooperation. The main issue during the Hopkins–Stalin meeting was Poland. Hopkins stated that the Americans 'would desire a Poland friendly to the Soviet Union and in fact desired to see friendly countries all along the Soviet borders'.[54] What the Americans were concerned about was the manner in which the Soviet Union was doing this. In Potsdam, the following month, Truman reminded Stalin that six million Poles lived in the United States. A free election reported by a free press would ensure that the American government could unequivocally recognise the new Polish government. Stalin, however, 'could not grasp that [the American and, indeed, British] objections ... were based on a genuine commitment to human rights, he inevitably sought some more sinister explanation'[55] – a point made to Truman by Harriman on 8 June:

I am afraid Stalin does not and never will fully understand our interest in a free Poland as a matter of principle. He is a realist in all his actions, and it is hard for him to appreciate our faith in abstract principles. It is difficult for him to understand why we should want to interfere with Soviet policy in a country like Poland, which he considers so important to Russia's security, unless we have some ulterior motive.[56]

This is a classic exposition of how suspicion leads to the creation of the security dilemma. Even though Stalin may not have been able to detect any tangible, hostile actions by Truman, his mistrust of the USA led him to suspect them. The presence of suspicion in the Grand Alliance ensured that accurate threat assessment was problematic. The suspicion with which the two European powers regarded each other ensured mutual mistrust and led to the assumption of malign intent.[57] In circumstances where neither state has malign intent, but they perceive each other as harbouring hostile intentions, the security dilemma will be in operation.

By the end of the Second World War the three characteristics of the security dilemma were in place. It has been suggested that while the USSR acted in a repressive and authoritarian manner in those countries that the Red Army liberated, it was primarily concerned with safeguarding its security. It did not harbour aggressive expansionist intentions towards the West immediately after the war. Second, with the exception of Roosevelt, the other two alliance members conceived of security as achievable via unilateral means. Consequently, they perceived their security as incompatible. Finally, the suspicious attitude of the leaders, most notably Stalin, ensured that accurate threat perception was difficult, thus guaranteeing a misperception of malign intent. How the security dilemma came into operation is the concern of the second part of this chapter.

The End of the Grand Alliance and the Start of the Cold War

In Chapter 1 it was shown that when a state seeks to achieve security via unilateral means, it can fall victim to the security dilemma. It was suggested that a state's action might be perceived by another as indicating hostile intent. In order to safeguard its own sovereignty, the action is reciprocated, inadvertently creating the same concerns in the first state. States perceive malign intent on the part of others and thus embark upon paradoxical policies which fuel their insecurity. This final section will examine the abandonment of Roosevelt's grand design by the United States, and the prevailing belief that a unilateral, not a mutual, approach to security best served their interests.

Although Truman had been Roosevelt's Vice-President, he was largely ill-informed of the direction in which Roosevelt was taking US foreign

policy.[58] He was therefore reliant upon members of Roosevelt's administration for advice and knowledge on how to deal with the Soviet Union.
The advisers that Truman inherited, however, were split on the question
of the danger posed by the Soviet Union and the best means of dealing
with that danger. Roosevelt's decision-making flourished in receiving conflictual advice, but Truman's floundered. Rather than revealing his own
ignorance of international affairs, Truman tended to agree with whomever
he was talking to and rarely thought issues through. According to Leffler,
'Almost everyone commented on his snap judgements. He conveyed a
sense of authority, but at the expense of thoughtful and consistent policy.' [59]
Averill Harriman was one of the presidential advisers who gained much
influence under Truman.[60] Harriman flew to Washington soon after
Roosevelt's death and warned Truman that 'our generosity and desire to
cooperate was being misinterpreted in Moscow' as a sign of weakness.[61]
According to Harriman, the United States was faced with a 'barbarian
invasion of Europe' and would need to adopt a much tougher stand with
Stalin. Truman agreed that a tougher stand was needed and thought that
'on important matters ... we should be able to get 85%' of what the USA
proposed.[62] With less willingness to make concessions, the two conferences
involving Foreign Ministers in London and Moscow in 1945 were to prove
unsuccessful. After the Moscow Conference, Truman wrote:

> Unless Russia is faced with an iron fist and strong language, another
> war is in the making. Only one language do they understand – 'how
> many divisions have you?' The United States should no longer 'play
> compromise'. And he concluded, 'I am tired of babying the Soviets'.[63]

This language was echoed by the US Republican Party: 'The wartime
policy of conceding whatever was necessary to reach agreement with the
Russians was no longer politically feasible.' [64]

Within the space of four weeks, between 9 February and 5 March 1946,
two speeches and one telegram were to mark the end of Roosevelt's grand
design. These three declarations can be said to represent the start of the
security dilemma which was to exist between East and West until the late
1980s. After the third declaration, American foreign policy was to move
away from conciliation to tenacious negotiation designed to secure only
US interests.

On 22 February, in response to a request from the State Department,
the US administration received George Kennan's famous 'long telegram'.
For Kennan, who had been at odds with US policy over cooperation with
the Soviet Union, here was an opportunity to give his own explanation
of Soviet behaviour. He had already been doing this for the past eighteen
months, but now 'they had asked for it ... [and] by God they would have
it'.[65] He presented a picture of continual conflict between the capitalist
and socialist camps. He wrote:

> [the] USSR still lives in antagonistic 'capitalist encirclement' with which in the long run there can be no permanent peaceful coexistence ... Soviet efforts ... must be directed toward deepening and exploiting of differences and conflicts between capitalist powers.[66]

The motives behind this aggressive Soviet attitude lay not in conditions outside the Soviet Union, but conditions within. According to Kennan, 'at [the] bottom of [the] Kremlin's neurotic view of world affairs is a traditional and instinctive Russian sense of insecurity'. He posited a Russian history where contact with western ideas was seen as threatening and destabilising because it could have revealed to the Russian populace the inadequacy of their own political system. Security was to be achieved not by seeking accommodation with others, but by seeking to refute their values; security was about struggle, not compromises.

Soviet policy was to be carried out on an 'official' and 'unofficial level'. Officially, this was to be achieved by an increase of Soviet power and influence through the development of armed forces, to extend interests to neighbouring countries, participate in international organisations for Soviet gain, and spread contacts to colonial peoples. Unofficially, Soviet power would increase by undermining the power of the western states and removing from office those governments that stood in the way of the Soviet Union. He summed up by claiming:

> we have here a political force committed fanatically to the belief that with [the] US there can be no permanent *modus vivendi*, that it is desirable and necessary that the internal harmony of our society be disrupted, our traditional way of life be destroyed, the international authority of our state be broken, if Soviet power is to be secure.[67]

From the security dilemma perspective, two crucial dynamics emanated from this telegram. The first was Kennan's startling revelation that Soviet foreign policy was formulated in response to conditions within the USSR, as opposed to events in the outside world. If this was true, then – no matter how well-intentioned – US foreign policy would not diminish Soviet hostility. The belief that states are hostile because of what they are (capitalist imperialists) as opposed to what they do can only fuel and exacerbate the security dilemma. It mattered little how the USA acted, if the Soviet Union viewed them as a threatening capitalist state that would inevitably cause war. Mitigation would only be possible if the Soviet Union altered its perception of international relations as a story of continual conflict between capitalism and communism.

The second dynamic was the enemy image that the telegram confirmed in the US administration. Stalin made his first postwar speech on 9 February, prior to Kennan's telegram.[68] He proclaimed that the Second World War had resulted from the uneven development of capitalist economies. 'As a result [of this uneven development] the capitalist world [had] split into two hostile camps at war.' The implication of this was that war was inevitable under capitalism, and not just between capitalist states. As in 1941, these capitalist wars could involve the USSR; as long as capitalist states existed, no peaceful international order was possible. In order to protect the Soviet Union, Stalin called for three five-year plans that would emphasise the development of heavy industry and rearmament.

The effect of Kennan's long telegram was to confirm the ominous interpretations of Stalin's speech. According to Gaddis, 'Kennan's telegram of the 22nd provided precisely the intellectual justification needed for [a] reorientation of policy.'[69] Such ominous interpretations included those of Elbridge Durbrow, Chief of the Division of Eastern European Affairs:

> It is felt that in view of the clear indication of the new Soviet line we should be most diligent to counteract Soviet propaganda and political moves in which all probability will be directed primarily at dividing the British and ourselves in order to give the Soviets a freer hand to attain their own aims.[70]

William Douglas, the Supreme Court Justice, simply thought of Stalin's speech as 'the Declaration of World War III',[71] while for James Forrestal, the Navy Secretary, it confirmed his view that democracy and communism could not coexist.[72] These interpretations of the speech were to prevail despite the existence of other less threatening explanations. According to *Time* magazine:

> Stalin's speech contained no threats. It was dry in tone, defensive in content. But its truculent exaggeration of the danger of attack from the capitalist world was the most warlike pronouncement uttered by any top ranking statesman since V-J Day.[73]

The magazine went on to suggest the reason for the speech:

> Stalin may have had purely Russian reasons for pointing outward toward imagined enemies. Restless Russians have been asking for more food, clothes and 'luxuries'. Although Stalin in his speech announced that food rationing would soon end, the foreign menace is still his handiest excuse for low living standards.

In other words – and it is important to note that the speech was given on the eve of the Soviet elections – there were domestic reasons why it was couched in such terms. This is also supported by *The Times*, which wrote: 'this was a domestic occasion, and, apart from the legitimate pride in the victory just achieved and in the new prestige won by the Soviet Union throughout the world, little or nothing was said that touched on international affairs'.[74] This lack of concern was shared by Henry Wallace, Secretary of Commerce, who called 'Stalin's speech a friendly challenge to prove that we can make our American system work without crises or depressions'.[75] Yet the image of the Soviet Union ensured that a more sinister interpretation of Stalin's speech was adopted. As Eric Sevareid said: 'If you can brush aside Stalin's speech of February 9, you are a braver man than I am.'[76] Since the security dilemma thrives on misperception and the difficulty of accurate threat perception, enemy imaging is a potent dynamic.

The third declaration to mark the end of Roosevelt's grand design was Churchill's Fulton speech, because it appeared to capture the changing mood in Truman's administration. This speech, tacitly endorsed by Truman, who introduced Churchill and had read the speech prior to its delivery, was the first public move away from the grand design by the US administration. The speech was to reiterate the dangers of Soviet communism and call for closer peacetime collaboration between the two countries. It was in this speech that Churchill introduced the famous 'iron curtain' metaphor, behind which the people were subject 'not only to Soviet influence but to [an] ... increasing measure of control from Moscow'.[77] He 'did not believe that Soviet Russia desired war. What they desired [was] the fruits of war and the indefinite expansion of their power and doctrines.' He noted that no one could know 'the limits, if any, to their expansive and proselytising tendencies ... [but] prevention is better than cure'. This prevention was to be a 'fraternal association of the English-speaking peoples'.

The Soviet reaction to Churchill's speech was reminiscent of the western reaction to Stalin's speech. That is, they considered it to signify western aggression. General Bedell Smith, the new United States Ambassador, recalled Stalin informing him that 'this speech ... was an unfriendly act; it was an unwarranted attack upon the USSR'. In his memoirs, Khrushchev wrote:

> [Churchill's] famous speech urging the imperialist forces of the world to mobilize against the Soviet Union served as a signal for the start of the Cold War ... Our relations with England, France, the USA, and other countries who had cooperated with us in crushing Hitlerite Germany were, for all intents and purposes, ruined.

From the Soviet perspective, it appeared that Churchill was casting the Soviet Union as the enemy against whom the western powers needed to combine their efforts. Their actions were being interpreted as indicative of malign intent and being used to justify the creation of an association directed against them. A division was being drawn in which the USSR was the enemy.[78]

The US administration's tacit support for the Fulton speech reveals the final break from Roosevelt's grand design. Churchill was clearly seeking greater cooperation between the United States and Great Britain because of concern about Soviet intentions. In other words, Britain was seeking to gain security by cooperating with America in order to balance Soviet power; security was to be achieved through the acquisition of power. The tacit support of the Truman administration signified that 'ganging up' was no longer an issue for the Americans; while they would continue to negotiate with the Soviet Union, the primary objective was the attainment of US interests, not maintaining collaboration with the USSR. In other words, US security interests could be achieved without cooperation with the Soviet Union. This belief that security could be attained unilaterally, and the fact that the relationship was perceived as an example of a deterrence model or power struggle, whereas it was actually a spiral model or security struggle, exacerbated the security dilemma.

Further evidence that the USA was beginning to view its relationship with the USSR as a power struggle is provided by the Clifford Report of September 1946.[79] The report claimed: 'the aim of current Soviet policy is to prepare for the ultimate conflict by increasing ... the relative power of the Soviet Union at the expense of her potential enemies'.[80] Clifford wrote that as long as this was the intention of the Soviet Union, 'it is highly dangerous to conclude that hope of international peace lies only in "accord", "mutual understanding", or "solidarity" with the Soviet Union'.[81] Although he believed that the ultimate objective of US policy should be to persuade the Soviet Union that war was not inevitable between them, this could only be done from a position of strength:

> The language of military power is the only language which disciples of power politics understand. The United States must use that language in order that Soviet leaders will realise that our government is determined to uphold the interests of its citizens and the rights of small nations. Compromise and concessions are considered, by the Soviets, to be evidence of weakness and they are encouraged by our 'retreats' to make new and greater demands.
>
> The main deterrent to Soviet attack on the United States, or to attack on areas of the world which are vital to our security, will be the military power of this country. It must be made apparent to the Soviet Government that our strength will be sufficient to repel any attack and sufficient to defeat the USSR decisively if a war should start. The prospect of defeat is the only sure means of deterring the Soviet Union.[82]

The rejection of compromises and concessions and their replacement with strength and deterrence reveal the report's emphasis on resolve. This is the primary requirement in a power struggle or deterrence model.

The Clifford Report's emphasis on strength, both militarily and diplomatically, set US foreign policy on a course that would confirm the Soviet preconception of collusion amongst the western powers. Indeed, the report noted that if cooperation with the Soviet Union was not possible, 'we should be prepared to join with the British and other Western countries in an attempt to build up a world of our own ... [and] recognise the Soviet orbit ... [as one] with which we cannot pursue common aims'.[83] The idea of mutual security was clearly extinct and, with its passing, the security dilemma loomed large.

Conclusion

The purpose of this chapter is to provide evidence of the security dilemma in the period immediately after the Second World War. It is noted that Soviet intentions during this period are something of an unknown and, therefore, it is difficult to determine whether they harboured hostile designs toward the West. Despite this, four broad arguments are advanced to imply that the USSR was primarily concerned with safeguarding its own security and that any fear the West might have had about the USSR was based upon an illusory incompatibility. These four reasons are: the USSR was exhausted after the Second World War; the USSR was concentrating on reconstructing its economy from the 'fruits of victory' in eastern Europe; the USSR was militarily inferior to the western powers; the Soviet leader was a pragmatic nationalist rather than a Marxist adventurist. They all illustrate the benign intent that is characteristic of the security dilemma. Another characteristic of the security dilemma is the pursuit of policies that, while perceived as necessary, are actually self-defeating because they fuel insecurity. It is suggested that the pursuit of unilateral policies by the European states – and, after the demise of Roosevelt's grand design, by the United States also – can be regarded in this light.[84] The final characteristic of the security dilemma is the uncertainty that states have about the intent of one another – and, as a result, the likelihood of the perception of malign intent. The existence of suspicion in the Grand Alliance is noted and it is argued that this made accurate threat perception even harder and the perception of malign intent more likely. It is therefore suggested that the three characteristics of the security dilemma were in existence during this period.

The adoption of a unilateral approach by the USA highlights the dynamics of the security dilemma. It is noted that enemy imaging and the apparent inability of statesmen to see their own actions as threatening are particularly important, since they appear to confirm the suspicions of malign intent. While the security dilemma would therefore appear to have been in operation during this time, it would be incorrect to consider it as the sole cause of the Cold War. It is more accurate to suggest that it played a contributing role. However, some authors believe the security dilemma to have been of utmost importance, as the following statements by Arthur Schlesinger and Robert Jervis illustrate. Schlesinger claims:

The Cold War ... was the product not of a decision but of a dilemma. Each side felt compelled to adopt policies which the other could not but regard as a threat to the principles of the peace. Each then felt compelled to undertake defensive measures. Thus the Russians saw no choice but to consolidate their security in Eastern Europe. The Americans, regarding Eastern Europe as the first step toward Western Europe, responded by asserting their interest in the zone the Russians deemed vital to their security. The Russians concluded that the West was resuming its old course of capitalist encirclement; that it was purposefully laying the foundation for anti-Soviet regimes in the area defined by the blood of centuries as crucial to Russian survival. Each side believed with passion that future international stability depended on the success of its own conception of world order. Each side, in pursuing its own clearly indicated and deeply cherished principles, was only confirming the fear of the other that it was bent on aggression.[85]

Robert Jervis states: 'The Cold War may ... have been an unavoidable tragedy rather than the result of an evil Soviet Union, as the orthodox school has it, or an evil United States, as most revisionists argue.'[86] It is, of course, contentious to conclude that the security dilemma had a role in the origins of the Cold War and, for as long as archival material from the former Soviet Union remains unavailable, it is likely to remain so. It is clear, however, that there is evidence of some weight to suggest that its detrimental effects were at play in the immediate postwar period.

Notes

1. There is a danger in assuming that one time period in the Cold War is a microcosm of the whole Cold War. Lynn Eden is probably right to claim that one 'cannot assume that US perceptions in one time period will be similar to those in' another. This, though, does not refute the claim that the period just after the Second World War established a relationship that would last until the late 1980s. Once western leaders perceived a threatening USSR, this image was to remain. John Lewis Gaddis claims: 'Trapped in their own rhetoric, leaders of the United States found it difficult to respond to the conciliatory gestures which emanated from the Kremlin following Stalin's death and, through their inflexibility, may well have contributed to the perception of the Cold War.' Robert Jervis also acknowledges this rigid mind-set: 'By logic that is now depressingly familiar, decision makers believed that a defeat in any area, no matter of how little intrinsic significance, would embolden adversaries and demoralize allies. Reputation and resolve were believed to be crucial.' See Lynn Eden, 'The End of US Cold War History', *International Security*, 18/1 (1993), p. 174; John Lewis Gaddis, *The United States and the Origins of the Cold War 1941–1947* (New York: 1972), p. 352; Robert Jervis, 'The End of the Cold War on the Cold War?', *Diplomatic History*, 17/4 (1993), p. 653.
2. Kathryn Weathersby of Florida State University is using Soviet declassified documents in her work on the Korean War. For evidence that, even with declassified documents, conclusions can be controversial, see the exchange between Weathersby and Adam

Ulam in *Cold War International History Project Bulletin*, Woodrow Wilson International Center for Scholars, Issue 4 (Fall 1994), p. 21.

3. William Burr has written: 'despite the significant openings in the files of the Foreign Ministry and the Central Committee of the Communist Party of the Soviet Union, the culture of secrecy continues to limit access to Soviet military records ... Thus, historians cannot investigate the way that the Soviet military leadership saw the world at the end of World War II': William Burr, 'Soviet Cold War Military Strategy: using declassified history', ibid., p. 9.

4. It is assumed that the US and west European intentions towards the USSR were benign, though of course the USSR would not neccessarily perceive this to be true.

5. For a succinct explanation of the differences between these Cold War historiographies, see Lynn Eden, 'The End', pp. 184–96. For a possible synthesis of the three positions, see Howard Jones and Randall B. Woods, 'The Origins of the Cold War: a symposium', *Diplomatic History*, 17/2 (1993), pp. 251–76.

6. Jones and Woods, 'The Origins of the Cold War', p. 253.

7. For figures, see George Kennan, *Memoirs 1925–1950* (London: 1967), p. 506; Vera Micheles Dean, *The United States and Russia* (London: 1947), p. 96; Isaac Deutscher, *Ironies of History* (London: 1966), pp. 149–50; Daniel Yergin, *Shattered Peace: the origins of the Cold War and the national security state* (London: 1978), p. 64; Adam Ulam, *Expansion and Coexistence: the history of Soviet foreign policy, 1917–67* (London: 1968), pp. 400–1.

8. Michael Cox, 'Western Intelligence, the Soviet Threat and NSC–68: a reply to Beatrice Heuser', *Review of International Studies*, 18 (1992), p. 76.

9. Deutscher, *Ironies of History*, pp. 150–1.

10. For details of the need to maintain control for fear of information reaching either the West or the Soviet people, see Ulam, *Expansion*, pp. 401–3.

11. Arthur Krock, *Memoirs* (New York: 1968), p. 261.

12. Michael Evangelista, 'Stalin's Postwar Army Reappraised', *International Security*, 7/3 (1982/3), pp. 114–19.

13. Soviet figures from Khrushchev quoted from Raymond Garthoff, *Deterrence and the Revolution in Soviet Military Doctrine* (Washington: 1990), p. 17 n11.

14. Ibid., p. 16.

15. Robert C. Tucker, *The Soviet Political Mind: studies in Stalinism and post-Stalin change* (London: 1972), p. 229.

16. Deutscher, *Ironies of History*, p. 154.

17. 'Stalin had been utterly indifferent to the fate of the Greek people, and repeatedly assured the English that he regarded the nation as within their sphere of interest and vital to their security ... [Indeed] neither British nor American experts found any evidence of Soviet material aid to the KKE [Greek Communists]:' Gabriel Kolko, *The Politics of War: allied diplomacy and the world crisis of 1943–1945* (London: 1969), p. 432.

18. For evidence suggesting a Soviet attack on Yugoslavia and the possibility that Stalin would launch a preventive war against the western states, see Beatrice Heuser, 'NSC 68 and the Soviet Threat', *Review of International Studies*, 17/1 (1991), pp. 33–40.

19. Gar Alperovitz, *Atomic Diplomacy: Hiroshima and Potsdam: the use of the atomic bomb and the American confrontation with Soviet power* (New York: 1985), p. 336.

20. 'The President Addresses the International Student Assembly, 3 September 1942', in Samuel I. Rosenman (ed.), *The Public Papers and Addresses of Franklin D. Roosevelt* (Pennsylvania: 1950), p. 353.

21. John Lewis Gaddis, *Strategies of Containment: a critical appraisal of postwar American national security policy* (New York: 1982), p. 9.

22. Ibid., p. 11.

23. For more details on these objectives, see Gaddis, *Origins of the Cold War*, ch. 1. See also Yergin, *Shattered Peace*, ch. 2.

24. Randall B. Woods and Howard Jones, *Dawning of the Cold War* (Chicago: 1994), p. 20.

25. 'Address at Annual Dinner of White House Correspondents' Association, 15 March 1941', in Rosenman, *Public Papers*, p. 69.
26. Don Cook, *Forging the Alliance* (London: 1989), p. 3.
27. Roosevelt's approach to the postwar period was a curious mixture of Wilsonian idealism and pragmatic realism. For example, while he sought a collective security arrangement in which the 'Four Policemen' would band together to deter aggression, he was not averse to using economic and political pressures to dismantle the British Empire and influence Soviet behaviour. Yergin has referred to him as a 'renegade Wilsonian' and Gaddis writes that he was seeking 'Wilson's goals by un-Wilsonian means': Yergin, *Shattered Peace*, pp. 10, 44; Gaddis, *Strategies of Containment*, p. 10.
28. Address by the President of the United States before a Joint Session of the Senate and the House of Representatives on the subject of the Yalta Conference. *Congressional Record*, 79th Congress 1st Session, vol. 91, part 2, p. 1619.
29. Ibid., p. 1622. This is not intended to imply that Roosevelt believed such 'expedients' were no longer relevant. Two days after his speech he talked of the territory liberated by the Soviet Union becoming its sphere of influence as opposed to its sphere of control, because of the collaborative international framework. See Yergin, *Shattered Peace*, p. 66.
30. Robert Sherwood, *Roosevelt and Hopkins: an intimate history* (New York: 1948), p. 870.
31. Stalin during the third plenary meeting at the Yalta Conference, 6 February 1945: *Foreign Relations of the United States (FRUS) – The Conferences at Malta and Yalta 1945*, p. 669. Hereafter referred to as *FRUS, Malta and Yalta*.
32. L. Churchward, *Contemporary Soviet Government* (London: 1975), pp. 253–4.
33. Cook, *Forging the Alliance*, p. 7.
34. Warren F. Kimball, *Churchill and Roosevelt*, III (New Jersey: 1984), p. 528.
35. Gaddis, *Origins of the Cold War*, p. 3.
36. While both Britain and the Soviet Union agreed on the need to defeat the Axis powers and, with varying degrees of commitment, the establishment of international organisations, neither fully supported self-determination or multilateral trading agreements. The British Empire was exempted from the Atlantic Charter's provisions and the Soviet Union added the reservation that the way in which the principles were adhered to was the concern of each individual country. Arthur Schlesinger writes: 'Moscow very probably, and not unnaturally, perceived the emphasis on self-determination as a systematic and deliberate pressure on Russia's Western frontiers': Arthur Schlesinger, Jr., 'Origins of the Cold War', *Foreign Affairs*, 46/1 (1967), p. 41. See also Gaddis, *Origins of the Cold War*, pp. 2–3.
37. Robert Rhodes James, *Winston S. Churchill, his Complete Speeches 1897–1963* (New York: 1974), vol. VI, p. 6428.
38. The old Balkan proverb is: 'My children, it is permitted you in time of grave danger to walk with the devil until you have crossed the bridge': see Gaddis, *Origins of the Cold War*, p. 3.
39. 'Radio Address at Dinner of Foreign Policy Association, 21 October 1944', in Rosenman, *Public Papers*, p. 352.
40. 'Informal, Extemporaneous Remarks to Advertising War Council Conference, 8 March 1944', ibid., p. 99.
41. In addition to listening devices planted in the delegates' residencies, two prominent members of the American team, Alger Hiss and Harry Hopkins, were NKVD and NKGB contacts. To what extent Hiss and Hopkins were Soviet spies is controversial, but they indubitably had access to US documents and, in Hopkins's case, direct access to the President. For details of NKVD and NKGB activity during the Yalta Conference, see Christopher Andrew and Oleg Gordievsky, *KGB: the inside story of its foreign operations from Lenin to Gorbachev* (London: 1991), pp. 343–7; for Hiss, see Allen Weinstein, *Perjury: the Hiss–Chambers case* (London: 1978), p. 354; for the closeness of Hopkins

and Roosevelt, see Dwight William Tuttle, *Harry Hopkins and Anglo–American–Soviet Relations 1941–1945* (New York: 1983), pp. 241–2.

42. Andrew and Gordievsky, *KGB*, p. 347.

43. 'In July 1952 Stalin assured the Italian socialist, Pietro Nenni, that the American Cardinal Spellman had been at the Yalta conference in disguise: it was he, Stalin said, who had hardened his friend Roosevelt against him': ibid., p. 348.

44. For the actual exchange between Molotov and the US Ambassador to the USSR, see Chapter 1. More details can be found in *FRUS – European Advisory Commission; Austria; Germany*, vol. III, 1945, pp. 736, 737. Hereafter referred to as *FRUS*, vol. III, 1945.

45. Ibid., p. 742.

46. Ibid., p. 746.

47. Ibid., pp. 746–7.

48. Kimball, *Churchill and Roosevelt*, p. 630.

49. *FRUS*, vol. III, 1945, p. 756.

50. Vojtech Mastny, *Russia's Road to the Cold War: diplomacy, warfare and the politics of Communism* (New York: 1979), p. 270.

51. Ibid., p. 272.

52. Gaddis, *Origins of the Cold War*, p. 94.

53. William Hillman, *Mr President* (London: 1952), p. 99.

54. Sherwood, *Roosevelt and Hopkins*, p. 890.

55. Andrew and Gordievsky, *KGB*, p. 347.

56. *FRUS – Conference of Berlin (Potsdam)*, vol. I, 1945, p. 61.

57. While Roosevelt had been President, the American attitude was to try and overcome the suspicion that was prevalent in the Soviet Union via conciliatory methods. However, by late 1944 a number of appointments to the US State Department suggested that US foreign policy was going to take a tougher stand with the Soviet Union; for example, the appointments of Dean Acheson to Congressional Relations and Charles E. Bohlen as White House liaison officer. Together with Harriman and Kennan in Moscow, 'the prejudices and perceptions shared by this group ... meant a harder line toward the Soviet Union, a softer one toward Britain, and confrontation with those who advocated appeasing Moscow': Woods and Jones, *Dawning*, p. 25. For more details, see Yergin, *Shattered Peace*, ch. 1; Schlesinger, 'Origins of the Cold War', pp. 22–52.

58. Melvyn Leffler has written: 'There was little affinity between the two men, and Roosevelt never confided in him. When the President died, Truman knew little about his diplomacy': Melvyn P. Leffler, *A Preponderance of Power: national security, the Truman administration, and the Cold War* (Stanford: 1992), p. 26.

59. Ibid., p. 30.

60. Gaddis, Leffler and Yergin consider Harriman to be very influential: Gaddis, *Origins of the Cold War*, p. 201; Leffler, *Preponderance of Power*, pp. 28, 32; Yergin, *Shattered Peace*, p. 74.

61. Memorandum of conversation by Charles Bohlen, *FRUS – Europe*, vol. V, 1945, pp. 231–4.

62. Woods and Jones comment: 'Grew, Bohlen, and the new regime in the State department, as well as Harriman, Deane, and Forrestal had decided, like Churchill, not only that the Soviet Union would prove uncooperative in the postwar period but also that it was bent on domination of the European continent. Responding to their urgings Truman during the first weeks of his presidency took a position so unyielding that it severely strained the Grand Alliance': Woods and Jones, *Dawning*, p. 36. By mid-May Truman was becoming more cautious as he accepted advice from those who had a more sympathetic view of Soviet foreign policy – most notably, Joseph Davies and Henry Stimson, the Secretary of War. However, Truman tended to favour the advice of those who urged a tougher stand, because it 'coincided with his instincts': Leffler, *Preponderance of Power*, p. 32.

63. Truman's letter to James Brynes, US Secretary of State 1945–7, quoted from Fraser Harbutt, *The Iron Curtain* (New York: 1986), p. 157. For details concerning the authenticity of Truman's letter, which was not actually sent, see Robert Messer, *The End of an Alliance: James F. Brynes, Roosevelt, Truman, and the origins of the Cold War* (Chapel Hill: 1982), pp. 157–66.

64. Gaddis, *Origins of the Cold War*, pp. 289–90.

65. Kennan, *Memoirs*, p. 293.

66. The Long Telegram, *FRUS – Eastern Europe*, vol. VI, 1946, pp. 697–8.

67. Ibid., p. 706.

68. For Stalin's speech, see 'Stalin takes Stock', *The Times*, 11 February 1946, p. 3.

69. Gaddis, *Origins of the Cold War*, p. 304.

70. *FRUS – Eastern Europe; The Soviet Union*, vol. VI, 1946, p. 695n. Hereafter referred to as *FRUS*, vol. VI, 1946.

71. James Gormby, *From Potsdam to the Cold War* (Delaware: 1990), p. 113.

72. Walter Mills (ed.), *The Forrestal Diaries: the inner history of the Cold War* (London: 1952), p 141.

73. *Time* (18 February 1946), vol. XLVII, No. 7, pp. 21–2.

74. *The Times* (editorial), 12 February 1946, p. 5.

75. 'Wallace lambasts "Soviet War" talkers', *New York Times*, 20 February 1946, p. 13.

76. Gaddis, *Origins of the Cold War*, p. 300.

77. Churchill's Fulton speech, 5 March 1946, quoted from Harbutt, *Iron Curtain*, pp. 186–7.

78. For more on this, see Harbutt, *Iron Curtain*, p. 196 and, for Smith's comment, p. 211. For Khrushchev, see Strobe Talbott, *Khrushchev Remembers: the last testament*, vol. 2 (London: 1974), p. 355.

79. The Clifford Report is quoted in full in Krock, *Memoirs*, Appendix A.

80. Ibid., p. 422.

81. Ibid., p. 476.

82. Ibid., p. 477.

83. Ibid., p. 476.

84. Jonathan Haslam writes: 'Soviet planning was predicated on a unilateral – rather than a multilateral – solution to the postwar security dilemma': Jonathan Haslam, 'Soviet Policy Toward Western Europe since World War II', in George W. Breslauer and Philip E. Tetlock, *Learning in US and Soviet Foreign Policy* (Boulder: 1991), p. 472.

85. Schlesinger, 'Origins of the Cold War', p. 45.

86. Jervis, 'End of the Cold War', p. 659.

Chapter Five

Intensification

The previous chapter has shown how the inferences made by the members of the Grand Alliance led the western democracies and the USSR to perceive a hostile intent on the part of one another. This misperception was based on the foreign policy actions that the Big Three (though increasingly just the USA and USSR) undertook. It was uncertainty regarding the intent behind each other's actions that led them to perceive hostility, even though – arguably – none existed. This in turn led to policies that were perceived as detrimental to each other's security and, thus, increased tension. The security dilemma was much in evidence. This chapter focuses on another period of the Cold War and is concerned with how the military postures adopted by the western powers, especially the USA, and the USSR exacerbated the security dilemma. As with the previous chapter, evidence of the security dilemma can be ascertained from the existence of three characteristics: benign intent, uncertainty of intent, paradoxical policies.

This chapter highlights the importance of uncertainty in fuelling the security dilemma by linking this characteristic to the other two. Thus, western uncertainty of Soviet intent is seen not only to confirm the USSR as harbouring aggressive designs, but also to influence the adoption of policies that heighten tension and increase mutual insecurity. The first part of the chapter is concerned with noting that there are good reasons for believing that the USSR did not harbour aggressive intent. However, there was such ambiguity in Soviet statements/military postures that the West could not be certain of this; indeed, a more ominous interpretation was given to these pronouncements. The second part is concerned with highlighting how the West's uncertainty led them to perceive malign intent behind Soviet action and how this in turn led the USSR to fear that the West intended them harm. Since the chapter is concerned with military postures, the adoption of strategies that manifest an offensive potential and are perceived to undermine mutual assured destruction (MAD) are considered to exacerbate the security dilemma. This chapter therefore relates to the offence/defence variable examined in Chapter 3.

Soviet Military Doctrine:[1] Uncertainty and Benign Intent

Soviet war-thinking displayed two types of duality that resulted in much ambiguity for the western powers. The first involved what the Soviet Union said about the use of nuclear weapons, while the second concerned the deployment of their military forces. It was this ambiguity or uncertainty that led the Western Alliance to perceive a Soviet attempt to gain superiority and hence undermine MAD. The only reason that the Soviet Union could have for undermining MAD, it was thought, was that they were unhappy with the existing status quo; Soviet military doctrine appeared to indicate a revisionist power that harboured malign intent.[2]

Soviet pronouncements on nuclear war

After the death of Stalin in 1953, the party leadership emphasised the unwinnable nature of nuclear war. At the 20th Party Congress in February 1956, Khrushchev began a retreat from the Marxist-Leninist thesis that 'wars are inevitable as long as imperialism exists'. Khrushchev asserted: 'Today there are mighty social and political forces possessing formidable means to prevent the imperialists from unleashing war, and if they start it, to give a smashing rebuff to the aggressors and frustrate their adventurist plans.' There is little doubt that this 'formidable' power with which to give a 'smashing rebuff' was the nuclear weapon. With this weapon available to both East and West, Khrushchev stated, 'war is not a fatalistic inevitability'.[3] By 1960 Khrushchev was claiming that the pre-eminence of nuclear weapons had instigated a revolution in Soviet military affairs. This was further enunciated by Brezhnev, who claimed at the 26th Party Congress: 'to try to prevail over the other side in the arms race or to count on victory in a nuclear war is dangerous madness'.[4] In October 1981, in response to Reagan's assertion that the Soviet Union did think a nuclear war was winnable, Brezhnev replied: 'The thoughts and efforts of the Soviet leadership, like those of the Soviet people as a whole, are directed toward preventing a nuclear war altogether and eliminating the threat that one will break out.'[5] Despite these political claims, the military gave what at first appear to be contradictory signals. Rather than note the unwinnable nature of nuclear war, the term 'victory' was commonplace in military writings. For instance, the former Chief of the Strategic Rocket Forces, Marshal of the Soviet Union N. I. Krylov, wrote in 1969:

> The imperialists are trying to lull the vigilance of the world's people by having recourse to propaganda devices to effect that there will be no victor in a future war. *These false affirmations contradict the objective laws of history* ... Victory in war, if imperialists succeed in starting it, will be on the side of world socialism and all progressive mankind [emphasis in original].[6]

According to Robert Arnett, statements such as this 'have been presented as evidence by some Western analysts that the Soviet military leaders believe they can win and survive a nuclear war, and therefore that they do not believe the US has an assured destruction capability'.[7] This would indeed appear to be a sensible deduction. If the Soviets refer to victory and winning, then they would not seem to be restrained, or deterred, by the Americans' secure second-strike capability; they do not subscribe to MAD logic. If this is true, the Soviet Union harboured malign intent and the Cold War was not a security dilemma.

Is this rather dire proposition an accurate reflection of Soviet thinking? There are two schools of thought on this. The first claims that it is accurate and has been best expounded by Richard Pipes. Pipes claims:

> Soviet doctrine ... emphatically asserts that while an all-out nuclear war would indeed prove extremely destructive to both parties, its outcome would not be mutual suicide: the country better prepared for it and in possession of a superior strategy could win and emerge a viable society.[8]

This assertion is based upon the Soviet use of Clausewitz's dictum that 'war is the continuation of politics by other means'. Pipes states that the Soviet use of this phrase proves that they believed they could use war, even in the nuclear age, to realise their political objectives. To support his opinion he quotes Marshal V. D. Sokolovskii: 'It is well known that the essential nature of war as a continuation of politics does not change with changing technology and armament.'[9] Pipes therefore asserts that 'as long as the Soviets persist in adhering to the Clausewitzian maxim on the function of war, mutual deterrence does not really exist'.[10]

The second school of thought, expounded in particular by Raymond Garthoff and Robert Arnett, holds that MAD was far from being dismissed by the Soviet Union. In fact, the various references to winning and victory can best be explained by three factors. The first is that of Marxist-Leninist ideology. With Soviet ideology viewing the fate of capitalism and socialism to be intertwined and historically predetermined, there was a need to address the outcome of any war within this ideological strait-jacket. Whether Marxist-Leninist ideology actually asserted that war between capitalism and socialism was inevitable is open to question, but what is clear was the belief that socialism would eventually emerge triumphant.[11] Thus, military officials needed to pay lip service to the idea that socialism would prevail in a nuclear war. According to Robert Arnett, 'to deny the possibility of a Soviet victory in any war, including a nuclear war, is to challenge, even if not intentionally, Marxist-Leninist ideology and the laws of history which are expressed by that ideology'.[12] It is not surprising, then, that members of the Military Political Academy criticised those who claimed that victory in a nuclear war was impossible. Major-General A. Milovidov wrote:

> Certain works by Soviet authors have made mistakes on the question of the essence and consequences of a nuclear-missile war. The authors

of these works have made absolutes of quantitative analysis and the arithmetic calculation of the destructive force of nuclear weapons. However ... the question of victory in war presupposes not only a quantitative but also a qualitative analysis.[13]

A second factor for this apparent contradiction lies with maintaining morale within the military and populace. Raymond Garthoff claims that 'the standard military statements implying Soviet victory in a nuclear world war ... have a number of purposes, prominently including indoctrination and morale-boosting of the armed forces and the public'.[14] Benjamin Lambeth also makes this point when he claims that, in Soviet writings, 'any rejection of the possibility of victory is harmful because it leads to moral disarmament, to a disbelief in victory, and to fatalism and passivity'.[15] The point is that not to have spoken of victory would have lowered confidence amongst the populace that they had 'caught up' with the West and that they no longer needed to fear an attack.

A third factor relates to the Clausewitzian notions that 'war is a continuation of policy by other means' and 'war is an instrument of policy'. Soviet military doctrine referred to these notions frequently, so it must be assumed that they considered these ideas to be correct. The question is to determine what they meant when they used them. As noted earlier, Pipes regards their usage as evidence of Soviet hostile intent. This appears less convincing, however, when it seems that Soviet military officials regarded nuclear war in much the same, apocalyptic, way that the West did. In 1973 Lieutenant-General P. A. Zhilin wrote: 'the contemporary revolution in means of conducting war ... has led to a situation where both combatants can not only destroy each other, but can also considerably undermine the conditions for the existence of mankind'. Four years later Major-General R. G. Simonyan concurred with this view by stating: 'both sides possess weapons which are capable of annihilating all life on earth many times over'.[16]

What did the Soviets mean, then, when they used these phrases? The most convincing rationale is that the Soviet Union agreed with the West that 'nuclear war precisely as a continuation of politics made no sense *as a policy option for the USSR*' (emphasis in original).[17] Stating that war was an instrument of policy was just reaffirming the obvious: war has no other function. Since nuclear war against another nuclear power cannot achieve any of the goals of socialism, it was not a viable option for Soviet policymakers. As Arnett concludes: 'the Soviet usage of the dictum "war is a continuation of politics" is a basic tenet of Marxist-Leninist theory explaining the cause of war and is not an expression of their views on survival or victory in a nuclear war'.[18] Victory for the Soviet Union, in this sense, would be to convince the imperialists of this fact. Thus, as Peter Vigor comments: 'Victory for [the Soviet Union] would therefore be the creation of battlefield conditions which made it impossible for the imperialists to achieve their wicked designs.'[19] Michael MccGwire and Raymond Garthoff concur by noting that, from the mid-1960s, the Soviet Union sought to prevent a nuclear war and planned to fight, if it was unavoidable, with non-nuclear means.[20]

So, while talk of victory may appear to manifest Soviet malign intent, this is far from being true and is actually highly misleading. For the Soviet Union, victory was inevitable because, ultimately, socialism would triumph over capitalism. If nuclear war occurred, however, then the best they could hope for was a pyrrhic victory. Holloway writes:

> It has been claimed that the Soviet Union and its allies would emerge victorious from such a war, but there is nothing to suggest that the Soviet leaders think that a general war would be anything other than catastrophic, for the victors as well as the vanquished.[21]

Lawrence Freedman concurs with this when he refers to the duality in Soviet writing:

> While it was true that careful reading of Soviet military writings left a clear impression of an expectation of the ultimate triumph of socialism, even through a victory in nuclear war, this was so far removed from actual capabilities that it was difficult to believe the Russians themselves took it seriously.[22]

In concluding this discussion of the first duality, it needs to be stressed that although there appears to be a convincing rationale to support the argument that there are no contradictions between the statements of Soviet military officials and Soviet politicians, this is not universally accepted. Raymond Garthoff notes that 'many in the West assumed and alleged that Soviet pronouncements on the political level were merely propaganda or deception, and not related to "real" Soviet military doctrine'.[23] With such uncertainty, it is not surprising that NATO remained wary of the benign interpretation.

The deployment of Soviet forces

If it is right to claim that the Soviet Union regarded the consequences of a nuclear war to be the same as the West, then it could be expected that their forces would be deployed in such a fashion as to support that conviction. In the West, the arrival of nuclear weapons had led to war prevention through deterrence by punishment rather than deterrence by denial. It was taken for granted that the Soviet Union would do likewise.[24] The fact that they did not was what caused the duality and ambiguity for the West. David Holloway asserts that:

the political aspects of [Soviet military] doctrine stresses the possibility, and the importance, of preventing a world war between capitalism and socialism. The military-technical aspects of doctrine attends to the question of fighting such a war 'if the imperialists should unleash it'.[25]

In other words, deterrence was a political term in Soviet thinking; should war occur, it was the military's responsibility to concentrate upon how best to wage it. This might appear contradictory, since the preparation for waging a war and the wish to avoid such an outcome seem strange bedfellows. However, far from being contradictory, they complement one another.[26] The preparation for waging war can be a good means of preventing, or deterring, an opponent from initiating hostilities. Indeed, it is the willingness to provide a force of such power as to appear insurmountable that lies behind the concept of deterrence by denial.[27] There are two main reasons why the Soviet Union adopted a war-fighting approach to war prevention: ideology and military experiences.

Ideology

When combined with the historical experiences of the USSR, the ideological factor appears to be of great importance. The prevailing belief that the imperialist powers would attack the Soviet Union was given credence in Soviet eyes by the western powers' involvement in the Russian Civil War and Hitler's 1941 invasion. It was this greater expectation of war that made reliance upon a war-fighting approach such an appealing policy for Soviet decision-makers. Unlike an all-out spasm attack, war-fighting promised a rational form of defence if deterrence failed. That is, keeping faith with the Clausewitzian notion that 'war is an instrument of policy', a war-fighting strategy sought not only to deter the West, but also, should deterrence fail, to achieve some semblance of victory.

Military experience

The second factor behind the war-fighting approach was the military's exclusive authority to determine how a war should be waged. Unlike the western states, and in particular the United States (RAND, Brookings), civilians had no input into Soviet decision-making on a deterrence posture for the nuclear age. The result of this was that there were few new or fresh approaches to the arrival of nuclear weapons. Consequently, Soviet strategic doctrine reflected the traditional concerns of the military and their responses to these concerns. Thus it was that they emphasised success in warfare through the traditional methods developed as a result of historical experience, most notably that of the Second World War. Michael MccGwire claims that the immediate postwar objectives of the USSR were to prevent the western powers from overthrowing the new socialist regimes in eastern Europe. This objective obviously required the forward deployment of Soviet forces, but it went further than that. If these forces failed to deter the West, a second objective was added, which was 'to repel the attack and then go on to defeat the aggressor'.[28] MccGwire posits four reasons for this second objective. The first is that the idea of victory in Soviet minds was conditioned by the successful offensive operations in the last years of the war – offensive operations that took the Soviet army into the capital of the Nazi aggressor. The second reason stemmed from the Soviet perception that the West sought the removal of the socialist system. The only means by which to counter this threat was to defeat the capitalist bloc and replace it with pro-Soviet regimes, much the same as they had done in eastern Europe after the Second World War. The third reason was that offensive operations would achieve the dual purpose of defeating the European powers and preventing the Americans from establishing a bridgehead in Europe. The fourth and final reason was that an offensive war would be fought on the enemy's territory. This was regarded as a positive consideration because Moscow believed that it would reduce the chances of defection by some east Europeans. The twin concepts of forward defence and offensive operations remained constant throughout the evolution of Soviet military doctrine.

The Soviet acceptance that a nuclear war was unwinnable led the military to highlight the importance of restricting any war between the East and West to the use of conventional weapons. By the 1970s, therefore, the Soviet military had added the requirement of neutralising NATO's nuclear forces, without resorting to nuclear means, to their offensive objectives. Thus MccGwire states:

> The defeat of NATO in Europe had to be accomplished without precipitating an intercontinental exchange. Thus the immediate objective was to inhibit NATO from resorting to nuclear weapons. The possibility of being able to do so was based in large part on NATO's adoption of flexible response, which meant that NATO would initially resist a Soviet offensive with conventional means only. If during this conventional pause the Soviets could neutralize NATO's nuclear forces by non-nuclear means, they would have removed the critical first rung of the ladder of escalation. Alternatively, if during this pause the Soviets could knock European NATO out of the war with a conventional blitzkrieg, then the question of escalation might become moot as Washington faced a fait accompli. A combination of both courses of action, with additional action designed to disrupt or paralyse the NATO decision making process, would increase the chances of taking over Europe without precipitating escalation to a full scale nuclear strike on Russia.[29]

The permanency of offensive operations in Soviet military doctrine led MccGwire to believe that its role had become, in Soviet military circles, 'a habitual frame of mind'; as such, MccGwire suggests that 'it is unlikely that any alternative to offensive operations in Europe was even considered'.[30]

The importance of offensive action directed specifically against military targets was highlighted by the Soviet ideas on pre-emption. The Soviets expected to be the victims of an imperialist attack; as a result, much emphasis was placed on responding to the attack quickly and gaining the initiative as soon as possible. Hence, in the early 1960s Colonel General N. A. Lomov, a professor of military sciences, wrote:

> Soviet military doctrine considers it to be the most important ... and foremost task of the armed forces ... to repel a surprise attack by the enemy. To stop the nuclear attack of the opponent and take the strategic initiative on one's own hands is therefore one of the main tasks in the initial period of war.[31]

By the 1980s, pre-emption and counter-force targeting were still much in evidence. David Glantz comments: 'the Soviets developed war-fighting approaches designed to preempt enemy nuclear use by the early destruction of enemy nuclear systems and the rapid intermingling of friendly and enemy forces by extensive manoeuvre in the initial period of war'.[32] This reliance on counter-force and pre-emption led Colin Gray to note that 'the Soviet strategic forces' posture ... is the posture of a state with a thoroughgoing "war-fighting" approach to deterrence'.[33] This approach is also acknowledged by Goure, Kohler and Harvey, who write: 'Soviet doctrine and military posture do not distinguish between deterrent and war-fighting nuclear capabilities, but appear to view them as "fused together" in dialectical unity.'[34] In other words, the Soviets may have emphasised traditional war-fighting roles for their forces, but, by doing this, they were seeking to strengthen deterrence rather than make a nuclear war winnable.

These two factors, considered in conjunction with the Soviet belief that nuclear war would be nothing other than apocalyptic, suggest a benign interpretation of Soviet intentions. The Western Alliance, however, could not be certain that such an interpretation was accurate. The use of the words 'winning' and 'victory' could easily suggest that the Soviet Union rejected the argument that nuclear weapons had had a major impact on the conduct of war. The difficulty in accepting a benign interpretation of Soviet intent was further compounded by the war-fighting approach that they adopted towards deterrence. It is not surprising, then, that in the mid-1970s an American lobby group known as the Committee on the Present Danger claimed: 'The Soviet Union has not altered its long-term goal of a world dominated from a single centre – Moscow.'[35] This ambiguity of Soviet declared policy and force posture was what led the West to perceive malign intent where, arguably, none existed.

Western Reaction: Uncertainty and Paradoxical Policy

In Chapter 3 it was demonstrated that where offence is perceived to hold the advantage in time of war and where offensive postures are favoured as the means of maintaining security, the security dilemma will operate at its highest pitch; such an approach to acquiring security cannot but appear threatening to other states. Conversely, where defence is perceived to hold the advantage and force postures are unambiguously defensive, the security dilemma can be mitigated. It was suggested that those nuclear doctrines that supported MAD could be considered as defensive and, therefore, mitigators of the security dilemma, while those which undermined MAD could be perceived as indicating aggressive designs and, therefore, inadvertently cause other states to feel insecure. Thus, a western perception that the Soviet Union sought superiority and an escape from MAD would exacerbate the security dilemma.

It was not until the mid- to late 1960s that the USSR acquired a secure second-strike capability.[36] The arrival of missile technology had effectively ended any hopes of defence against a nuclear attack, and mutual assured destruction became a reality.[37] Despite this, however, the Soviet Union adopted a war-fighting approach towards deterrence. Why, though, given MAD's compelling logic, did the Western Alliance also adopt a war-fighting approach during the 1970s/early 1980s and thereby exacerbate the security dilemma?

For the West, MAD's shortcoming was that it did not take into account the problem of extended deterrence (ED). Although MAD produced a convincing rationale for paralysis between the two superpowers, it left much ambiguity over its paralysing effect in relation to secondary security interests. So, while it was credible for the USA to threaten assured destruction if the USSR attacked it, it was not so credible for the USA to threaten this if the USSR attacked western Europe. Threatening assured destruction in a world of secure second strikes is a suicidal policy: to commit suicide when the homeland is attacked has a degree of credibility; to do so when another state is attacked has less credibility. If the threat is incredible, then its deterrent power is severely weakened. The implication of this is that the USSR would not feel restrained or paralysed with respect to western Europe. Once the Soviet Union had achieved nuclear parity, the Western Alliance sought to overcome the problems that ED had created. This, it has been argued, was the main underlying theme in the evolution of nuclear strategy.[38] It was the Western Alliance's attempts to overcome NATO's ED problem that led the West to adopt the force postures that exacerbated the security dilemma. Before examining the inappropriateness of this, however, it is necessary to note that there is a counter-argument which holds that ED does not undermine MAD.

This counter-argument is that ED has more theoretical than practical significance and that the role of escalation will ensure that deterrence is successful for secondary issues as well as for primary or core values.[39] This is especially true, so the argument goes, where American interests/ commitments are very strong – such as in western Europe. Accordingly, America's deterrence by punishment remains credible because the USSR could not be certain of two factors: first, that the USA would refrain from carrying out its threat; and, second, that the conflict would not become uncontrollable and unintentionally force the USA to escalate to strategic nuclear use. In other words, the infinite costs of a nuclear war are such that the Soviet Union could not risk calling America's bluff. While this view may well be true, it is vital to note that it is based upon a large assumption – namely, that aggression is usually the result of opportunism and not fanatical zeal. This argument claims that 'opportunists are, by definition, calculating, and are therefore more likely to be impressed by the possibility of infinite costs than are zealots'.[40] The reason why ED lacks practical significance, therefore, issues from the assumption that the USSR is, at worst, opportunistic in its motivation towards aggression.[41] One of the security dilemma's premises is that states have benign intent, so, in the absence of a master plan for the eventual downfall of the West, MAD, even with the theoretical weaknesses of ED apparent, would have deterred the USSR. So long as MAD endured, the Soviet Union would not have been tempted into indiscretions.

The argument that ED did not create a problem because the Soviet Union was not pursuing a sophisticated long-term strategy to defeat the western democracies did not prevail in NATO circles. Rather than viewing the Soviets as opportunists, the impression in the West was that Soviet doctrine rejected MAD logic. This rejection appeared to be manifest in three developments. The first was the build-up of forces and their counter-force characteristics, the second was an interest in civil defence measures, and the third was the Soviet concern that MAD may not be permanent.

The growing unease of the Atlantic Alliance concerning the Soviet build-up was expressed in various NATO communiqués. At the Washington Summit in May 1978 the North Atlantic Council:

> expressed their concern at the continual expansion of Warsaw Pact offensive capabilities. Faced with this situation, and notwithstanding Soviet statements that these massive military resources are not designed to threaten the security of the Allied countries, the latter have no option but to continue two complementary approaches: on the one hand, strengthen their defensive capabilities and on the other, seek to promote negotiations on arms control and disarmament agreements.[42]

General Alexander Haig, the Supreme Allied Commander Europe (SA-CEUR), 1974–9, noted in 1978 that the Soviet Union's investment in defence enabled them to:

> add 100,000 men to those forces facing NATO in Western Europe, to increase its tank inventories by 40 percent, to augment substantially its deployed firepower, and to change fundamentally the character of its air forces in Eastern Europe. It has transformed its navy from a coastal defensive force to an offensive arm of global proportion.[43]

In December 1979 concerns regarding the offensive orientation of the Warsaw Pact were reiterated by the Defence Planning Committee, and the deployment of the new Soviet SS-20 missile and Backfire bomber warranted a special meeting of the alliance's Foreign and Defence Ministers. It was from this meeting that NATO's famous 'dual-track' decision was announced. It confirmed the two approaches noted in the North Atlantic Council's communiqué in 1978. The ministers noted:

> Soviet superiority in theatre nuclear systems could undermine the stability achieved in the inter-continental systems and cast doubt on the credibility of the Alliance's deterrent strategy by highlighting the gap in the spectrum of NATO's available nuclear responses to aggression ... [Therefore] Ministers concluded that the overall interest of the Alliance would best be served by pursuing two parallel and complementary approaches of TNF modernization and arms control.[44]

This last statement is highly revealing when viewed in the context of ED creating a large hole in MAD logic. By the end of the 1970s, NATO had become convinced that Soviet force deployments and increasing capabilities were exposing 'the gap in the spectrum of NATO's available nuclear responses to aggression' – the ED problem. The fear was the 'decoupling' of the Europeans from the Americans. Robert Spencer quotes a Canadian spokesman who in 1979 explicitly highlighted the doubt over MAD's paralysing effects on secondary security issues:

> There is a political concern in Europe that this growing imbalance could (a) in the absence of response at a level short of intercontinental missiles weaken the United States guarantee that underpins the Alliance, and (b) lead to miscalculation by the Soviet Union that it could threaten Western Europe without running an unacceptable risk in terms of a United Sates response.[45]

The Soviet war-fighting approach was undermining MAD and exacerbating the security dilemma. Their emphasis on offensive action ensured that they perceived offence as holding the advantage in time of war, and their emphasis on counter-force weapons ensured that their weapon characteristics appeared offensive.

A second development that suggested that the Soviets were undermining MAD was their apparent interest in passive and civil defence measures. The deployment of an ABM-type system and the education of the public in civil defence measures would have had the effect of taking their populations out of hostage and, as such, were to be regarded as offensive.[46] The entire Soviet attitude towards deterrence therefore undermined the logic of basing a doctrine on MAD. As Jervis claims: 'Russian declaratory policy as well as its military posture seem to reject the logic of MAD.'[47] Indeed, the result of a Soviet approach 'designed to deter war by developing counterforce capabilities [can only] exacerbate the security dilemma'.[48] The third reason why the Soviets did not appear to accept MAD was that they did not appear to accept it as a permanent reality. The permanency of MAD was dependent upon the continuing vulnerability of both sides to counter-city strikes. If that should change and mutual vulnerability were to end, then one side would be in an extremely weak and inferior position. The Soviet concern was that, with the USA's superior scientific/technological prowess, they would be the ones feeling vulnerable. Denis Ross quotes a Soviet spokesman who in 1972 outlined this concern explicitly: 'new scientific discoveries could lead to the creation of essentially new types of weapons, which could sharply upset the "balance of fear" [mutual vulnerability] and create a state of general instability'.[49] The American announcement of the SDI project eleven years later would seem to validate their concern.

These three developments appeared to confirm for the West that the Soviet Union rejected MAD and was in fact adopting force postures that indicated aggressive intent.[50] If the Soviet Union believed that its build-up could provide political and military advantages, then an American reliance on MAD would appear to be an inadequate approach to maintaining security: ED was a real difficulty which the Soviet Union appeared to be exploiting. While this may have been an understandable interpretation of Soviet actions, there are reasons for thinking it inaccurate, as noted above. If this is true, then the western reaction to the Soviet build-up was based upon a misperception. Not to respond to the Soviet build-up may have been considered inappropriate, but the actual western response of a warfighting approach increased tension and fuelled the security dilemma. Perceived as prudent, the preferred option was in fact paradoxical.[51]

Reliance on the threat to annihilate Soviet cities in response to a Soviet attack on western Europe had not been regarded as satisfactory by many US Presidents. Nixon spoke for many when he asked: 'should a President, in the event of a nuclear attack, be left with the single option of ordering the mass destruction of enemy civilians, in the face of the certainty that it would be followed by the mass slaughter of Americans?'[52] The Soviet Union's apparent move to exploit this 'suicide or surrender' dilemma, as it was known, coincided with an American disillusionment with assured destruction as the basis for US nuclear strategy. In 1975 the US Secretary of Defence, James Schlesinger, began a reorientation of US nuclear strategy that would culminate in the early 1980s with Reagan's 'prevailing' nuclear war-fighting strategy. Schlesinger noted that:

> there are many ways, other than a massive surprise attack, in which an enemy might be tempted to use, or threaten to use, his strategic forces to gain a major advantage or concession. It follows that our own strategic forces and doctrine must take a wide range of possibilities into account if they are successfully to perform their deterrent functions.[53]

Schlesinger implied that the 'other ways' in which the Soviet Union might threaten nuclear use was to exploit ED; the US needed to 'couple' its nuclear forces to the defence of Europe.[54] The prudent policy for the Western Alliance, therefore, was to base its strategy on a mixture of denial and punishment; denial to deter Soviet 'salami' tactics, and punishment to remind the Soviet Union of the cost of any adventurism.[55] The result of this deterrence mix, NATO's 'seamless web', was that although MAD continued to exist as a strategic reality, it would no longer act as a basis for western strategy. The mix of denial and punishment forces to secure deterrence was not new for the NATO Alliance.[56] Indeed, it was the ability of NATO to respond flexibly to an attack that gave its strategy, MC 14/3, the name 'Flexible Response'. The arrival of Soviet parity, however, together with the concern that they were seeking superiority, brought a war-fighting approach to NATO that was new.

The intention is not to provide an account of NATO's war-fighting doctrine as it developed during the 1980s; rather, it is to note that by adopting this approach, NATO exacerbated the security dilemma. The decision to deploy intermediate-range nuclear force (INF) systems in Europe, part of the dual-track approach, was 'believed to be critical to restoring the credibility and viability of Flexible Response, as interpreted from the warfighting strategy's perspective'.[57] Thus cruise and Pershing II missiles were deployed in Europe during the early 1980s. INF systems were not adequate on their own, however, and they were 'to be part of a more general increase in the US and NATO capacity for selective nuclear employment'.[58] Thus the USA continued development of the LANCE, MX, Trident D-5 and nuclear artillery pieces. The objective of this was to match Soviet capabilities across the board, thus filling in any gaps, and gain escalation dominance.[59]

The concern that escalation dominance would not actually work and that, once nuclear weapons were used, escalation would rapidly become uncontrolled resulted in a call for more emphasis to be placed on conventional forces.[60] 'No longer [was] conventional war [to be] seen in terms of early defeat leading to nuclear escalation, [instead] the conventional battle [was] a battle NATO believe[d] it [could] now win in its early stages.'[61] As such, much effort was put into developing a military doctrine that would deny the Soviet Union the option of waging a conventional war in Europe. The result was 'follow on forces attack' (FOFA) that called for 'deep strikes' against second-echelon Warsaw Pact forces in times of war. The adoption of FOFA by NATO in 1984, Bagnall's reforms in the northern army group, and the US 'airland battle' concept all emphasised an offensive means of achieving victory.[62] While McInnes is right to claim that this offensive potential was at the 'tactical and operational not strategic level', such a means of achieving defence was likely to be considered by the Soviet Union as providing an offensive potential at the strategic level.[63] As Buzan comments: 'Declarations by the country acquiring counterforce options that it intends to limit their use, and that no first strike threat is contemplated, are unlikely to provide significant reassurance to those responsible for national security in the rival power.'[64] By acquiring the weapons necessary to carry out such an approach towards deterrence, NATO inadvertently exacerbated the security dilemma. Thus NATO strategy was in danger of creating just the sort of security concerns in the Soviet Union that the Soviet approach to deterrence had created in the West. It is to this situation that Buzan is referring when he notes that:

> In following the warfighting logic of Soviet strategic doctrine, Third Wave theory opens itself to the same criticism of *apparent* aggressiveness that has so often been levelled at the Soviet Union. Where a state's military capability exists in a warfighting mode, other states have no way of determining its intention from its capability. Armed forces configured for warfighting can support either non-aggressive deterrence intentions or aggressive expansionist ones. Such capabilities therefore heighten the security dilemma for other states, forcing them to respond to the visible reality of the capability rather than to the possibly more benign, but hidden, reality of intentions [emphasis in original].[65]

Evidence that the Soviet Union had become very concerned about the direction of western strategy, and the intent that this indicated, has been provided by the KGB defector Oleg Gordievsky. Gordievsky claims that the arrival of the US President, Ronald Reagan, in 1980 exacerbated Soviet paranoia of western intentions:[66] 'Andropov saw the policy of the Reagan administration as based on an attempt to give the United States the power to deliver a successful nuclear first strike.'[67] As a result, Andropov announced Operation RYAN (an acronym for Raketno-Yadernoye Napadenie – Nuclear Missile Attack).[68] The objective of RYAN was to collect intelligence on the threat of nuclear attack from the USA and NATO. According to Gordievsky, 'paranoia in the Centre [KGB headquarters in Moscow] reached its peak during the NATO command post exercise Able Archer83, held from 2 to 11 November to practice nuclear release procedures'.[69] In other words, from a security dilemma perspective, although there was no danger of the West launching an attack against the Soviet Union (the incompatibility was illusory), the perception in the Kremlin was that the exercise might be a cover for a surprise attack.[70] MccGwire writes:

> Given that the NATO exercise ran its full course, it seems likely that Western command authorities were not aware of the Soviet reaction at the time ... If this was an intelligence failure, it was probably a fortunate one ... There is no knowing what escalatory process might have been triggered if NATO authorities had understood the implications of the Soviet response at the time.[71]

Gordievsky shared this concern by concluding: 'The world did not quite reach the edge of the nuclear abyss during operation RYAN. But during Able Archer83 it had, without realising it, come frighteningly close – certainly closer than at any time since the Cuban missile crisis of 1962.'[72]

By late 1983 it would appear that the security dilemma was operating at its highest pitch. Both East and West perceived each other as harbouring hostile intentions and embarked upon strategies that, while designed to provide security, were creating insecurity in one another. The seeming inability of statesmen to realise that their actions might be having this effect is neatly captured in a statement by Casper Weinberger, the US Secretary of Defence, in March 1983; eight months before Able Archer83: 'The other reason they have no need to worry [about SDI] is that they know perfectly well that we will never launch a first strike on the Soviet Union.'[73] However, if the Gordievsky account is to be believed, then Weinberger was simply wrong and the bellicose approach of the Reagan administration very nearly brought about exactly what it was trying to avoid – a nuclear war (Herz's tragedy). Jervis notes: 'if the state believes that others know that it is not a threat, it will conclude that they will arm or pursue hostile policies only if they are aggressive'.[74] Weinberger confirmed Jervis's opinion by continuing: 'And all of their attacks, and all of their military preparations – I should say, and all of their acquisitions in the military field in the last few years have been offensive in character.'[75]

Conclusion

This chapter has sought to provide evidence that, before Gorbachev's arrival in 1985, a security dilemma was much in evidence between the Western Alliance and the Soviet Union. The three criteria of benign intent, uncertainty regarding intention, and pursuit of paradoxical policies all appear to be evident. The Soviet achievement of nuclear parity in the

1970s led the USA to perceive that, rather than accepting the existence of MAD, the USSR was seeking superiority. While several Soviet statements and its deployment of forces suggested that this may be true, there are a number of reasons why we should believe that the USSR did accept MAD and sought no change in the status quo. Thus, the first part of this chapter exposes two dualities in Soviet war-thinking. The first is the apparently contradictory statements by the Soviet military concerning victory in a nuclear war and the Soviet politicians' pronouncements that no victory was possible. It is suggested that, rather than the latter being merely propaganda, many in the military acknowledged the reality of an unwinnable nuclear war but used such terms because they felt constrained by Marxist-Leninist ideology. To highlight military pronouncements of victory in a nuclear war as an indication of Soviet malign intent is understandable, therefore, but it is to misunderstand and misinterpret those pronouncements. The second duality concerned the offensive potential indicated by Soviet force posture and the Soviet claims of defensiveness. It is suggested that two reasons (ideology and military experience) can be marshalled to explain this duality; while the Soviet Union certainly did adopt a war-fighting strategy, this did not necessarily indicate malign intent.

Faced by these contradictory signals, however, the western states remained uncertain as to Soviet intentions and responded by matching the Soviet build-up across a range of weaponry. The West's uncertainty led them to perceive malign intent and, as a result, to adopt policies, based upon a misperception, that were self-defeating and thus paradoxical. By the early 1980s both East and West conceived of deterrence in war-fighting terms and adopted clearly offensive stances in order to manifest their ability to deny each other victory. This resulted in a heightening of tension and a deterioration in relations that became known as the Second Cold War. Operation RYAN revealed the degree of mistrust and suspicion that characterised the superpowers' relationship; according to Gordievsky, nuclear war was a distinct probability. Yet within five years of Gorbachev's arrival, the Berlin Wall had collapsed, the Warsaw Pact was no more and the Cold War had officially ended. Part III will examine whether the means of mitigating the security dilemma that were discussed in Chapter 3 played a role in the end of the Cold War, and whether in post-Cold War Europe the security dilemma has been escaped or is now re-emerging.

Notes

1. The Soviet concept of military doctrine is highly confusing. David Holloway writes that it 'cannot be properly understood without reference to the concepts of military science and military art'. Military science involves preparing the forces for war and the methods for waging it, while military art encompasses the conduct of military operations;

military art is thus a part of military science. Military doctrine, on the other hand, is defined by the politicians who take account of economic and political factors. Military doctrine is thus an expression of the purposes of the state, and military science is the means of waging war in accordance with that purpose. This distinction, though, is often fudged. Holloway notes 'that their apparent precision becomes blurred when one tries to distinguish the substance of doctrine from that of military science', a point illustrated by Peter Vigor, who comments: 'Doctrine is concerned with formulating who the Soviet Union's most likely enemies are, and how the Soviet armed forces will conduct their operations against those enemies in the event of war.' The latter would appear to be the preserve of military science, though military doctrine would clearly have a role in this – after all, if war is a continuation of policy, then the politicians need to control the execution of the war. Since there appears to be overlap, I use the term 'doctrine' to cover all aspects of Soviet military thinking, unless it is obviously an issue of military science. A very clear exposition of this is given by Christoph Bluth, but even he acknowledges that 'the distinction between doctrine and strategy is at times confused; since one is the implementation of the other, their content is often similar': Christoph Bluth, *Soviet Strategic Arms Policy before SALT* (Cambridge: 1992), pp. 84–7; David Holloway, *The Soviet Union and the Arms Race* (London: 1986), p. 30; Peter Vigor, 'Western Perceptions of Soviet Strategic Thought and Doctrine', in Gregory Flynn (ed.), *Soviet Military Doctrine and Western Policy* (London: 1989), p. 33.

2. Not all political commentators believed the Soviet build-up indicated a desire for superiority. George Kennan thought 'there is no reason for persuading oneself that ... the strengthening of the strategic nuclear "deterrent", is necessitated by changes in Soviet political and military intentions for which there is no adequate evidence': George F. Kennan, *The Cloud of Danger: current realities of American foreign policy* (London: 1978), p. 171. Other writers, however, perceived a more ominous reason: 'Many explanations have been developed for the continuing Soviet military build-up. It has, however, become harder to believe that purely defensive aims explain the extraordinary size and continuity of the Soviet effort': Amos A. Jordan, William J. Taylor, Jr., Lawrence J. Korb, *American National Security: policy and process* (Baltimore: 1990), p. 368. Paul Nitze believes that if the Soviet build-up had achieved superiority, 'the Soviet Union would adjust its policies and actions in ways that would undermine the present détente situation, with results that could only resurrect the danger of nuclear confrontation or, alternatively, increase the prospect of Soviet expansion through other means of pressure': Paul H. Nitze, 'Assuring Strategic Stability in an Era of Détente', *Foreign Affairs*, 54/2 (1976), p. 207.

3. 'Khrushchev's Report to the Party Congress – 1', *Pravda*, 15 February 1956, pp. 1–11, trans. in *The Current Digest of the Soviet Press*, 8/4, p. 11. Hereafter known as the *CDSP*.

4. 'Brezhnev's Report to the Congress – 1', *Pravda* and *Izvestia*, 24 February 1981, pp. 2–9, trans. in *CDSP*, 33/8, p. 11.

5. 'Brezhnev: No One Would Win in a Nuclear War', *Pravda*, 21 October 1981, p. 1, trans. in *CDSP*, 33/42, p. 13.

6. Quoted from Robert Arnett, 'Soviet Attitudes Towards Nuclear War: do they really think they can win?', in John Baylis and Gerry Segal (eds), *Soviet Strategy* (London: 1981), p. 59.

7. Ibid., pp. 63–4.

8. Richard Pipes, 'Why the Soviet Union Thinks It Could Fight and Win a Nuclear War', *Commentary*, 64/1 (1977), p. 21.

9. Quoted from ibid., p. 30.

10. Ibid., p. 34.

11. Khrushchev's speech to the 20th Party Congress in 1956 suggested this by stating that war was no longer to be considered 'fatalistically inevitable'. Prior to this, it was thought that Marxist-Leninist ideology had considered war between the East and West to be

inevitable. Yet this is not very clear. In Lenin's writing, the inevitability of war was referring to war amongst capitalist powers; the closest that Lenin came to war being inevitable between capitalist and communist states was in his report to the 8th Party Congress in 1919. Here he said: 'the existence of the Soviet Republic side by side with imperialist states for long-time is unthinkable'. For more on this, see Frederic S. Burin, 'The Communist Doctrine of the Inevitability of War', *American Political Science Review*, 57/2 (1963), pp. 334–54.

12. Arnett, 'Soviet Attitudes', p. 59.

13. 'Marxism-Leninism and Military Affairs', *Krasnaya zvezda*, 17 May 1973, pp. 2–3, trans. in *CDSP*, 25/25, p. 14.

14. Raymond Garthoff, 'START and the Soviet Military', *Problems of Communism*, 24/1 (1975), p. 33.

15. Benjamin S. Lambeth, 'How to Think about Soviet Military Doctrine', in John Baylis and Gerry Segan (eds), *Soviet Strategy* (London: 1981), p. 112.

16. Arnett, 'Soviet Attitudes', p. 65; for more examples, see ibid., pp. 61–6.

17. Raymond L. Garthoff, 'Mutual Deterrence, Parity and Strategic Arms Limitation in Soviet Policy', in Derek Leebaert (ed.), *Soviet Military Thinking* (London: 1981), p. 94.

18. Arnett, 'Soviet Attitudes', p. 66.

19. Vigor, 'Western Percpetions', p. 52.

20. See Michael MccGwire, *Military Objectives in Soviet Foreign Policy* (Washington: 1987), esp. ch. 4; Raymond Garthoff, *Deterrence and the Revolution in Soviet Military Doctrine* (Washington: 1990), ch. 3.

21. Holloway, *The Soviet Union*, p. 43.

22. Lawrence Freedman, *The Evolution of Nuclear Strategy* (London: 2nd edn, 1989), p. 258.

23. Garthoff, *Deterrence*, p. 51.

24. There existed an arrogance which thought that Soviet nuclear thinking was less sophisticated and lagged behind its western equivalent. In due course, they were expected to understand MAD and act in accordance with the restraints that the West prescribed the MAD era had created. Lawrence Freedman refers to this as the 'strategic learning curve': see Freedman, *Evolution*, pp. 257–9.

25. Holloway, *The Soviet Union*, p. 32.

26. Colin Gray and Keith Payne claim that deterrence would be strengthened by an American willingness to plan for nuclear victory. They write: 'Soviet leaders would be less impressed by American willingness to launch a LNO (Limited Nuclear Options) then they would be by a plausible American victory strategy': Colin S. Gray and Keith Payne, 'Victory is Possible', *Foreign Policy*, 39 (1980), pp. 20–1.

27. There is some contention over the use of deterrence by denial to describe the Soviet approach to war prevention. Raymond Garthoff contends: 'Some observers have posited a possible Soviet conception of "deterrence by denial", as contrasted with the American conception of "deterrence by punishment" ... Soviet force posture and "war-waging" military doctrine have suggested the possible applicability of this idea, but Soviet statements on deterrence have invariably been couched in terms of retaliatory punishment, and there is no indication that such a distinction reflects a Soviet way of thinking.' It would seem, therefore, that while the Soviets preferred a war-fighting approach, they did not consider that those forces had a deterrent function. I will therefore refer to the Soviet posture as a war-fighting one and only use 'denial' where other authors use this term: Raymond L. Garthoff, 'The Tightening Frame: mutual security and the future of strategic arms limitation', in Derek Leebaert and Timothy Dickinson (eds), *Soviet Strategy and New Military Thinking* (Cambridge: 1992), p. 59.

28. MccGwire, *Military Objectives*, p. 70.

29. Ibid., p. 76.

30. Ibid., p. 75.

31. Quoted from Christoph Bluth, *Soviet Strategic Arms Policy*, p. 102.

32. David M. Glantz, *The Military Strategy of the Soviet Union: a history* (London: 1992), p. 203.

33. Colin S. Gray, 'Soviet Nuclear Strategy and the New Military Thinking', in Derek Leebaert and Timothy Dickinson (eds), *Soviet Strategy and New Military Thinking* (Cambridge: 1992), p. 33.

34. Leon Goure, Foy D. Kohler, Mose L. Harvey, *The Role of Nuclear Forces in Current Soviet Strategy* (Florida: 1974), p. 8.

35. *New York Times*, 11 January 1977, p. 33. The Committee on the Present Danger was dominated by conservative hawks and its dire warnings were not necessarily representative of all US thinking. However, three members of this committee (Paul Nitze, Richard Pipes, William Van Cleeve) were part of the influential 'Team B'. Team B was comprised of outside experts who provided an alternative analysis of Soviet intentions to that provided by the CIA. Team B considered the Soviet Union to be a real threat to the United States; far from being a status quo benign power, it was perceived to be a revisionist power harbouring expansionist ambitions. This interpretation of the Soviet Union continued into the 1980s, when a number of Team B members gained top posts in Ronald Reagan's administration. The Committee on the Present Danger might not have been representative of all US thinking, but its view was most influential in US decision-making circles. For more on this, see Anne Hessing Cahn and John Parados, 'Team B: The Trillion Dollar Experiment', *The Bulletin of Atomic Scientists*, 49/3 (1993), pp. 23–31.

36. Barry Buzan claims that 'although the United States still had a substantial advantage in nuclear strength over the Soviet Union by the mid-1960s, the Soviet Union had clearly reached the point where it could inflict a devastating blow on the United States in return for any attack the Americans might make on them': Barry Buzan, *Introduction to Strategic Studies: military technology and international relations* (London: 1987), p. 146.

37. While a nuclear attack relied upon bombers as the means of delivery, there remained a degree of optimism that such an attack could be defended. With the arrival of missiles, such optimism was dispelled. As Brodie states: 'with the very short flight times involved, a defence system that detected an enemy missile on the way has little room to permit human judgment and decision to intervene. A system with enough built-in sensitivity to react promptly to any real attack must be sensitive enough to respond also to false alarms or deliberate enemy "spoofing".' Such a defence system has not been created. See Bernard Brodie, *Strategy in the Missile Age* (Princeton: 1965), p. 221.

38. For instance, Lawrence Freedman writes: 'if there is an underlying theme it is the attempt to develop a convincing strategy for extended deterrence, to make the United States' nuclear guarantee to Europe intellectually credible rather than just an act of faith': Freedman, *Evolution*, p. xix.

39. Barry Buzan refers to this school of thought as the 'easy' school; see Buzan, *Introduction to Strategic Studies*, pp. 168–9.

40. Ibid., p. 169.

41. The idea of the Soviets even being opportunists is difficult to accept. Opportunism suggests the rapid adjustment of policy to take advantage of temporary factors. It is, then, a risky policy. Soviet policy tended to reflect evolutionary as opposed to revolutionary change, and was rarely embarked upon as a gamble. Indeed, there were many reasons to suggest that the Soviets were content with the status quo and, hence, neither opportunists nor zealots: the Cold War era saw a continuation of the Soviet Empire, its sphere of influence and the rise of its power and status.

42. North Atlantic Council Communiqué, *NATO Review*, 26/4 (1978), pp. 28–9.

43. General Alexander Haig, SACEUR, 'NATO and the Security of the West', *NATO Review*, 26/4 (1978), p. 8.

44. Foreign and Defence Ministers' Communiqué, *NATO Review*, 28/1 (1980), p. 25.

45. Robert Spencer, 'Alliance Perceptions of the Soviet Threat, 1950–1988', in Carl-

Christoph Schweitzer (ed.), *The Changing Western Analysis of the Soviet Threat* (London: 1989), p. 40.

46. The Soviet interest in ABM and civil defence after SALT I is difficult to gauge. In 1974 Colonel General A. Altunin, Chief of Civil Defence of the USSR and a Deputy Minister of Defence, wrote: 'The preparation of the country's rear for the defence against means of mass destruction has become, without a doubt, one of the decisive strategic factors ensuring the ability of the state to function in wartime ... Civil Defence, by carrying out protective measures and the thorough preparation of the population, seeks to achieve the maximum weakening of the destructive effects of modern weapons.' As regards the offensive connotations of these measures, Altunin stated: 'Soviet civil defence does not incite, does not promote and does not provide impetus to war.' However, writing with hindsight in 1990, Jeanette Voas claims that although 'the ABM Treaty did not entirely quash support for an accelerated BMD effort in the Soviet Union, nor completely prevent supporters from expressing continuing interest in BMD ... these expressions of interest were exceptional. They were not taken up widely, and seem to have had little appeal in political circles.' Much as this may have been the case, however, the perception in the United States at the time was that 'newly developed guided missiles, a vast programme of underground shelters and a continuing buildup of air defences' were being constructed by the Soviet Union: David Binder, 'CIA Believes Russia Seeking Arms Lead', *International Herald Tribune*, 27 December 1976, p. 1. For the Altunin quotes, see Goure, Kohler and Harvey, *The Role of Nuclear Forces*, pp. 118–20; for Voas, see 'Soviet Attitudes Towards Ballistic Missile Defence and the ABM Treaty', *Adelphi Paper 255* (Winter 1990), p. 14.

47. Robert Jervis, 'Security Regimes', *International Organization*, 36/2 (1982), p. 375.

48. Robert Jervis, 'Realism, Game Theory, and Cooperation', *World Politics*, 40/3 (1988), p. 333.

49. Denis Ross, 'Rethinking Soviet Strategic Policy: inputs and implications', *Journal of Strategic Studies*, 1/2 (1975), p. 11.

50. In addition to the many NATO utterances expressing concern over the continuing build-up of Warsaw Pact forces, the CIA explicitly stated: 'the Soviet Union is seeking superiority over US forces': David Binder, 'CIA', p. 1. There also appeared to be a growing Soviet assertiveness in the Third World: Egypt 1973, Angola 1975–6, Middle East and Africa 1977–9, Afghanistan 1979.

51. Beatrice Heuser supports this assertion when, in reference to the nuclear war-fighting school, she writes 'that variation on the nuclear theme produced by these strategies contributed greatly, as we now know, to Soviet paranoia about Western intentions, and seems to have had little but counter-productive consequences': Beatrice Heuser, 'The Development of NATO's Nuclear Strategy', *Contemporary European History*, 4/1 (1994), p. 65.

52. Richard Nixon, 'US Foreign Policy for the 1970s', in Philip Bobbitt, Lawrence Freedman and Gregory F. Treverton (eds), *US Nuclear Strategy: a reader* (London: 1989), p. 387.

53. James R. Schlesinger, 'Annual Defence Department Report 1975', ibid., p. 368.

54. See Freedman, *Evolution*, p. 383.

55. This is referred to as 'the difficult school' by Buzan: see Buzan, *Introduction to Strategic Studies*, pp. 153, 182–90.

56. The denial forces have been variously referred to as 'shield' and 'trip-wire' forces. The term 'shield' was originally used by General Norstad, SACEUR, 1956–62, to differentiate between the denial and punishment forces. The shield was made up of the ground troops designed to meet a less than ultimate threat with a less than ultimate response. The punishment, or strategic reserve, forces were known as the 'sword'. For more on this, see David Schwartz, *NATO's Nuclear Dilemmas* (Washington: 1983), pp. 57–9. The term 'trip-wire' is an unofficial name used to express the widely held belief that the

denial forces were inadequate to defend against an attack, and the presence of nuclear weapons would ensure that they merely acted to 'trip' the sword into action. As Robert Osgood explains: 'Presumably – although this point was never publicly explained – tactical nuclear weapons [part of the denial forces armoury] were a useful supplement to massive retaliation because it was more credible that, in the event of a conventional attack, NATO would employ them as a means of resistance on the battlefield than that the United States or Great Britain would immediately drop hydrogen bombs as a means of reprisal on the Soviet Union, even though the employment of tactical weapons would probably lead to a disastrous war of annihilation by a natural process of escalation': Robert E. Osgood, *NATO: the entangling alliance* (Chicago: 1962), p. 120.

57. Ivo H. Daalder, *The Nature and Practice of Flexible Response* (New York: 1991), p. 208.

58. Ibid., p. 213.

59. Escalation dominance refers to a state acquiring superiority over its adversary on all 'rungs' of an escalation ladder; as the conflict escalates, the state with superiority can match and dominate its opponent, thereby forcing the opponent to either back down or escalate the conflict further. If the adversary chooses to escalate, then – even at this higher 'rung' – it will still be in an inferior position. A state with escalation dominance should not therefore be placed in a position where it has to back down and concede an issue of vital importance to an adversary.

60. In 1985 a West German White Paper on Defence stated: 'the continued evolution of NATO strategy requires a strengthening of NATO's conventional forces in order to reduce the possibility that NATO may be compelled to resort early to the use of nuclear weapons'. This line of argument resulted in December 1985 in the Defence Planning Committee stating: 'we are determined to strengthen the credibility of our strategy by avoiding an undue reliance on the early use of nuclear weapons through the special effort to improve our conventional capabilities'. Both quotes are from Jane Stromseth, *The Origins of Flexible Response: NATO's debate over strategy in the 1960s* (Hong Kong: 1988), p. 206.

61. Colin McInnes, 'The Rediscovery of Conventional War: NATO strategy and conventional defence', Conference paper at BISA/ISA, London, March 1989, p. 1.

62. See Colin McInnes, *NATO's Changing Strategic Agenda: the conventional defence of Central Europe* (London: 1990), pp. 116–62.

63. Colin McInnes, 'NATO Strategy and Conventional Defence' in Ken Booth (ed.), *New Thinking about Strategy and International Security* (London: 1991), p. 180.

64. Buzan, *Introduction to Strategic Studies*, p. 187.

65. Ibid., p. 201. The term 'Third Wave' belongs to Colin Gray; he is referring to the questioning of MAD as a means of achieving strategic stability. Buzan notes that this questioning or challenge involved 'extending the logic of limited nuclear war into a full-scale denial doctrine of extended deterrence by threat of warfighting' (ibid., p. 155). For Third Wave, see Colin S. Gray, *Strategic Studies: a critical assessment* (London: 1982), pp. 16–17.

66. See Christopher Andrew and Oleg Gordievsky, *KGB: the inside story of its foreign operations from Lenin to Gorbachev* (London: 1991), pp. 582–605.

67. Ibid., p. 583.

68. The fact that the KGB and GRU were asked to cooperate on this operation, the first time that this had been ordered, highlighted the seriousness of the operation in the eyes of leading Politburo members.

69. Andrew and Gordievsky, *KGB*, p. 599.

70. Soviet paranoia existed despite the presence of Soviet observers at a NATO exercise in 1983. See *NATO Review*, 3 (1984), p. 13.

71. Michael MccGwire, *Perestroika and Soviet National Security* (Washington: 1991), pp. 390–1.

72. Andrew and Gordievsky, *KGB*, p. 605.

73. Quoted from Charles L. Glaser, *Analyzing Strategic Nuclear Policy* (Princeton: 1990), p. 77.
74. Robert Jervis, *Perception and Misperception in International Politics* (New Jersey: 1976), p. 71.
75. Glaser, *Analyzing Strategic Nuclear Policy*, p. 77.

III

Gorbachev and Mitigation

Chapter Six

Recognition

Although a state will not be able to judge the other's intentions from the kinds of weapons it procures, the level of arms spending will give important evidence. Of course a state that seeks a high level of arms might not be an aggressor but merely an insecure state, which if conciliated will reduce its arms, and if confronted will reply in kind. To assume that the apparently excessive level of arms indicates aggressiveness could therefore lead to a response that would deepen the dilemma and create needless conflict. But empathy and skilful statesmanship can reduce this danger.[1]

It has been argued so far that, by the time Mikhail Gorbachev became General Secretary of the Communist Party (CPSU) in March 1985, the security dilemma was operating at its highest pitch; the world had reached the brink of nuclear disaster in late 1983, according to KGB defector Oleg Gordievsky. Yet within five years the Cold War, which had structured superpower relations since the late 1940s, was over. The purpose of this chapter and the succeeding one is to examine Gorbachev's administration to determine whether mitigating the security dilemma played a role in ending the Cold War: was Gorbachev Jervis's 'skilful statesman'?

Chapter 7 will concentrate on the policies that Gorbachev pursued in foreign and defence policy to see whether they related to the ideas of common security and force postures noted in Chapter 3. This chapter is concerned with what can be regarded as the first step towards mitigation: the realisation by at least one state that it is a victim of a security dilemma. If a state is able to appreciate that its policies have not only failed to achieve security but are part of the existing problem, then it might be possible for that state to change its policy and thereby mitigate the security dilemma. Realisation that the state is a victim of a spiral/security dilemma is therefore the necessary first step towards mitigation, and so this chapter will examine whether Gorbachev was aware that the USSR was a victim of the security dilemma.

The claim that Gorbachev was aware of the security dilemma and that this lay behind the changes he introduced is a controversial one. Far from accepting that Gorbachev initiated the changes, it has been argued that the western world used competitive policies to bankrupt the Soviet economy and forced Gorbachev into introducing change. This argument provides a double challenge to the claim that the security dilemma was in existence. First, if western policies explain the changes that Gorbachev introduced, then they cannot be considered self-defeating; while western policies may have raised tension, they ultimately proved successful in winning the Cold War and, therefore, were not paradoxical. Second, Gorbachev's desire for better international relations reflected a need for conditions conducive for domestic reform and nothing else; the need to maintain the superpower status of the USSR, not reduce tension and expose an illusory incompatibility, lay behind the change.

The chapter is divided into two sections, with each analysing these challenges in turn. The first section suggests that there is no conclusive evidence to support the claim that the Soviet economy became bankrupt because of western policy, while the second claims that the changes introduced by Gorbachev suggest that he was seeking more than just domestic reform. In other words, it is not the condition of the Soviet economy that is questioned; rather, did its failings result from external pressure and did its stagnation provide the sole reason for the policies that Gorbachev embarked upon? The answers to these questions will reveal whether Gorbachev was aware of the security dilemma and how far this awareness explains his actions.

Did the West Win the Cold War?

There exists a school of thought that the West won the Cold War because of the policies it pursued. According to this view, the ideological resolve and military build-up by the West brought the Soviet economy to its knees. The Reagan administration then 'delivered the knock-out punch to a system that was internally bankrupt and on the ropes';[2] with the collapse of the old enemy, the West could celebrate its 'great victory in the Cold War'.[3] According to this view, NATO was a key player in the grand strategy. Sir Michael Alexander, UK Permanent Representative to the North Atlantic Council (1986–91) claims:

> the Alliance did much more than contain Soviet imperialism and deter aggression. Its refusal to be either brow beaten or out built by the Soviet military/industrial complex eventually brought the whole edifice of state socialism to its knees. It provided a framework within which the nuclear and conventional defence requirements of Western Europe's states could be satisfied. It thus allowed those states to concentrate on creating the prosperity which eventually forced even Moscow's diehards to acknowledge the bankruptcy of the Soviet system.[4]

Put quite simply, 'NATO played a decisive role in determining the outcome of the Cold War.'[5] This would suggest that the policies pursued by the West, and in particular NATO, ultimately proved successful. The security concerns of the NATO members were satisfactorily resolved when the Cold War ended and the West was victorious. If this view is correct, then it raises serious doubts about NATO being a victim of the security dilemma; the policies of the Western Alliance proved satisfactory and, therefore, were appropriate. Was this true?

The suggestion that the Soviet economy was in decline is not in question. The growth rate of the Soviet economy began to slow down in the 1960s and by the 1970s it was stagnating. By the late 1980s there was 'wide agreement among both Soviet and Western economists that the Soviet economy ha[d] ceased growing and ha[d] begun to shrink'.[6] It is not the state of the Soviet economy that is at issue, but the extent to which western policies were directed at exhausting the Soviet economy and were western policies responsible for its eventual collapse?

The West's policy throughout the Cold War remained consistent. Regardless of President and rhetorical calls for 'rollback', the policy of containment remained the focal point of western strategy *vis-à-vis* the USSR. According to Nigel Hawkes, 'the liberation of Eastern Europe ... was the ultimate aim of the policy of containment adopted in the Forties. And the lesson of Soviet policy in the past few years is that containment has triumphed.'[7] This analysis is challenged by William Pfaff, however, who claims that, by pursuing the policy of containment, 'Washington had not only accepted the Soviet Union's domination of Eastern Europe for more than 30 years but, at the cost of a not inconsiderable hypocrisy, had contributed to maintaining it throughout that period'.[8] What did containment seek to achieve?

George Kennan, the father of containment, introduces the policy in his famous 'X' article. He writes: 'the main element of any United States policy toward the Soviet Union must be that of a long-term, patient but firm and vigilant containment of Russian expansive tendencies'. He goes on to argue that this containment should be achieved 'by the adroit and vigilant application of counterforce at a series of constantly shifting geographical and political points corresponding to the shifts and manoeuvres of Soviet policy'.[9] Although Kennan comments on the deficiencies of the Soviet economy, it was clear that 'the objective of containment should be to limit Soviet expansionism'.[10] He identifies three steps to this objective: first, restore the power lost during the war to those states that were threatened by Soviet expansion; second, exploit tension between Moscow and the international communist movement; third, modify the Soviet concept of ideological struggle in international relations. In other words, waiting for the Soviet economy to 'crack' was not one of his steps.

The policy of containment that was implemented differed from Kennan's prescription. It highlighted the need to strengthen the USA and its allies, but not to alter the Soviet concept of international relations as a class struggle. 'Strength came to be viewed almost as an end in itself, not as a means to a larger end; the process of containment became more important than the objective that process was supposed to attain.'[11] Seeking to alter Soviet behaviour was largely demoted to the sidelines of rhetoric. 'Containment meant building up the military strength of America and her allies, and a willingness to stand up to the Russians wherever they applied pressure.'[12] Its objective was not the ultimate demise of the Soviet economy. However, even if the West did not intend to crack the Soviet economy, it has been suggested that it was still responsible for this, because the Soviet Union had to respond to the West's military build-up. By responding, the USSR placed an intolerable burden on its own economy; the policy was unintentionally appropriate because it exhausted the Soviet economy through a crippling arms race.

The problem with this argument is determining whether the arms race was the cause of the collapse or just an exacerbating factor in the collapse. The burden of the military on the Soviet economy is not in question. Although it was notoriously difficult to determine how much the Soviet Union spent on defence, it is widely accepted that its primacy was to the detriment of the Soviet economy.[13] However, was the collapse the result of the strain that the defence industries placed on the economy as the military attempted to compete with the USA, or did the economy collapse because it was poorly managed?

The centrally planned economy of the Soviet Union, despite attempts at reform in the 1960s, 1970s and 1980s, became increasingly inefficient. The primary target for industry was total output, a measure of performance that led to ridiculous economic activities. For example, during the 1930s and 1940s the Soviet Union produced the heaviest furniture in the world (bed-frames were constructed from lead), because furniture factories were judged on total weight produced. When this was changed under Khrushchev to quantity produced, the furniture was made out of lightweight plywood. Such economic activity was endemic in the Soviet economy. Housing construction firms were rated by how many houses that they had started. This led to firms laying foundations for houses they never intended to build. Since total output was the most important criterion, some factories would continue to produce even though they did not have all the necessary materials. It was not unusual for Soviet cars to be sold without headlamps, rear lights or windscreen wipers because the automobile plant had run out of those parts (often due to theft by the workers). The customer, having waited up to three years for the car, was unlikely to refuse the vehicle and would 'simply try to acquire the missing parts on the black market'.[14]

The acquisition of spare parts or the exchanging of goods on the black market was known as the 'second economy'. The second economy was illegal, but it was tolerated by Soviet officials because they used it to supplement their incomes and achieve their targets. A tacit acknowledgement developed in the Soviet Union of officials being drawn into corrupt practices involving patronage and bribery. In an attempt to save the sagging economy, Yuri Andropov (General Secretary of the CPSU from November 1982 to February 1984) launched a campaign against corruption, notably in the power bases of his leading rival, Konstantin Chernenko. In 1984, after a two-year investigation, the Minister of Finance, Minister of Internal Affairs, Chairman of the State Committee for Publishing, the First Secretary of the Dzhizak City Party Committee, and 59 deputies of local soviets in the Uzbek Republic were removed from office.[15] In addition, in Tashkent '1056 employees of stores, wholesale depots, pharmacies and hospitals [were] removed from their positions and had charges brought against them' for accepting bribes and other forms of corruption.[16] Another investigation in Bukhara resulted in 461 party members being expelled for corruption.[17] With such widespread corruption, the economy's efficiency obviously suffered. Edward Acton claims: 'with the state's own servants failing to implement orders and deliberately misleading the centre, rational planning and coordination of different branches of the economy was quite simply impossible'.[18] Corruption had become an inherent feature of the Soviet economy.

The worst aspect of central planning and corruption, however, was that it inhibited development. An industry that sought to introduce new techniques, increase labour productivity through training schemes, but declined in total output was reprimanded, while a factory that failed to modernise but reached its goal was rewarded, regardless of the quality or saleability of the product. As Gorbachev said: 'how can the economy advance if it creates preferential conditions for backward enterprises and penalizes the foremost ones?'[19] The realisation by Gorbachev that 'mere tinkering with the planned and state-owned economies would not only fail to solve the difficulties, but could in fact make matters worse', led him to pursue the policy of *perestroika*, or restructuring.[20] In the end, his efforts proved too late and the economy ground to a halt. The defence industries had certainly been a drain on the economy, but they only exacerbated what was a fundamentally corrupt and inefficient process.

There would appear to be valid reasons for questioning whether the Western Alliance intended to crack the Soviet economy or did so unintentionally. However, it has been argued that the Reagan era brought a more competitive approach which did have an effect upon the Soviet economy. According to this view, it was the Reagan administration that administered the fatal dose to the crumbling Soviet Empire. This view became known as the 'Reagan victory school' and claims: 'President Ronald Reagan's military and ideological assertiveness during the 1980s played the lead role in the collapse of Soviet communism and the "taming" of its foreign policy.'[21] Reagan's policies sought to go beyond containment, which was deemed to be soft. He began a massive military build-up and the administration made remarks about surviving a nuclear war. In addition to this, the USA unveiled the SDI project; successfully deployed, this

would have undermined the assured destruction concept which under-
pinned the superpowers' mutual deterrence. Reagan also challenged the
Soviet Union on the ideological front.

> According to the Reagan Right, the supreme vulnerability of the Soviet
> Union to ideological assault was greatly under appreciated by Western
> leaders and publics. In that view, the Cold War was won by the West's
> uncompromising assertion of the superiority of its values and its com-
> plete denial of the moral legitimacy of the Soviet system during the
> 1980s.[22]

The Reagan victory school proponents, who – not surprisingly – were
mostly Republicans and members of his administration, claimed that
Reagan's policies were intended to achieve, and resulted in, the defeat of
communism through the undermining of the Soviet economy and political
philosophy. In other words, Reagan's policies were not paradoxical and
they won the Cold War.

The belief that Reagan had sought to undermine communism is itself
undermined by the failure of the administration to predict the collapse.
Far from predicting the demise of the USSR, most US–Soviet analysts
saw the bipolarity of the Cold War as a permanent feature. As former
National Security Advisor Zbigniew Brzezinski put it in 1986: 'the American–Soviet contest is not some temporary aberration but a historical rivalry
that will long endure'.[23] Indeed, it has become clear that the administration's intent to end the Cold War has only become apparent since it
ended. As Deudney and Ikenberry note: 'the Cold War's end was a baby
that arrived unexpectedly, but a long line of those claiming paternity has
quickly formed'.[24] However, supporters of the Reagan victory school still
see the collapse as the result, if not the intent, of Reagan's policies.
Vice-President Dan Quayle (1988–92) claimed: 'we were right to increase
our defence budget ... Had we acted differently, the liberalization that
we are seeing throughout the Soviet bloc would most likely not be taking
place.'[25] Did the US military build-up cause the Soviet economy to
collapse?

The contention that the Soviet military had to respond to the West's
increase in military capabilities during the 1980s is known as the 'build-up
argument'. If it does explain the Soviet collapse, then one would expect
the military spending of the USSR to have risen during the 1980s in an
attempt to match Reagan's build-up. In other words, it is an *increase* in
the defence budget, not the overall defence budget, that interests us. The
figures, however, do not appear to support the build-up argument. Fred
Chernoff and John McCain compared increases in US and Soviet military
spending and found no discernible Soviet reaction to Reagan's build-up.
According to Chernoff, the USA's annual military spending rose from
2.79% to 8.42% between 1980 and 1983, while the Soviet annual military

spending increased at a consistent 2.5%. Indeed, throughout the 1980s Soviet military spending increased by more than 2.5% only once, in 1986, to 3% where it remained until 1989. This 0.5% rise accounted for an extra 1.7 billion roubles per year. Chernoff asserts: 'this sum is far too small to account for any meaningful added strain on the Soviet economy'.[26] John McCain also notes that while Soviet expenditure on military pro-grammes was higher than that of the USA, the relative increase favoured the Americans. In overall costs of military programmes, the USA showed an increase from $175 billion in 1978 to $275 billion in 1987 (dollars at 1986 value), while the Soviet Union showed a much slower rate of increase which did not respond to the dramatic US rise – $270 billion in 1978 to $300 billion in 1987.[27] The data simply do not support the build-up argument; hence Chernoff's claim that 'the contention that the US military buildup had an effect on the end of the Cold War by damaging the Soviet economy is ... unsupportable'.[28] This assertion is supported by Richard Ned Lebow and Janice Gross Stein, who write: 'the proposition that American defence spending bankrupted the Soviet economy and forced an end to the Cold War is not sustained by the available evidence'.[29]

It would appear that the West did win the Cold War despite, rather than because of, the policies it pursued. This is extremely important from the security dilemma perspective, since the argument that western policies lay behind the Soviet change is strong evidence that they were ultimately appropriate and, hence, that there was no security dilemma. However, it would appear that the policies pursued by the West were to strengthen their position *vis-à-vis* the Soviet Union rather than to induce change.

> To the extent that the US has had a grand strategy for foreign policy over the past 40 years, it has been to promote economic prosperity and political stability in Western Europe and Japan and to maintain close alliances with them.[30]

The effect that these policies had was to exacerbate the security dilemma; they were not intended to bankrupt the Soviet economy nor were they responsible for its collapse. As Lebow and Stein conclude: 'the critical factor in the Soviet economic decline was the rigid "command economy" imposed by Stalin in the early 1930s'.[31] While this may confirm that the changes that Gorbachev introduced were for internal reasons, it does not yet prove that they were the result of an awareness of the security dilemma; the changes may simply have been a response to a declining Soviet economy.

Was the End of the Cold War Solely Attributable to the Need for Better International Relations to Aid Domestic Reform?

The USSR that Gorbachev inherited was in a state of malaise. The stagnation of the Brezhnev era had retarded the economy, witnessed a decline in social values, stifled ideological debate, and damaged the Soviet image abroad with the protracted occupation of Afghanistan.[32] A change was needed and, with Gorbachev's arrival, a new term entered the political vocabulary – 'new thinking'. New thinking, and the related concepts of perestroika (restructuring) and glasnost (openness), were applied to all aspects of Soviet society. According to Christoph Bluth, 'the driving force behind the "new thinking" was the long-term unsustainability of competing with the USA for military power on the basis of a weak economy'.[33] In other words, it was not the dangers of the security dilemma but the relative decline of the socialist economy in comparison to the West that lay behind the change in Soviet policy. This opinion has been challenged by Janice Gross Stein, however, who notes that the US economy was also in decline and, therefore, the relative decline of the Soviet economy would not have been great enough to warrant such far-reaching changes. Stein writes:

> If the changes in Gorbachev's concepts that spilled over into Soviet doctrine and behaviour were a straightforward response to relative economic decline, then 'new thinking' is an epiphenomenal and unnecessary component of an explanation of the change in Soviet foreign policy.[34]

In other words, a response to economic decline would not require such a fundamental reappraisal of Soviet political thinking; something else, an awareness of the security dilemma perhaps, must also explain the changes. This is not intended to imply that concerns about the Soviet economy were not important; clearly they were. Seweryn Bialer is right to comment that 'there can be little doubt that Gorbachev's top priority [was] the reconstruction of the Soviet Union's domestic well-being'.[35] Gorbachev and Shevardnadze both made reference to the importance of domestic concerns in shaping foreign policy.[36] The difference, though, is that Soviet decision-makers were concerned with their *absolute* economic decline, rather than the relative decline of the Soviet economy *vis-à-vis* the West. Bluth is right to note, therefore, that Gorbachev sought better relations, amongst other reasons, to divert resources away from the military towards civilian usage, but that this was due to the absolute rather than the relative decline of the Soviet economy.[37]

Bluth was not alone in noting that the desperate state of the Soviet economy acted as the catalyst for change; indeed, many, if not all, commentators emphasise the stagnation and retardation of the Soviet economy. However, although the Soviet economy might have been the primary force behind the change in policy, and thus explains why the change was necessary, it does not necessarily explain why Gorbachev sought change in the way that he did. Stein comments:

> Domestic politics, however, cannot address the important question of why Gorbachev began to think differently about security, why he rejected the conventional wisdom of the time, and how and why he developed new concepts to organise his thinking about foreign and defence policy.[38]

Stein repeats this claim with Lebow, when they assert: 'the need to arrest economic decline and improve economic performance cannot by itself explain the scope of reforms or the kind of relationship Gorbachev tried to establish with the West'.[39] If it was also an awareness of the security dilemma that lay behind Gorbachev's changes, then this would initially manifest itself in a Soviet rejection of traditional foreign and defence policies. That is, the ability of states to change a paradoxical policy is the necessary first step towards mitigating the security dilemma.

This first step towards mitigation is extremely important and deserves repetition. A state must believe that its foreign and defence policies have failed to provide security and that, far from making the outbreak of war less likely, they have actually, in conjunction with the other state, made war more likely; it has been pursuing a paradoxical policy, or, as Jervis refers to it, the 'policy will lead down a blind alley'.[40] Unfortunately, if that policy has been perceived as keeping a revisionist state at bay – and, therefore, as appropriate – enlightenment as to the real situation is difficult to imagine. Where foreign and defence policy are treated as sacrosanct and discussion on their merits is taboo, as in the pre-Gorbachev USSR, such enlightenment becomes even harder to imagine. If the security dilemma is to be mitigated, however, decision-makers must realise that they are pursuing paradoxical policies. It is precisely this point to which Jervis is referring when he writes: 'The first step must be the realisation, by at least one side but preferably by both, that they are, or at least may be, caught in a dilemma that neither desires.'[41] Only by taking this first step can states alter their policies and break away from the ever-tightening spiral to which they have fallen victim and, hence, reverse their deteriorating relationship.

Indication of an awareness of the security dilemma requires a number of factors to be prevalent in the changes that Gorbachev introduced. First, the realisation that Soviet foreign and defence policy did create insecurity in the West and, thus, that western fear of the USSR was understandable. Second, that the Soviet perception of threat from the West was exaggerated and that the West was not seeking to invade the USSR. Third, that Soviet foreign and defence policies were exacerbating the first two factors and, thus, were causes, not solutions, to the problems that the USSR faced.

Foreign policy

Gorbachev's rejection of traditional Soviet foreign policy can be witnessed in three key areas – the role of ideology in foreign policy, the external threat, and the relationship with the United States – all of which highlight a movement towards mitigating the security dilemma.

The role of ideology in foreign policy

Not surprisingly, the western perception of an inherently aggressive communist bloc that espoused the downfall of the capitalist system exacerbated the security dilemma. Gorbachev's rejection of traditional interpretations of Marxist-Leninist ideology signalled that new thinking would challenge this ideological element which had characterised Soviet foreign policy during the Cold War. As such, Gorbachev would have the effect of de-demonising the Soviet Union in the eyes of the West and, as a result, reduce the Soviet image of being the enemy.

Whereas previous interpretations of Marxism-Leninism had led the USSR to view international relations as a class struggle, Gorbachev sought to prioritise common interests and universal values and minimise the conflictual nature of the class struggle. He wrote:

> Ideological differences should not be transferred to the sphere of inter-state relations, nor should foreign policy be subordinate to them, for ideologies may be poles apart, whereas the interest of survival and prevention of war stand universal and supreme.[42]

Gorbachev frequently made reference to reducing the importance of the class struggle and emphasising the value of common concerns:

> Yes, we remain different as far as our social system, ideological and religious views and way of life are concerned. To be sure, distinctions will remain. But should we duel because of them? Would it not be more correct to step over the things that divide us for the sake of the interests of all mankind, for sake of life on Earth?[43]

This new emphasis on common values received support from Anatoly Dobrynin, who wrote: 'the interdependence of survival – the indissoluble unity of the historical destinies of all states of the world in the face of a possible nuclear conflict – is of cardinal importance'. Eduard Shevardnadze was even more blunt: 'The struggle between two opposing systems is no longer a determining tendency of the present era.'[44]

The subordination of class differences to universal values was most marked in the redefinition of peaceful coexistence. During the Brezhnev era, peaceful coexistence was regarded as a continuation of the class struggle under the condition of assured destruction. Gorbachev rejected this definition and stated: 'we deem it no longer possible to retain ... the definition of peaceful coexistence of states with different social systems as a "specific form of class struggle" '.[45] Instead, peaceful coexistence was to be regarded as a description of the 'permanent *condition* of international life in the age of deterrence and interdependence, and that the communists must adjust accordingly' (emphasis in original).[46] Hence Shevardnadze's comment: 'New political thinking views peaceful coexistence in the context of the realities of the nuclear age. We are fully justified in refusing to see it as a special form of class struggle. Coexistence ... cannot be equated with the class struggle.'[47]

While it is undoubtedly correct to emphasise that Gorbachev sought a relaxation of international tension for domestic and, specifically, economic needs, it is important to note the way in which he chose to achieve this goal. By targeting the conflictual aspect of class struggle in Marxist-Leninist ideology, Gorbachev was addressing and challenging an aspect of Soviet foreign policy that had been a source of western fears about Soviet intentions. To challenge an aspect of policy that gives rise to insecurity in others can only help to ameliorate the security dilemma.

The nature of the threat

Where the ideological aspect of Soviet foreign policy had generated an aggressor in the minds of the western states, so that same ideology was responsible in the Soviet Union for characterising all capitalist states as imperialist enemies.[48] Whether this is a correct interpretation of Marxism-Leninism is questionable. However, the belief that imperialist states are inherently aggressive does explain the paranoiac tendencies of the Soviet Union and their susceptibility to the security dilemma.[49] While believing that the history of the twentieth century had 'served to reinforce the Marxist-Leninist logic that imperialism inevitably generates major armed confrontations', Gorbachev questioned whether this remained true.[50] He raised four questions on this matter in his speech to commemorate the 70th anniversary of the Bolshevik Revolution on 3 November 1987.[51]

Gorbachev's first question was whether it was possible to exert an influence on the nature of imperialism which would block its most danger-ous manifestations. Although he did not reply with an unambiguous 'yes', he certainly implied that it was possible. He implied that an interdependent world, where the common value of survival was the priority, would limit the 'destructive action' of the capitalist system. His second question was whether capitalism could function without militarism. To this he suggested that the answer was 'yes'. With reference to West Germany, Japan and Italy, he wrote: 'whatever the contributory factors were, there was a period of rapid development of a modern capitalist economy in a number of countries with minimal military expenditures'.[52] His third question concerned neocolonialism and whether capitalism could function without its support. Although he did emphasise that the developing world was the 'life support' of the capitalist system, he nevertheless concluded that 'the situation does not appear to be *unresolvable* ... the contradictions [in the capitalist system] will yield to *modification*' (emphasis added).[53] His final question addressed the threat of nuclear war and whether the western states, which he believed were aware of the danger, would embark upon practical policies to eradicate the threat. Whilst Gorbachev did not answer this question directly, he did indicate an affirmative response to all four questions – and hence, indirectly, to this last question. While he believed that the contradictions in the capitalist system had led to imperialistic actions causing war, 'the situation is different now' and cooperation between the two systems was possible.[54] He claimed that because they had cooperated in the past to defeat a fascist threat, it might be possible for them to cooperate to defeat such present-day threats as a nuclear catastrophe.

This speech was of great importance; by raising the possibility that imperialism may not require militarism, neocolonialism and war, Gorbachev was suggesting that the nature of imperialism was changing. By questioning whether imperialism led inevitably to conflict, Gorbachev was challenging the way in which the USSR perceived the international environment. In other words, he was challenging the central Leninist tenet of the aggressiveness of the capitalist system and, thereby, suggesting that the nature of the threat that the USSR perceived was diminishing.[55] This is clearly of great importance in mitigating the security dilemma. If the Soviet Union began to regard the NATO members as status quo powers, then embarking upon conciliatory policies became a viable objective.

The effect of Gorbachev's questions was to raise the subject of imperialism for debate. In the first issue of *Kommunist*, Vitalii Zhurkin, Sergei Karaganov and Andrei Kortunov, three specialists from the Institute of US and Canadian Studies, subjected the Soviet assumption of imperialist threat to a rigorous analysis. They noted that circumstances in the late 1980s were very different from those in 1941, when Nazi Germany had attacked the USSR. They wrote: 'one could say with a sufficient degree of confidence that no single aggressor, with a sane mind, would attempt something against [the USSR]'.[56] The obvious consequence of such a position is that the USSR need not fear an attack from the West. It was this proposition that lay at the heart of the article. They went on to argue that contemporary internal factors inhibited the imperialist powers from seeking conflict. They claimed: 'the very nature of industrial society operates here as a war restraining factor', and 'bourgeois democracy provides a certain obstacle to the outbreak of ... war'.[57] Such comments clearly support Gorbachev's suggestion that the Soviet Union has little reason to fear the West and, as such, support the prospect of security dilemma mitigation.

US–Soviet relations.

One of the most important psychological dynamics to exacerbate the security dilemma is the inability, or unwillingness, of states to appreciate that what they see as benign actions and statements might be interpreted as aggressive. This is what Butterfield referred to as self-righteousness. That this psychological dynamic afflicted the USA and the Soviet Union during the Cold War would appear to be beyond doubt. Marantz captures the dynamic when he writes:

> In the past, Soviet officials have refused to admit that Soviet foreign policy was ever in error or that Soviet actions might have contributed to an increase in international tension. Western mistrust of the Soviet Union was said to be the product of bourgeois class hatred for a rival system rather than a consequence of anything the Soviet Union might have done, and Western fears of Soviet aggression were dismissed as totally groundless.[58]

An important step in mitigating the security dilemma, therefore, is to appreciate that actions with benign intent can be misinterpreted as aggressive. Under Gorbachev, Soviet foreign policy became, albeit slowly, open to discussion and criticism.[59] As with imperialism, it was Gorbachev who engineered debate on past Soviet policies. In the CPSU Central Committee's theses for the 19th All-Union Party Conference in 1988 he wrote:

> A critical analysis of the past has shown that dogmatism and a subjective approach left an imprint on our foreign policy. It was allowed to lag behind fundamental changes in the world, and new possibilities for the lessening of tension and for greater mutual understanding among the peoples were not fully realised. In striving for military-strategic parity, we did not always take advantage of opportunities to ensure the state's security by political means, and, as a result, we allowed ourselves to be drawn into the arms race, which could not help but have an effect on the social and economic development of the country and on its international position.[60]

The introduction of glasnost on past Soviet foreign policies produced a number of articles denouncing the invasion of Afghanistan and the deployment of the SS-20 missile. Alexander Bovin, an ardent critic of the Afghan invasion, borrowed Gorbachev's phrases to state what Gorbachev had implied: 'It is not hard to understand that a foreign policy that bore the "imprint" of dogmatism and a subjective approach ... was accompanied by mistakes and misunderstandings.'[61] The most eloquent criticism, however, was written by Professor Dashichev on 18 May 1988.[62]

Dashichev's article, which has been regarded as 'the most fundamental critique of Soviet foreign policy to have been published in the USSR in more than half a century', suggests that Soviet foreign policy bore some responsibility for exacerbating tensions between the two superpowers.[63] Dashichev criticises Stalin's post-war policy as 'alien to the nature of socialism'. He raises the question of whether the division of Europe was the sole responsibility of the West, and concludes that 'the hegemonistic, great-power ambitions of Stalinism, becoming deeply rooted in foreign policy, repeatedly jeopardized the political equilibrium among states, especially the East–West equilibrium'. Dashichev acknowledges that the West was right to perceive hegemonistic tendencies in Soviet foreign policy. With regard to the Brezhnev era, he notes the western position and agrees with its concerns:

> As the West saw it ... the Soviet leadership actively took advantage of détente to build up its military forces, striving for military parity with the US and with all the opposing powers combined – a fact unprecedented in history ...
>
> In Western eyes, the expansion of the sphere of Soviet influence reached critical dimensions with the introduction of Soviet troops in Afghanistan ...
>
> Could such a great exacerbation of tensions in the USSR's relations with the West in the late 1970s and early 1980s have been avoided?
>
> Yes, certainly. It is our conviction that the crisis was caused mainly by errors and the incompetent approach of the Brezhnev leadership to the accomplishment of foreign policy tasks.[64]

Such a frank admission that not only could Soviet action be perceived as threatening by the West, but that it was so incompetent that the West's interpretation was understandable, signifies a vital first step in mitigating the security dilemma. Dashichev is explicitly acknowledging that the Soviet Union bore some responsibility for the Cold War by making the West feel threatened, even though no threat existed. Appreciation that one's policies or actions, regardless of the benign nature of their intent, can be misinterpreted as aggressive enables one of the exacerbating psychological dynamics in the spiral model/security dilemma to be mitigated.

These key areas of Soviet foreign policy reveal the dramatic extent of Gorbachev's changes. While the driving force behind the changes was the dire state of the economy, the changes reveal an appreciation that existing foreign policy was not providing security and, therefore, required alteration. They indicate that Gorbachev was aware of the security dilemma.

Defence policy

Gorbachev's rejection of traditional Soviet defence policy can be witnessed in two key areas: prevention of nuclear war, and preparation for war. Both of these areas highlight a movement towards mitigating the security dilemma. As with foreign policy, the driving force was the stagnation of the Soviet economy. In this instance, though, there appears to be a direct correlation between high defence spending and poor economic growth. Thus Michael MccGwire notes: 'the new Soviet leadership saw the high level of investment in defence as one of the main obstacles to renewed economic growth and modernizing the Soviet industrial base'.[65] However, as was the case with foreign policy, it is unlikely that economic considerations alone explain why Gorbachev chose to change Soviet military doctrine in the way that he did. To appreciate fully why the changes occurred, it is also necessary to understand that Gorbachev realised that Soviet defence policy had been an exacerbating factor in the security dilemma and needed to change. This is noted by Roy Allison, who writes:

> A re-evaluation of the basis of security under the Gorbachev leadership, and a sober appraisal of the Soviet military-technological base, resulted in a determination to reject the traditional extensive approach to en-suring defence, which was open-ended in its military requirements, in favour of 'reasonable sufficiency' in defence and an unequivocal com-mitment to war prevention.[66]

As before, it is not intended to imply that economic considerations were unimportant; rather, that the changes signalled an awareness of the security dilemma.

Prevention of nuclear war

The Soviet leadership sought nuclear parity throughout the Cold War, believing that, by doing so, they could deter the West and achieve security. Once parity was achieved during the Brezhnev era, security could be maintained by maintaining equivalence with the West. Maintaining parity with the West in nuclear forces was concomitant with maintaining mutual deterrence in Soviet military thinking. While Gorbachev shared the ob-jective that such thinking sought (i.e., to prevent nuclear war), he did not agree that it should be attained through parity.[67] The maintenance of parity (e.g., by the modernisation of forces) merely legitimised the arms race, according to Gorbachev, and was thus a source of destabilisation. In other words, rather than providing security, the continuing procurement of arms actually reduced security. In true security dilemma/spiral model terminology, Gorbachev stated that: 'from the security point of view the arms race has become an absurdity because its very logic leads to the de-stabilization of international relations and eventually to a nuclear conflict'.[68] Gorbachev was to reiterate the dangers of the arms race on numerous occasions, often with implicit reference to the security dilemma.

> The 'balance of fear' is ceasing to be a deterrent factor. And not only for the reason that fear in general does not counsel reason and can be an impetus to action with unpredictable consequences. It, this fear, is a direct participant in the arms race: By increasing distrust and suspicion, it forms a vicious circle of aggravated tension.[69]

While continuing the Soviet policy that nuclear war must be prevented, Gorbachev appreciated that maintaining parity with the West was not necessarily going to achieve that objective. Indeed, it was his belief that the maintenance of parity actually increased the likelihood of war. Such reasoning clearly manifests an awareness of the security dilemma.

Preparation for war

Soviet military doctrine had long been based on the adage that 'if you want peace prepare for war'. Nuclear war was deterred by preparing to devastate the opponent's homeland, and victory was to be achieved at the conventional level by overrunning western Europe. Christoph Bluth writes:

> The public position of the Soviet leadership in the 1970s emphasized the reality of nuclear strategic parity and mutual assured destruction (MAD) ... The 1970s saw the development and strengthening of theatre conventional and nuclear capabilities. The primary objective in a war in the European theatre would now be to deny NATO the option of mobilizing its resources and exercising its options for escalation. This could be done only by the rapid occupation of Western Europe and the elimination of American bases, thus presenting the United States with the *fait accompli* of having been excluded from Europe.[70]

This inevitably resulted in the Soviet Union maintaining a huge standing army.[71] Thus, when Gorbachev came to power, scarce resources were being expended on weapons for a war that the Soviet Union did not want to fight and actively sought to prevent. At best, this was an extravagant waste of resources; at worst, it was dangerously destabilising. With the military emphasis placed upon seizing the initiative in war, it was quite plausible that, in a crisis, the political decision-makers would have been under tremendous pressure to implement the strategy before it was too late. This scenario is not too dissimilar to Germany prior to the First World War – hence Lebow's reference to the Soviet strategy as 'the Schlieffen Plan revisited'.[72]

The idea that preparing for war was a means of achieving security was rejected by Gorbachev on two counts. The first was that he viewed the outcome of a conventional war in Europe in much the same apocalyptic fashion as a nuclear war.[73] Even if the war could be kept to the conventional level – an extremely dubious 'if' – there were reasons to believe that victory would be as meaningless as it would be in a nuclear war. Blagovolin, while head of the Institute of World Economics and International Relations (IMEMO), claimed:

> The fact of the matter is that for the industrially developed countries [conventional war] has become unacceptable. For example, in Western Europe, which is full of chemical plants, petroleum refineries, and atomic and other power plants, even a conventional conflict would bring destruction fully comparable to the consequences of a nuclear war.[74]

General Yazov also noted that a conventional war 'would have catastrophic consequences comparable to a nuclear cataclysm', while Alexi Arbatov confirmed Blagovolin's concerns and raised doubts as to the feasibility of keeping a war non-nuclear:

> Victory would also be out of the question in a large-scale conventional war in Europe between the WTO and NATO because of the disastrous consequences which even conventional hostilities would have for the population, economy, and environment of the continent and in view of the practically inevitable nuclear escalation of such a conflict.[75]

The implication that even a conventional war could not achieve victory in any meaningful sense was of fundamental importance for the technical aspect of the Soviet military doctrine. The Soviet Union had hoped that mutual deterrence would prevent war, but planned on the assumption that it might fail. As Donald Kelley claims:

> This conclusion led inevitably to greater Soviet emphasis on conventional war-fighting forces and on strategies that stresse[d] the necessity of Soviet preparations for massive and prolonged conventional warfare in the European theatre where the probability of war was the greatest.[76]

Since conventional war was now considered to be as dangerous as nuclear war, it was no longer viable to plan for waging war; the military doctrine would have to change. The importance of this is examined in Chapter 7; it is sufficient at this point to note that the guiding principle of the technical aspect of the military doctrine had been removed. Given that a war-fighting strategy that emphasises taking the offensive is an exacerbating factor in the security dilemma, such a change promises a move towards mitigation.

The second reason for Gorbachev's rejection of the idea that preparing for war was the best way to keep the peace is closely associated with his belief that security is indivisible. Since he perceived security as indivisible, he concluded that the Soviet Union should not seek to acquire security at the expense of others. He rejected the traditional Soviet perception of a direct correlation between increased military capability and enhanced security. While Gorbachev agreed that Soviet military power made others feel insecure, he rejected the view that this enhanced Soviet security because insecure neighbours would not contemplate threatening the USSR. Instead, Gorbachev noted that such insecurity bred tension, distrust and suspicion and, therefore, was not conducive to feeling secure. Rather than enhancing security, Soviet military posture was, at best, not improving security and, at worst, was decreasing security. Gorbachev's awareness of the security dilemma led to his belief that the latter was closer to the mark. Primakov articulated this point in explicit security dilemma terminology:

> the security of some cannot be ensured at the expense of the security of others. Searches for military superiority will inevitably backfire against those who make them – after all, the other side will inevitably search and find countermeasures, and, in critical situations, it may even not want to be 'driven into a corner'.[77]

The criticism of the SS-20 deployment provides a good example of 'countermeasures' producing detrimental effects. Geoffrey Ponton comments that 'the deployment of medium range SS-20 missiles not only "intimidated" West Europeans, but diminished Soviet security by provoking NATO to deploy Pershing and Cruise missiles'.[78] MccGwire supports this analysis by noting NATO's reaction, and claims that the deployment 'served as the catalyst for Western concerns ranging from the Soviet conventional buildup in Europe to Soviet "adventurism" in the Third World'.[79] The inappropriateness of the SS-20 decision was also acknowledged by the Soviet political commentator Alexander Bovin. He referred to the decision as 'kicking balls into our own goal', and said that it 'was detrimental to our prestige in the international arena'.[80]

The SS-20 deployment, however, was only symbolic of the far greater Soviet concern that an emphasis on offence was resulting in a depreciation of Soviet security. This realisation has been noted by a number of Soviet experts. Paul Marantz claims:

> To a far greater extent than ever before, Soviet policy-makers seem to understand the interactive quality of international politics and recognise that their actions – especially in the military realm – have a direct effect on Western policies. The West, it is now recognised, is hostile to the Soviet Union not just because of what it is (i.e., a socialist state) but because of what it does.[81]

MccGwire also notes 'the [Soviet leadership's] admission that the Soviet force posture facing NATO could be seen as threatening', and that it had 'faced up to the fact that in covering the ever more remote contingency of world war it had raised international tension, fostered distrust, and made world war more likely'.[82] Craig Nation also claims that Gorbachev was aware 'that real security could not be built upon an accumulation of military capacity that contributed to a feeling of insecurity among one's neighbours'.[83] Not surprisingly, Gorbachev questioned the military rationale of maintaining equality with the combined strength of all potential enemies. Shevardnadze supported Gorbachev by noting that the idea 'that the Soviet Union can be just as strong as any possible coalition of states opposing it is absolutely untenable'.[84] That Gorbachev was aware that previous Soviet military thinking was a contributing factor in East–West tensions clearly signals his awareness of the security dilemma.

Conclusion

The first step towards mitigating the security dilemma is the realisation by at least one state that it is a victim of a security dilemma. This realisation can be manifest in an awareness that previous policies, perceived as maintaining security and, therefore, appropriate, have in fact fuelled insecurity and are therefore paradoxical. This chapter has sought to provide ample evidence that Gorbachev was aware of the security dilemma and that this awareness played a role in changing Soviet policies. He appreciated that foreign and defence policies created insecurity in the West, that Soviet fear of the West was exaggerated, and that Soviet foreign and defence policies had exacerbated the security dilemma and did not solve the problems that the USSR faced. Two counter-claims to this argue that the Cold War was brought to an end because, first, the western policies were successful in bankrupting the Soviet economy, and, second, Soviet decision-makers needed to create better relations to save their economy and not for any other reason. These counter-claims provide two different challenges to the existence of the security dilemma.

The first argument that the West was victorious because its policies defeated the USSR indicates the western pursuit of appropriate policies. Since the security dilemma is a tragedy, this would appear to indicate that no security dilemma was in operation; where is the tragedy for the West if its policies explain the collapse of the USSR? However, it was shown that there are good reasons for believing that although the West did win, it did so regardless of the policies it pursued. The tragedy, therefore, is that the policies pursued by the superpowers only heightened tension; they did not solve or address the source of their differences.

The second argument is that the changes that Gorbachev introduced were based solely on the need for better international relations so that domestic economic reform was more likely to succeed. In other words, the need to maintain Soviet superpower status, not to expose an illusory incompatibility, lay behind the changes. It has been suggested, however, that Gorbachev's reforms went much further than simply creating more conducive conditions for economic reform. They indicated a desire to alter the perception of the way in which long-term security can be attained. Thus, not only did he engineer the change in the USSR's perception of international relations, but he also sought a fundamental change in Soviet military doctrine. These steps go beyond those needed for domestic reform and would appear to indicate that Gorbachev was aware of the security dilemma. Awareness is only the first step, however; the next chapter will chart the perilous steps that the USSR and the Western Alliance had to undertake subsequently in order to mitigate the Cold War security dilemma. It is sufficient here to note that one state in the Cold War did realise that it was a victim of a security dilemma – and thus conclude that Gorbachev took the first step towards mitigation.

Notes

1. Robert Jervis, 'Cooperation under the Security Dilemma', *World Politics*, 40/1 (1978), p. 212.
2. Daniel Deudney and G. John Ikenberry, 'Who Won the Cold War?', *Foreign Policy*, 87 (Summer 1992), p. 124.
3. Colin L. Powell, 'US Forces: challenges ahead', *Foreign Affairs*, 71/5 (1992/3), p. 44.
4. Sir Michael Alexander, 'NATO's Future Challenges', *RUSI Journal* (April 1992), p. 13.
5. Ibid.
6. Daniel Deudney and G. John Ikenberry, 'The International Sources of Soviet Change', *International Security*, 16/3 (1991/2), p. 99.
7. 'The Dawn of a New Age', *The Observer*, 5 March 1989.
8. 'The Revolutions of 1989 Owe Nothing to the West', *International Herald Tribune*, 4 May 1990.
9. 'X', 'Sources of Soviet Conduct', *Foreign Affairs*, 65/4 (1987), pp. 861–2.
10. John Lewis Gaddis, *Strategies of Containment: a critical appraisal of postwar American national security policy* (New York: 1982), p. 34.
11. Ibid., p. 83.
12. Stephen E. Ambrose, *Rise to Globalism: American foreign policy since 1938* (New York: 5th edn, 1988), p. 98.
13. For the difficulties in measuring military spending, see Fred Chernoff, 'Ending the Cold War: the Soviet retreat and the US military buildup', *International Affairs*, 67/1 (1991), pp. 115–18; Franklyn D. Holzman, 'Politics and Guesswork: CIA and DIA estimates of Soviet military spending', *International Security*, 14/2 (1989), pp. 101–31. With regard to the primacy of the Soviet defence industries, the CIA were estimating between 1967 and 1977 that 12% of the USSR's GNP went on defence. When the economy slowed in the 1980s, this rose to between 15% and 17%. In comparison, the USA's defence budget was 6%–7% of GNP.
14. Gorden B. Smith, *Soviet Politics: continuity and contradiction* (London: 1988), p. 199.
15. 'Corruption, Mismanagement in Uzbekistan', *Pravda Vostoka*, 24 June 1984, p. 1, and *Izvestia*, 29 June 1984, p. 2, trans. in *The Current Digest of the Soviet Press*, 36/26 (25 July 1984), pp. 1–6, 13–14, 24. Hereafter known as *CDSP*.
16. 'More Uzbek Party, State Officials Replaced', *Pravda Vostoka*, 15 July 1984, p. 1, trans. in *CDSP*, 36/33 (12 September 1984), p. 9.
17. 'Bukhara: police corruption; three district party heads out', *Pravda Vostoka*, 31 July 1984, p. 2, trans. in *CDSP*, 36/33 (12 September 1984), p. 10.
18. Edward Acton, 'The Russian Experience: decoding a cautionary tale', *Fin de Siècle: the meaning of the twentieth century*, a seminar series at the University of Keele (2 December 1992), p. 4.

19. Mikhail Gorbachev, *Perestroika: new thinking for our country* (London: 2nd edn, 1988), p. 85.

20. Valerie Bunce, 'The Soviet Union under Gorbachev: ending Stalinism and ending the Cold War', *International Journal*, 46/2 (1991), p. 223.

21. Deudney and Ikenberry, 'Who Won', p. 124.

22. Ibid., p. 133.

23. Quoted in ibid., p. 124.

24. Ibid., p. 125.

25. Dan Quayle address to the National Defence University, 17 November 1989; reprinted in Chernoff, 'Ending the Cold War', p. 114 n9.

26. Ibid., p. 126.

27. John McCain, 'Weapons and Budgets', *Orbis*, 33/2 (1989), p. 184.

28. Chernoff, 'Ending the Cold War', p. 126.

29. Richard Ned Lebow and Janice Gross Stein, *We All Lost the Cold War* (Princeton: 1994), p. 372. The revelation that Soviet defence spending did not rise in response to American defence spending may initially be seen as evidence against the existence of a security dilemma. After all, the logic of the security dilemma is that the Soviet Union should have feared the US action and responded by providing additional forces for security, thereby confirming in American eyes the malign intent of the USSR. It would appear, though, that the Soviet Union did not respond, their increase remained consistent; is this evidence against the security dilemma? This relates to the action–reaction model issue noted in the introductory chapter, and the criticism that because there is no reaction, the security dilemma is not in existence. It was noted that the security dilemma does not require a rigid sequence of actions, reactions and counteractions and that although a response would be expected, it could occur in other areas of their relationship. It would appear that while Soviet decision-makers did not raise their defence spending above its annual increase, they did respond to the American build-up, especially the SDI project, by allocating more rubles to countermeasures. The Soviet Union did respond, therefore, and it is known from the Oleg Gordievsky revelations that the Reagan build-up did cause consternation in the USSR; it would appear that the security dilemma was in existence.

30. Joseph S. Nye, Jr., 'American Strategy after Bipolarity', *International Affairs*, 66/3 (1990), p. 517.

31. Lebow and Stein, *We All Lost*, p. 372.

32. Gorbachev referred to this retardation as the 'braking mechanism': see Gorbachev, *Perestroika*, pp. 14–25.

33. Christoph Bluth, 'Military and Security Issues', in Alex Pravda (ed.), *1991 Yearbook of Soviet Foreign Relations* (London: 1991), p. 227.

34. Janice Gross Stein, 'Political Learning by Doing: Gorbachev as uncommitted thinker and motivated learner', *International Organization*, 48/2 (1994), pp. 157–8.

35. Seweryn Bialer, 'The Soviet Union and the West: security and foreign policy', in Seweryn Bialer and Michael Mandelbaum (eds), *Gorbachev's Russia and American Foreign Policy* (Boulder: 1988), pp. 474–5.

36. Shevardnadze commented that the chief goal of foreign policy was 'to create the maximum favourable external conditions needed in order to conduct internal reform': Eduard Shevardnadze, *The Future Belongs to Freedom* (London: 1991), p. xi. In an interview with *Time* magazine, Gorbachev said: 'You know our domestic plans, draw your own conclusions about what kind of a foreign policy this plan requires': quoted from Bialer, 'The Societ Union and the West', p. 468.

37. Bluth writes: 'enduring relaxation of tension in East–West relations and a significant restraint in the arms competition is an important prerequisite for the success of the policy of domestic perestroika': Bluth, 'Military and Security Issues', p. 227.

38. Stein, 'Political learning', pp. 161–2.

39. Lebow and Stein, *We All Lost*, p. 373.
40. Robert Jervis, *Perception and Misperception in International Politics* (New Jersey: 1976), p. 77.
41. Ibid., p. 82.
42. Gorbachev, *Perestroika*, p. 143.
43. Ibid., p. 139.
44. For both quotes, see Peter Zwick, 'New Thinking and Foreign Policy under Gorbachev', *PS: Political Science and Politics*, 22/2 (1989), p. 216.
45. Gorbachev, *Perestroika*, p. 147.
46. Yevgeny Primakov, quoted from Allen Lynch, *The Soviet Study of Intentional Relations* (Cambridge: 1987), p. 31.
47. 'Soviet Foreign Policy's New Look', *Pravda*, 26 July 1988, p. 4, trans. in *CDSP*, 40/30 (24 August 1988), pp. 13–14.
48. The western perception of Soviet aggression was based not only on the ideological aspect of class struggle in Soviet foreign policy, but also on the immense size and offensive stance of Soviet military forces.
49. The reason why this enhances the prospect of a security dilemma is that those states that perceive another state as aggressive are likely to interpret that state's actions as evidence of aggressive intent. As such, they are vulnerable to the spiral model/security dilemma.
50. Gorbachev, *Perestroika*, p. 147.
51. 'Gorbachev, "New Thinking" in World Affairs', *Pravda* and *Izvestia*, 3 November 1987, pp. 2–5, trans. in *CDSP*, 39/45 (9 December 1987), pp. 12–16.
52. Ibid., p. 14.
53. Ibid.
54. Ibid., p. 13.
55. The primary needs of the Soviet economy were also evident in this respect. Gorbachev suggested that imperialism might be restrained by internal factors (he refers to the drain on the US economy by the military-industrial complex), as opposed to external factors (the deterrent effect of a huge Soviet military), thereby paving the way towards reducing the burden of the military on the economy.
56. Quoted from Paul Marantz, 'Changing Soviet Conceptions of International Security', in Sylvia Woodby and Alfred B. Evans, Jr. (eds), *Restructuring Soviet Ideology* (Boulder: 1990), p. 125.
57. Ibid., p. 124.
58. Ibid., p. 113. US pronouncements include that of John Foster Dulles, who said: 'Khrushchev does not need to be convinced of our good intentions. He knows we are not aggressors and do not threaten the security of the Soviet Union': quoted from Jervis, *Perception*, p. 68.
59. Shevardnadze noted the sacrosanctity of foreign policy and on 27 June 1987 sought to alter this by implicitly welcoming criticism. He said: 'Bold, interesting and controversial articles have appeared on many basic questions of domestic life in all its manifestations, party and state construction, the economy, culture, art and science. But there is nothing like it in the field of foreign policy. Is it really because everything is correct with us and variants other than those which are being implemented do not exist?: quoted from Marantz, 'Changing Soviet Conceptions', p. 114. Gorbachev's speech on the 70th anniversary of the Bolshevik Revolution also provided an opportunity for discussion on Soviet foreign policy: see 'Yakovlev, Historians React to Speech', *Pravda*, 4 November 1987, p. 8, trans. in *CDSP*, 39/44 (2 December 1987), p. 11.
60. 'Party Approves Theses for the 19th Conference', *Pravda* and *Izvestia*, 24 May 1988, p. 1, trans. in *CDSP*, 40/21 (22 June 1988), p. 9.
61. 'Restructuring and Foreign Policy', *Izvestia*, 16 June 1988, p. 5, trans. in *CDSP*, 40/24 (13 July 1988), p. 5.
62. 'Wrong Turns in Soviet Foreign Policy Seen', *Literaturnaya gazeta*, 18 May 1988, p. 14, trans. ibid., pp. 1–5.

63. Marantz, 'Changing Soviet Conceptions', p. 115.
64. 'Wrong Turns in Soviet Foreign Policy Seen', p. 4.
65. Michael MccGwire, *Perestroika and Soviet National Security* (Washington: 1991), p. 241.
66. Roy Allison, 'Introduction', in Roy Allison (ed.), *Radical Reform in Soviet Defence Policy: selected papers from the Fourth World Congress for Soviet and East European Studies* (London: 1992), p. xiii.
67. 'Parity' became an ambiguous term, with military and civilian experts disagreeing over what it actually meant. Thus, while Gorbachev disagreed with the traditional Soviet concept of parity, it was not unusual for him and his supporters to use the term. 'Parity' was not alone in this respect; such phrases as 'reasonable sufficiency' and 'defensive defence' also became subject to various interpretations. The implication of this is discussed in Chapter 7.
68. Gorbachev, *Perestroika*, p. 141.
69. 'Gorbachev Extends Test Ban until January 1', *Pravda* and *Izvestia*, 19 August 1986, p. 1, trans. in *CDSP*, 38/33 (17 September 1986), p. 5.
70. Christoph Bluth, *New Thinking in Soviet Military Policy* (London: 1990), pp. 10–11.
71. In addition to increasing the number of divisions (175 in mid-1960s to 200 by mid-1980s), there was a rise in the number of conventional artillery pieces and a change in training which gave greater attention to fighting in a non-nuclear war: see Raymond L. Garthoff, *Deterrence and the Revolution in Soviet Military Doctrine* (Washington: 1990), pp. 70–1. Richard Ned Lebow has quoted V. Ye. Savkin as estimating a Soviet superiority of '3–5 : 1 in infantry, 6–8 : 1 for artillery, 3–4 : 1 for tanks and a self-propelled artillery, and 5–10 : 1 in aircraft': Richard Ned Lebow, 'The Soviet Offensive in Europe: the Schlieffen Plan revisited?', *International Security*, 9/4 (1985), p. 51.
72. Lebow, 'The Soviet Offensive in Europe', pp. 44–78.
73. Gorbachev has stated that 'military technology has developed to such an extent that even a non-nuclear war would now be comparable with a nuclear war in its destructive effect': see Gorbachev, *Perestroika*, p. 141.
74. 'A Call to De-emphasize Military Strength', *Izvestia*, 18 November 1988, p. 5, trans. in *CDSP*, 40/46 (14 December 1988), p. 3.
75. Alexi Arbatov, 'How Much Defence Is Sufficient?', *International Affairs (Moscow)*, 4 (April 1989), p. 34. The Yazov quote is from Garthoff, *Deterrence*, p. 103.
76. Donald R. Kelley, 'Gorbachev's "New Political Thinking" and Soviet National Security Policy', in Woodby and Evans, Jr., *Restructuring Soviet Ideology*, p. 137.
77. 'New "Flexibility" in Soviet Foreign Policy', *Pravda*, 10 July 1987, p. 4, trans. in *CDSP*, 39/28 (12 August 1987), p. 4. The 'driven into a corner' remark is rather confusing, but it probably refers to the state being left with little choice but to initiate hostilities.
78. Geoffrey Ponton, *The Soviet Era* (Oxford: 1994), p. 153.
79. MccGwire, *Perestroika*, p. 248.
80. 'Restructuring and Foreign Policy', *Izvestia*, 16 June 1988, p. 5, trans. in *CDSP*, 40/24 (13 July 1988), p. 5.
81. Marantz, 'Changing Soviet Conceptions', p. 122.
82. Michael MccGwire, 'A Mutual Security Regime for Europe?', *International Affairs*, 64/3 (1988), pp. 361, 378.
83. Craig Nation, *Black Earth, Red Star: a history of Soviet security policy 1917–1991* (Ithaca: 1992), p. 294.
84. 'The 19th All-Union CPSU Conference: foreign policy and diplomacy', *International Affairs (Moscow)*, 10 (October 1988), p. 18. By questioning the need to accumulate so much military capacity, Gorbachev and his supporters were not only redefining the method of achieving security, but also seeking to reduce the defence burden on the economy.

Chapter Seven

Resolution

In the previous chapter it was suggested that Gorbachev appreciated that the USSR was a victim of a security dilemma. He realised that past policies were failing to achieve their objectives and, therefore, were paradoxical. This awareness of their self-defeating nature revealed that change was needed; however, this is only the first step towards mitigation. In itself, realisation of the security dilemma does not mitigate its effects. In order to halt the downward spiral of insecurity, it was necessary for Gorbachev to implement changes in Soviet foreign policy and military force posture. In order for these changes to mitigate the security dilemma, as explained in Chapter 3, it is necessary to witness the embodiment of common security, non-offensive defence (NOD), and minimum deterrence in Soviet new thinking. This is the yardstick by which new thinking can be assessed as a mitigator of the security dilemma. However, while this may reveal that Gorbachev pursued a policy that *could* have mitigated the Cold War security dilemma, it does not necessarily follow that it *did* mitigate the Cold War security dilemma. This is examined in the final section of the chapter. Before examining Gorbachev's implementation of new thinking, it is necessary to outline the ways in which the security dilemma can be mitigated. By drawing on analysis from previous chapters, the difficulties involved in mitigating the security dilemma – and the solutions to these difficulties – can be placed in a context that will aid the examination of the late 1980s.

How to Mitigate the Security Dilemma

Dangers and difficulties

The problem of changing policy in order to mitigate the security dilemma is that such change will invariably appear to be a sign of weakness. This is what Jervis is referring to when he writes: 'one side must take an initiative that increases the other state's security'.[1] This is taken as a sign of weakness because the state will be seeking a conciliatory approach instead of showing its traditional resolve over an issue.[2] The danger for the initiating state is twofold. First, the other state must be a status quo power, since a revisionist power will take advantage of the initiator's weakness in order to change the current status quo. Indeed, if the other state is a revisionist power, then the initiator is not in a security dilemma and should not seek to alter its policy. Of course, determining whether the other state is a revisionist or a status quo power is extremely difficult; hence the first problem in mitigating the security dilemma is the initiator's uncertainty regarding the other state's intentions – the possibility of being taken advantage of by a revisionist power. The second danger is that while it is essential for the other state to be a status quo power, it does not necessarily follow that the initiator will not be threatened. While the incompatibility between states in a security dilemma is illusory, the heightened tension, suspicion and distrust indicate that their relationship is marred by real hostility. Jervis recognises this when he writes:

> If the prophecy of hostility is thoroughly self-fulfilling, the belief that there is a high degree of conflict will create a conflict that is no longer illusory. Overtures that earlier would have decreased tensions and cleared up misunderstandings will now be taken as signs of weakness.[3]

The implication of this is that a sign of weakness may invite an attack by the other status quo power as it seeks to solve the conflict while it is in a superior position. Herein lies the second danger: even a status quo power may take advantage of a conciliatory gesture. Given these two dangers, is it possible to follow the advice of spiral model theorists (i.e., reassure the other state of your benign intention by pursuing a conciliatory policy) when the other state is blatantly hostile? Indeed, is mitigation of the security dilemma possible?

The answer lies in understanding the nature of the conflict between the two status quo powers in the security dilemma. Jervis's use of the term 'conflict' is misleading; although both states are hostile to one another, this does not necessarily mean that they are a threat to one another. It is important to be aware of the reason for hostility in a security dilemma. The cause of the hostility is that, despite their efforts to show that the other state has little to gain and much to lose from attacking it, the other state continues to ignore these efforts and pursues threatening policies. Butterfield refers to this pattern as 'each side [being] locked in its own system of self-righteousness'.[4] According to Butterfield, this pattern is likely to result in war; hence the tragedy of the security dilemma. However, Jervis argues that if the pattern is interrupted and one side does not respond, then, in its moment of weakness, it could be attacked. Yet it does not follow logically that this will happen. The hostility that the state feels towards the other is based purely on the mistaken belief that the other means it harm, not on the fact that the other is preventing an aggressive action. For one of the states to take advantage of a conciliatory gesture would indicate the adoption of malign intent (a complete reversal of its previous objective). Thus, although Jervis writes that 'even a status quo power may interpret conciliation as indicating that the other side is so weak that expansion is possible at little risk', this might not always be true.[5] Not all status quo powers will take advantage of a conciliatory gesture, even if the relationship is marked by real hostility. This will be reinforced if the risks of adopting a malign objective could rebound on the state (for instance, in a nuclear war). While this may indicate that mitigation is possible, it does not lessen the perceived dangers that the initiator faces. How does a state that wants to break away from the spiral of insecurity determine the trustworthiness of the other state? In the language of the prisoner's dilemma game, how can the state ensure against becoming a 'sucker'?

If the hostility is the result of the other state's aggressive intentions, then the likely outcome is that the state embarking on conciliation will suffer defection. However, if the hostility is not the result of aggressive intent, but mistrust and suspicion, then defection might not be the outcome. In this scenario, which is the spiral model/security dilemma, a reduction of distrust and suspicion may produce a cooperative response from the other state because the cause of hostility is being addressed. Thus, determining whether the other state can be trusted is ascertained when the state responds in a cooperative fashion. However, the distrust and suspicion that mars the relationship may affect the willingness of the other state to risk cooperation; after all, the other state is also faced with the problem of determining trustworthiness. The onus to overcome the other state's understandable suspicion rests with the initiator. How can the initiator convince the other state or states that its new policies are conciliatory and are not a ruse to lull the state into a false sense of security? It is the ability to overcome both of these problems (i.e., determine trustworthiness, convince others of good intentions) that determines whether the security dilemma can be mitigated.

A course of action that might overcome these problems is the pursuit of common security. In Chapter 3 it was noted that common security policies emphasise security as interdependent; states have a common interest in survival and it is believed that they cannot achieve security at the expense of one another. Common security, therefore, is relevant to both of the difficulties that the initiator faces: first, by emphasising the shared interest in survival, common security reduces the likelihood of either state gaining from defection; second, it reduces the likelihood of defection by highlighting that, because security is a mutual concept, it can only be achieved via cooperative enterprises. Was new thinking a common security approach to achieving security?

New thinking as a common security policy

It is evident that new thinking did share the core themes of common security. Underpinning Gorbachev's new thinking on security was the theme that the problems that affect the security of all nations – and are thus a threat to universal values – are common problems that can only be solved by all states cooperating together. Although Gorbachev did mention such issues as the environment, population expansion and a collapse of the international economy, the most obvious common problem is the existence, and potentially devastating effects, of nuclear weapons. According to Gorbachev, it is the existence and global effects of these weapons that have made security interdependent. Gorbachev likened the situation to that of mountain climbers: 'the nations of the world resemble today a pack of mountaineers tied together by a climbing rope. They can either climb on together to the mountain peak or fall together into the abyss.'[6] The interdependent theme led Gorbachev to voice two assumptions about security. The first was that security could no longer be acquired through the use of military force. Gorbachev wrote:

> *Nuclear war cannot be a means of achieving political, economic, ideological or any other goals* ... Nuclear war is senseless; it is irrational. There would be neither winners nor losers in a global nuclear conflict; world civilization would inevitably perish. It is suicide, rather than a war in the conventional sense of the word ...
>
> The only way to security is through political decisions and disarmament [emphasis in original].[7]

Gorbachev was reiterating the Palme Commission's point that nuclear war was unwinnable.[8] The second assumption was that, in accordance with common security ideas, security had become indivisible and, therefore, 'there should be no striving for security for oneself at the expense of others'.[9] Gorbachev claimed: 'the new political outlook calls for the recognition of one more simple axiom: security is indivisible: It is either equal security for all or none at all.'[10] These assumptions led Gorbachev to share the Palme Commission's view of the dangers of nuclear weapons and the need for a nuclear-free world. He wrote: 'In our age genuine and equal security can be guaranteed by constantly lowering the level of the strategic balance from which nuclear and other weapons of mass destruction should be completely eliminated.'[11] Since new thinking and common security shared the same core assumptions about security, the implementation of new thinking was the implementation of common security. As such, it did address the difficulties outlined above and, therefore, provided an opportunity to mitigate the security dilemma. Of course, actual mitigation would depend upon overcoming those difficulties via the implementation of new thinking and the western response to this new Soviet foreign policy.

Western recognition of new thinking as a common security policy

The initiating state may be able to convince other states of its benign intentions if the other states recognise the conciliatory nature of a policy. It has been suggested that the western peace community introduced the Soviet leadership to common security and, therefore, influenced the development of new thinking.[12] If this is true, then it might help to explain why new thinking was recognised by certain members of the Western Alliance as a sincere attempt to improve relations; familiarity breeds confidence regarding other states' intentions. The key to this 'familiarity factor' is whether the West recognised new thinking as a conciliatory as opposed to a deceptive policy. This does not mean that the origins of new thinking had to be found in the West, but if the West were harbingers of change, they would be quicker to respond in a positive fashion. The argument that new thinking became Soviet policy because of western influence has been articulated by Thomas Risse-Kappen and Janice Gross Stein. Thomas Risse-Kappen writes: 'common security [was] new to the Soviet security debate, [its] intellectual origins must be found outside the country and its foreign policy institutes'.[13] Janice Gross Stein supports this by claiming that 'the ideas that informed the reconceptualization of Soviet security interests and centred around notions of "common security" and "reasonable sufficiency" originated in the Western liberal internationalist community'.[14] If it is true that Gorbachev was influenced by western common security advocates, then this would ensure that new thinking was recognisable for what it was or, even more importantly, for what it was not – a malicious attempt to lull the West into a false sense of security.[15]

Whether the origins of new thinking can be found in the western liberal community is contentious. While its advocates highlight the contact that Gorbachev had with social democratic leaders like Willy Brandt and Egon Bahr,[16] as well as the ideas of close advisers,[17] others have argued that the origins of new thinking were home-grown. According to this view, new thinking emanated from Soviet Third World specialists in the 1970s;[18] they note that other close advisers to Gorbachev had little contact with western ideas, yet still articulated common security ideals.[19] With regard to mitigating the security dilemma, and specifically the role of familiarity, the key is not whether the West influenced new thinking, but whether the ideas embodied in new thinking were familiar to the West. If the ideas were recognisable, then this might reduce western fears of being lulled into a false sense of security – a situation often referred to as fooled by Soviet propaganda. Of course, the 'West' as a bloc of similar ideas did not actually exist. The result of this was that new thinking was not familiar to all western countries. If familiarity did breed confidence, however, then it might be expected that those countries that did recognise new thinking as a common security approach would be quicker to understand, embrace and reciprocate Gorbachev's policies than those that did not.

Graduated reciprocation in tension reduction (GRIT) and institutionalised security regimes

In order to mitigate the security dilemma, a state needs to overcome the two difficulties of determining trustworthiness and convincing others of its benign intent. For the USSR, this meant overcoming their own fear of defection by witnessing a western willingness to reciprocate their initial conciliatory policies. The crucial ingredient for this reciprocal response from the West was for the Soviet Union to overcome the West's distrust of their motives. Familiarity would only be able to help once Gorbachev began to implement new thinking. Ultimately, the success of new thinking would depend upon whether Gorbachev's implementation of a common security policy would induce reciprocation from the Western Alliance. It is the uncertainty that states have about each other's intentions that lies at the heart of the security dilemma, so the ability of new thinking to reduce that uncertainty and allay the West's fear of Soviet duplicity would determine its success.

How could Gorbachev embark upon conciliatory policies to prove that he was sincere in his desire to escape the spiral of insecurity when those same policies could also expose the USSR to western defection? The answer may lie with institutionalised security regimes, since these are capable not only of encouraging reciprocation, but also of reducing the likelihood of defection. This is because they clarify and operational-ise the accepted norms and rules that guide state behaviour over a particular issue. By clarifying these procedures, states are better able to understand why another state is acting in particular fashion. In other words, uncertainty regarding the state's true intentions is replaced by confidence regarding the state's true intentions. Janice Gross Stein makes reference to this when she writes:

> Insofar as agreed procedures are in place, individual decision-making is both constrained and predicable. It is constrained insofar as norms and rules are reflected in the collective procedures, and it is predicable insofar as governments are committed to known rules and procedures ... It is precisely these constraints and commitments, both of which reduce uncertainty, which make the management of conflict easier among regime members.[20]

This awareness of what states are doing – and why – is referred to as 'transparency'. This transparency reduces the likelihood of misperception of state action and, therefore, contains the solution to the two problems of avoiding defection and persuading others to reciprocate conciliatory gestures. By reducing misperception, states become more confident about the expected behaviour of one another and are therefore more likely to reciprocate conciliatory policies. In addition, by enabling states to determine intent more accurately, transparency makes it much easier for states to detect defection. Institutionalised security regimes may also make defection a less appealing option by containing built-in forms of punishment for states that defect. It was this ability to induce reciprocation and reduce defection that Robert Axelrod and Robert Keohane refer to when they claim:

> International institutions may therefore be significant, since institutions embody, and affect, actors' expectations. Thus institutions can alter the behaviour of others on future issues. The principles and rules of international regimes make governments concerned about precedents, increasing the likelihood that they will attempt to punish defectors. In this way, international regimes help to link the future with the present. [This is] true of arms control agreements in which [the] willingness to make future agreements depends on others' compliance with previous arrangements.[21]

Institutionalised security regimes would appear to be ideal mechanisms for mitigating the security dilemma and are therefore a useful criterion for examining the Gorbachev era. However, if security regimes can provide this benefit, why have so few been established between the superpowers?

The most obvious reason is that security regimes are attempting to constrain state activity on an issue that is of paramount importance to a state's national interest (i.e., security). Whereas defection in the prisoner's dilemma game results in a prison sentence, defection in the superpowers' relationship could result in national destruction. The stakes are very high; if there is an element of doubt regarding the true intentions of the other state, then prudence dictates that a security regime is not in the state's best interests. Given that, during the Cold War, both superpowers believed that the other was seeking to change the existing status quo (the worldwide Marxist revolution/the inevitable war between capitalism and socialism), it is not surprising that they were reluctant to create security regimes. The two notable exceptions to this – Strategic Arms Limitation Treaty (SALT) and Non-Proliferation Treaty (NPT) regimes – were both concerned with maintaining and strengthening the current status quo. Prior to Gorbachev's arrival, attempts to establish regimes to deal with issues which, if defection occurred, might alter the status quo in favour of one of the superpowers were floundering (intermediate-range nuclear forces (INF), Strategic Arms Reduction Treaty (START), Mutual Balanced Force Reductions (MBFR)).

If Gorbachev was to achieve security regimes in these areas, he needed to convince the West of his sincerity.

Forming a security regime raises a puzzle for mitigation. In order to escape the spiral of insecurity/security dilemma, Gorbachev needed to induce reciprocation of conciliatory policies from the West while also seeking to maintain Soviet security in cases of western duplicity. Institutionalised security regimes, by reducing the fear of defection and enhancing the prospects of cooperation, appear to provide the solution. However, security is of such vital importance that states need to be convinced that defection is extremely unlikely. Given the suspicious nature of the Cold War relationship, the superpowers' fear of defection, most evident in their poor record of arms control reduction talks, mitigated against the prospect of such a regime being formed. How, then, is it possible to create institutionalised security regimes in order to mitigate the security dilemma?

The answer lies in the incremental approach noted in Chapter 3. It is suggested that the initial areas in which conciliation can occur will be those in which the state's vital interests are not at stake. If such limited conciliation is reciprocated, then it is suggested that states will be more willing to cooperate on reducing the threatening aspects of their policies. In other words, the approach to building trust between adversaries is an incremental one. As they become more confident about each other's intentions, so the fear of defection lessens and they feel more able to tackle those issues which, while perceived as vital for national security, induce the greatest fear in each other. If Gorbachev was able to establish security regimes on issues that were not of vital importance, then a security regime on arms reduction might follow which would mitigate the security dilemma.

This still leaves the question of how Gorbachev was supposed to induce the creation of security regimes – even on issues that would not give rise to monumental consequences if defection occurred. An answer can be found in the 1960s writings of Charles Osgood and Amitai Etzioni. Osgood introduces a process whereby the two superpowers could reverse the spiral of increased tension by embarking upon conciliatory policies; the process is called 'graduated reciprocation in tension-reduction' (GRIT).[22] Osgood claims:

> being unconventional in nature – and worse, being conciliatory – GRIT is open to suspicion abroad and resistance at home, particularly under the conditions of the Cold War mentality. Therefore ...
>
> The unilateral initiatives that give substance to Graduated Reciprocation in Tension-reduction must be shown to satisfy reasonable requirements of national security, while at the same time risking enough of it in small bits to induce reciprocation from opponents and thereby reduce world tension.[23]

Osgood highlights the need to maintain security (i.e., avoid defection) while also inducing reciprocation (i.e., overcome suspicion) of conciliatory policies.

The achievement of GRIT requires the initiating state to show a large degree of persistence and fortitude. According to Osgood, the acronym is appropriate; it suggests the type of national determination that is required in order to implement the strategy. The essence of the GRIT strategy is that the initiator needs to undertake a number of explicit, unilateral steps to indicate a willingness to reduce tension. If the steps are not immediately reciprocated, then the initiator will continue to take conciliatory steps in other areas of their relationship and will explicitly encourage the other state to respond in kind. Osgood suggests that in order to pre-empt the cry of 'trickery', one of the first steps could even be a fairly dramatic initiative. The need for persistence is emphasised most acutely by Osgood's insistence that conciliatory moves should continue even if tension rises in other areas of the relationship. He is aware of the need to maintain security, however, and advocates retaining a nuclear capability, at least until fears of defection have receded.

Osgood's GRIT strategy was the basis of a similar strategy prescribed by Amitai Etzioni in his book *The Hard Way to Peace*.[24] Etzioni refines GRIT into a 'gradualist' approach to reducing tension. Etzioni suggests that GRIT can be acquired via three stages. The first requires the initiator to embark upon unilateral 'psychological' measures that will help open communication between the two states: in other words, to engage in dialogue or, as Etzioni writes, 'to calm jittery nerves and tone down the interbloc argument so that the sides can again hear what they are saying to each other'.[25] If, and only if, there has been success at this stage, does Etzioni prescribe that the subsequent steps should be embarked upon. The second stage still requires unilateral initiatives, but, unlike the 'symbolic' nature of the first stage, these will be 'comparatively important political and military concessions' which require some form of reciprocation from the other side.[26] The final stage, which is dependent upon success at the previous stage, will occur when 'suspicion and fear [have been] reduced to a level where fruitful negotiations are possible'.[27] The final stage therefore involves bilateral agreements as a means of achieving further concessions. This three-staged gradualist approach clearly supports the incremental approach noted earlier. Etzioni believes that it is necessary to conduct these threat reduction measures in a negotiated format because the fear of defection ensures that unilateral initiatives will only involve minor concessions. Thus, gaining the type of reciprocated measures necessary to mitigate the security dilemma requires negotiated agreements. Such an agreement on arms control/disarmament would be concomitant with the establishment of institutionalised security regimes.

These two strategies clearly relate to the establishment of security regimes, with their emphasis on reciprocity reducing the fear of defection and enhancing the possibilities of cooperation. Joshua Goldstein and John Freeman introduce another variant on GRIT – 'super-GRIT'. In essence, their model is little different to Osgood's GRIT or Etzioni's 'gradualist' or progressive GRIT (PGRIT). They reiterate the need to show persistence and to strengthen reciprocity by responding to the concessions of by the other state, but they state that the unilateral initiatives should be of a permanent and sporadic nature. According to Goldstein and Freeman, GRIT-type strategies are relevant to the Gorbachev era. They state that 'the Soviet Union since 1985 has implemented a strategy that strongly resembles super-GRIT'.[28] This is also supported by Richard Bitzinger, who claims: 'whether he knew it or not, Gorbachev was practising classic "graduated and reciprocated initiatives in tension reduction"'.[29] If this is true, then the implementation of new thinking can be seen as a mitigator of the security dilemma, though this does not in itself prove that new thinking *did* mitigate the security dilemma. Ascertaining the answer to this requires an examination of the Gorbachev era from the perspective of GRIT-type strategies and the establishment of institutionalised security regimes.

Gorbachev's Foreign Policy Initiatives, 1985–1988

Nuclear moratorium

At the end of 1985 the superpowers met in Geneva. This was regarded by Soviet decision-makers as an important summit where they would ascertain the United States' views on peace and war – and thus whether common security was an objective which could realistically be achieved with the USA. In security dilemma terminology, it was Gorbachev's attempt to determine if the USA was a status quo power, in which case GRIT-type strategies might work, or whether the USA was a revisionist power, in which case new thinking was inappropriate.

In true GRIT fashion, Gorbachev announced a number of unilateral initiatives that would 'pave the way [for the Geneva meeting] by creating a more favourable climate'.[30] As would be expected in a GRIT-type strategy, these initiatives were on issues carrying minor risks to Soviet security, but with a larger political impact. Thus, in April 1985 Gorbachev announced a halt in the deployment of SS-20 missiles in Europe, following this in October by a reduction in the number facing Europe to 243. In July Gorbachev announced a unilateral moratorium on nuclear testing. This latter initiative was specifically intended to induce reciprocation. Gorbachev said:

> out of a desire to set a good example, the Soviet Union has decided to

unilaterally halt all of its nuclear explosions ... The Soviet Union anticipates that the United States will respond favourably to this initiative and halt its nuclear explosions.[31]

This moratorium on nuclear testing was a classic example of a GRIT-type strategy in action. It had been announced publicly, so as to give the USA time to evaluate the significance of the initiative and also to influence the administration's interpretation of the initiative. The announcement had included an unequivocal invitation to reciprocate on an issue that would not compromise either state's security if defection occurred. The US response was negative; they rejected the Soviet offer on three counts. The first was that the American administration believed that it was in their interest to modernise their nuclear armoury in order to strengthen their bargaining position in arms control talks or future crises. As such, the initiative was regarded as a pressurising tactic rather than a cooperative venture. The second reason was that the Americans did not think that a test ban would be verifiable, and the final reason centred on their belief that the Soviet Union had already completed its testing, making the initiative nothing more than a ploy to disrupt US nuclear testing.

If the last two reasons are correct, then Gorbachev's unilateral initiative was not an example of a GRIT-type strategy.[32] However, there appears to be some contention regarding their validity. In May 1986 American and Soviet scientists privately monitored US tests and, although their findings are contentious, claimed them to be verifiable. There is also reason to doubt that the USSR had completed its nuclear testing.[33] Despite Gorbachev's willingness to allow on-site verification, however, the Reagan administration remained firm in its determination to continue nuclear testing. Secretary of State Shultz claimed that 'as long as there are nuclear weapons, there is a need to conduct tests'.[34] Despite this negative response, the Soviet Union continued to extend the moratorium (January 1986, August 1986 and January 1987) before curtailing the experiment after nineteen months when the USA tested a nuclear weapon in February 1987. Was the moratorium a failure as a GRIT strategy?

In so far as the USA failed to reciprocate the Soviet initiative, it would appear to have been a failure. Gorbachev had stated that 'we expect the US leadership to make a concrete and positive decision that would have a very favourable effect on the entire situation, would change it greatly and build up trust between our countries'.[35] As a criterion for judging success, this was expecting too much too soon, a point that even Gorbachev must have accepted, as he continued to extend the ban despite the lack of US reciprocation.[36] However, the failure of the Americans to reciprocate means that it is difficult not to concur with Bitzinger when he writes: 'GRIT simply did not work here.'[37] But this conclusion fails to appreciate the broader impact of the moratorium on the superpowers' relationship.

The willingness of the Soviet Union to persist with the ban in the face of US resistance did begin to dismantle the western suspicion and distrust of Soviet motives that exacerbated the security dilemma. Soviet observer N. V. Shishlin claims:

> the Soviet initiative has been rejected by the United States ... [But this does not] mean that this Soviet step was useless ... In shaping the political climate in the middle of 1985 this step, perhaps, is the most significant intervention ... designed to change this climate for the better.[38]

This is supported by Goldstein and Freeman, who note that the 'initiative did succeed in promoting a peaceful image of the Soviet Union among the American public and among US allies, as well as among a few Reagan administration officials'.[39] While not having the effect for which Gorbachev had initially hoped, the moratorium did begin, albeit in a limited fashion, to reduce tension.

The Geneva summit at the end of 1985 was disappointing for the Soviet Union in that it failed to produce anything concrete, but it nevertheless produced some valuable insights for Soviet decision-makers into the way in which the Reagan administration saw the East–West conflict.[40] Thus, while Gorbachev failed to convince Reagan that his Strategic Defense Initiative (SDI) project was destabilising, he did come to believe that Reagan saw SDI as a purely defensive weapon. In addition, on the issue of nuclear weapons, Gorbachev found in Reagan a kindred spirit. The two sides agreed in the Geneva Accords that nuclear war was inadmissible and that neither side should seek military superiority.[41] The summit appeared to confirm that a strategy based on conciliation could improve East–West relations and, as a result, mitigate the security dilemma. MccGwire confirms this when he writes:

> This whole process seems to have provided Gorbachev and Shevardnadze with the confirmation they needed that the new political thinking about international relations was indeed the correct approach and that President Reagan offered an avenue for making progress in this direction.[42]

Dramatic initiative: eliminate nuclear weapons

The beginning of 1986 was to witness an example of Osgood's 'dramatic initiative' from the Soviet Union. Undaunted by the lack of reciprocation from the West on the nuclear test moratorium, Gorbachev announced a plan to free the world of nuclear weapons within fifteen years or, failing that, at least by the end of the century. The proposal was divided into three stages. The first, to be completed by 1990, applied to the superpowers.

It included a 50% reduction in ICBMs, as agreed at Geneva, the elimination of ICBMs in Europe, and the renunciation of the development,
testing and deployment of space-based weapons. The second stage would
last for 5–7 years and involved the elimination of all tactical nuclear
weapons and a ban on the creation of new weapons of mass destruction.
The final stage would involve the elimination of all remaining nuclear
arms. In keeping with GRIT expectations, Gorbachev announced the
extension of the unilateral moratorium on nuclear testing and a proposal
to eliminate chemical weapons and the industrial bases that created them,
and he also expressed support for reducing conventional forces at the
Conference on Confidence- and Security-Building Measures and Disarmament in Europe (CDE) that was being held in Stockholm.

The response by the West was negative. The British were not prepared
to freeze their nuclear capability while the superpowers cut theirs by 50%,
and Gorbachev said of the American response that the 'positive expressions
[were] lost in various sorts of reservations ... that, to all intents and
purposes, block[ed] the resolution of the fundamental questions of disarmament'.[43] The West clearly remained sceptical of Gorbachev's initiatives.
Having reached a temporary dead end on nuclear issues, Gorbachev turned
his attention to the arms control talks at the CDE.

An institutionalised security regime

Prior to new thinking, the Soviet objectives for the CDE differed from
those of the western states. However, the Soviet position changed with
Gorbachev's arrival and began to resemble the western preference for
initiating CSBMs that would engender more transparency in military
activities and thereby reduce tension. The breakthrough occurred in
August 1986, when the Soviet Union announced its willingness to accept
mandatory on-site inspections of CSBMs. According to Stefan Lehne,
'the decision to accept on-site verification in Stockholm was the clearest
signal so far of the new Soviet leadership's changing approach to military
security and its determination to achieve progress in arms control'.[44] With
the Soviet turn-about, a new CSBM regime quickly fell into place. On
22 September 1986 the Stockholm Document was adopted, the first
agreement in the area of arms control in the 1980s. The document
included, among other things, the following provisions:

> *Notification*: Prior notification of exercise activities, troop transfers, and
> concentrations involving at least 13000 troops or 300 battle tanks, or
> amphibious landing and parachute assaults involving at least 3000
> troops; notification of the participation of airforces, if at least 200 sorties
> take place during the activity; notification is required 42 days in advance
> and must include detailed information on the activity.

Observation: Observers are required to be invited from all CSCE states to all notifiable activities involving at least 17000 troops.

Annual Calendars: By November 15 of each year all states will exchange lists of notifiable military activities forecast for the subsequent year, including information on these activities.

Constraining Provisions: Notifiable activities exceeding 75000 troops must not take place unless they are announced two years in advance. Activities exceeding 40000 troops are prohibited unless they are included in the Annual Calendar.

Verification: On-site inspections, on the ground, from the air, of three inspections per year.[45]

While this agreement on CSBM was not the first of its type between East and West, the measures were significantly better than those agreed in the Helsinki Document of 1975. They provided longer notification times, increased information exchange, and an obligatory system for verification. The requirement for notification of military activity, combined with the presence of observers at an exercise, reduced the likelihood of the activity being perceived as a precursor to an act of aggression. Sverre Logaard refers to this when he writes: 'there will be less scope for biased perception of regular [military] activities'.[46] These CSBMs are clearly of relevance in mitigating the security dilemma; by creating transparency, they are re-ducing the uncertainty factor that is of such importance in the formation of a security dilemma. These measures are also of particular value because they form an institutionalised security regime, thereby further enhancing trust and reducing defection. This is clearly expounded by Lehne when he writes:

> Implementation of the Stockholm measures contributes to greater open-ness and predictability. The exchange of annual calendars and the notification regime helps to establish a stable pattern of routine military activities. Together with the invitation of observers, this reduces the risk of misunderstandings and promotes confidence. But the Stockholm measures also have a dissuasive effect. They make it more difficult to mass military forces in order to intimidate or attack others because any state that deviates from the normal pattern will be promptly subjected to inspections and held accountable for its behaviour. This might also complicate the planning of surprise attacks.[47]

The document did contain a number of ambiguities and important measures were omitted, such as the exchange of information on the structure of military forces, but it was an important breakthrough and became a symbol of a renewed and productive East–West dialogue.

Reykjavik

The Reykjavik Mini-summit of 11–12 October 1986 was regarded as a success, a failure and even a 'strange interlude'.[48] For Gorbachev, the summit provided the opportunity to confirm that Reagan was a kindred spirit on nuclear matters. The year that had passed since Geneva had witnessed very little reciprocation from the West and, therefore, had proved disappointing for Gorbachev. Despite Reagan's agreement that nuclear war was inadmissible, no attempt had been made by the USA to halt nuclear testing or to respond positively to Gorbachev's plan to eliminate nuclear weapons by the year 2000.[49] Reykjavik was therefore an important opportunity for Gorbachev to reaffirm his belief that the Americans were prepared to cooperate.[50]

In order to regain the impetus towards arms reduction, Gorbachev came to Reykjavik with a number of proposals and concessions. Once again, the similarities between these unilateral initiatives and a GRIT-type strategy are quite marked. Osgood makes the point that the initiatives should 'be announced publicly at some reasonable interval prior to their execution'.[51] While such a public announcement had been the case with the nuclear moratorium, Gorbachev decided this time to inform the US administration privately, with a letter to Reagan. This letter outlined his specific proposals.[52] He was prepared to exclude British and French strategic nuclear weapons from the negotiations, eliminate all INF weapons from Europe, and place limits on the number of warheads (100) on INF systems based in the USA and USSR. He was also prepared to adopt the US definition of a strategic nuclear delivery vehicle (SNDV) and have the 50% cut in SNDVs apply to heavy missiles, and he was prepared to allow work to continue on SDI so long as the work was confined to a laboratory and the ABM Treaty was extended for an additional fifteen years. Unfortunately for Gorbachev, the Americans did not take his proposals seriously. According to MccGwire:

> the president's advisers [believed that because] Gorbachev had written to Reagan of the need to provide an 'impulse' to the stalled negotiations [this was evidence that] he had for some reason jettisoned the arms control objectives he had been proclaiming continually during the previous eighteen months.[53]

As a result, the Americans were quite unprepared for what was to occur at Reykjavik.

The American attitude towards Reykjavik ensured that nothing tangible was likely to result from the meeting. The Americans regarded the mini-summit as a 'last base camp' before the two sides would meet for a 'real' summit in Washington. This attitude goes a long way towards explaining why the Americans did not bring any proposals to Reykjavik and why they felt that they had been ambushed by the Soviet Union.[54] After the summit, this attitude was prevalent in the American newspapers. Philip Taubman quoted an American official who said: 'they are trying to lay the foundations for a public relations campaign that will denigrate the United States'. Taubman claimed that the superpowers 'have now been thrown into a period of heightened mistrust'.[55] Others saw the Soviet proposals as traps to ensnare Reagan, while others, noting Soviet failures to comply with agreements in the past, questioned the reasons behind the Soviet proposals.[56]

Given this American response and Gorbachev's disappointment that the Americans had not come to Reykjavik with any proposals, why did Gorbachev regard Reykjavik as a 'turning point' from which 'we became convinced that our course was correct and that a new and constructive way of political thinking was essential'?[57] The answer probably lies in a rather enlightening episode that occurred during the meeting. On 12 October Reagan proposed the elimination of all ballistic missiles within ten years. This would leave the USA in a commanding position, retaining an advantage in nuclear bombers and cruise missiles. Gorbachev responded by proposing the elimination of all nuclear weapons in ten years, to which Reagan is reputed to have replied: 'suits me fine'.[58] This was the type of frank discussion that Gorbachev had sought and, as a result of the meeting in Reykjavik, he became convinced that Reagan was serious about reducing nuclear weapons. In addition, the very fact that they *contemplated* such proposals suggested that they could be implemented.[59] While Gorbachev may have considered Reykjavik to be a turning point, however, the European response highlighted just how difficult it would be to mitigate the security dilemma. In Europe the summit appeared to be a clandestine attempt by Gorbachev to decouple the USA from Europe and divide the NATO Alliance.

Gorbachev's call for total nuclear disarmament would effectively have nullified NATO's Flexible Response strategy by removing the concept of nuclear deterrence. With Soviet conventional forces remaining untouched in eastern Europe, the western governments' alarm was easy to understand. The fact that Reagan had agreed with Gorbachev, albeit in an ambiguous manner, to the elimination of nuclear weapons ran counter to the British and French insistence that nuclear deterrence had a role to play in the future. It also suggested that their own independent nuclear forces were temporary. As if this was not bad enough, Reagan's proposal to eliminate all ballistic missiles was a 'bolt out of the blue'. General Hans-Joachim Mack, the West German Deputy Supreme Commander, speaking on behalf of General Rogers, SACEUR, claimed: 'it was unacceptable that SHAPE should be still largely in the dark four days after the Iceland summit'.[60] This apparent lack of consultation, and the fact Reagan was prepared to scrap ballistic missiles, raised serious doubts about the American commitment to the use of nuclear weapons in the defence of Europe. According to Jonathan Dean, because the 'Europeans had grown accustomed to thinking of nuclear deterrence in terms of ballistic missiles', it appeared as if America was decoupling itself from Europe.[61] To the governments of western Europe, it seemed as though the President of the United States was being taken down a dangerous road to nuclear disarmament by the leader of a country who would gain most from it, a conventionally superior Soviet Union.[62]

At the meeting of NATO's Nuclear Planning Group at Gleneagles, NATO ministers 'gave only half-hearted approval of the Reykjavik package'.[63] British Defence Secretary George Younger claimed that the US proposals were 'very questionable', while the West German Foreign Minister, Hans-Dietrich Genscher, claimed that many of the supporters of a zero–zero INF agreement had only supported it on the assumption that the USSR would reject it.[64] The first European leader to visit America after Reykjavik was Chancellor Kohl, who, while publicly approving Reagan's initiatives, cautioned against further reductions. Friedhelm Ost, Kohl's spokesman, stated: 'discussions in Reykjavik for greater reductions could be a danger for Western Europe', and warned that 'further cuts ... would require an improvement in NATO's conventional forces'.[65] As Kohl aired European concerns regarding the strategic consequences of Reykjavik, Mrs Thatcher stressed the possibility of Soviet deception. At a banquet given by Sir David Rowe-Ham, the Lord Mayor of London, she claimed: 'there is a world of difference between what they mean by peace and what we understand by it'. She mentioned those who had died in the Budapest uprising, the Berlin Wall as a symbol of the Cold War erected by the Soviet Union, the invasion of Afghanistan, 'and the broken promises of Helsinki'. She denounced the Soviet Union for its human rights' record and warned the Americans not to give up the nuclear weapon.[66] The French view summed up the European position quite succinctly: 'the area of real disagreement lies in the ultimate objective ... Reagan's proposal [was] heresy and the Soviet plan ... pure fantasy.[67] Clearly, if Gorbachev was going to acquire the trust of the west Europeans, he would need to tackle the issue of conventional as well as nuclear arms control.[68] For the Europeans, the willingness of the Soviet Union to give up its superiority in conventional forces was the test of Gorbachev's true intentions.

Intermediate-Range Nuclear Forces (INF) Treaty

In April 1987, when George Shultz visited Moscow, Gorbachev offered to eliminate intermediate-range missiles (a range of 1,000–5,500km) and those with a range of 500–1,000 kilometres without linking the deal to SDI. Gorbachev was again providing the impulse for the negotiations, as he was seeking to reduce military expenditure and adjust the Soviet military doctrine. The change in attitude regarding SDI was due to a number of reasons. First, as already stated above, Gorbachev believed that Reagan saw the project as a purely defensive system; he had even offered to sell it to the Soviet Union when it became available. Second, the 1983 version appeared technologically impossible; a more limited missile, or point defence system that could be overwhelmed cheaply appeared the most likely outcome for SDI. Finally, SDI seemed to be Reagan's 'pet' project; another President would not be so attached to it. Throughout the summer and autumn of 1987 the USA and the Soviet Union worked on the negotiations that would result in the signing of the INF Treaty in Washington on 8 December. The agreement was a clear watershed for nuclear arms control. For the first time the superpowers eliminated a whole class of weapons (ground-based weapons in Europe with a range between 500–55,000km), and this included asymmetrical reductions (931 US missiles compared with 1,836 Soviet missiles) and intrusive verification procedures (both were new and vital concessions from the Soviet Union).[69] The immediate reaction was euphoric, as Gorbachev claimed that the treaty 'offers us a chance to embark on a new direction that leads away from catastrophe', and Reagan, who had stated that Soviets would cheat, lie and commit any crime to further their goals, was now saying that he felt 'our people should have been better friends long ago'. In fact, Reagan 'sounded positively chummy at times', reciting Russian proverbs and informing Gorbachev that the American people felt only goodwill towards him.[70]

The role of GRIT in the successful completion of the INF Treaty is difficult to discern. Richard Bitzinger claims that the 'INF Treaty ... was not the result of any GRIT strategy but rather the end-product of years of good, old fashioned, hardball negotiations';[71] whereas Daniel Druckman, referring to a stream of initiatives taken by Gorbachev, claims: 'the successful outcome of these initiatives – an INF agreement – was due to the willingness by the other nation to reciprocate'.[72] The reason for these contradictory comments probably lies in the emphasis that the authors are placing on two different types of cooperative strategies.[73] Thus, while Bitzinger is right to note the role of 'bargaining' strategies in the successful completion of the INF talks, Druckman is also right to note the importance of 'reciprocity' strategies in influencing the negotiations by improving the relationship between the participants. Druckman receives support from Thomas Risse-Kappen, who notes:

> a 'good' bargaining strategy cannot make up for a 'bad' environment that is not conducive to cooperation. Bargaining strategies alone are rarely able to induce cooperative behaviour unless the target is perceptive to external influences and already prepared to respond positively.[74]

This complementary approach is very important and receives more attention in the analysis of 1989–90. The INF Treaty constituted contradictory evidence as a means of mitigating the security dilemma. The elimination of a class of nuclear weapons that were procured to perform a war-fighting role was certainly a positive step towards mitigating the security dilemma, but, after the treaty, there was an attempt by the NATO allies to 'plug' the gap created by their removal. This indicates that the West's willingness to enter into the agreement reflected a long-standing desire born during the suspicious days of the 'second Cold War' as much as any new-found optimism resulting from Gorbachev's arrival.[75] The one notable exception on the western side was West Germany, which, after the INF Treaty, was to become a valuable ally for Gorbachev in mitigating the security dilemma.

One of the methods by which the NATO allies sought to 'plug' the gap was an increase in conventional forces, especially with new 'smart' systems. This had not been unexpected by Soviet arms control experts, who, in parallel to the INF negotiations, had also sought to reach an agreement in the conventional field.[76] Victor Karpov, the Chief of the Arms Control Directorate of the Soviet Foreign Ministry, had stated in March 1987 that an INF agreement would enable 'drastic reductions in conventional forces'.[77] During 1987 the Soviet Union made a number of concessions in the negotiations on the mandate for what was to become the Conventional Arms Forces in Europe Treaty (CFE). With the conclusion of the INF Treaty, according to Roy Allison, 'Soviet efforts to dampen down the NATO drive for reinvigorated conventional forces were intensified'.[78]

More Soviet unilateral initiatives

Throughout 1988 and 1989 Gorbachev continued to push the arms control process along; once again, the similarities with a GRIT-type strategy are quite marked. At the superpower summit in Moscow in May 1988 Gorbachev presented a three-point plan for conventional arms reduction. Gorbachev proposed data exchange and verification during the first phase, a reduction in NATO and Warsaw Pact strength by 500,000 troops in the second stage, and the creation of defensive military structures in the final stage. The plan therefore involved a steady increase in the level of cooperation in order to achieve each subsequent step. The first stage, which sought to build upon the CSBMs agreed at Stockholm, would lessen the fears of a sudden unilateral action by either side. As a result, East and West would become more confident about the benign intentions of one another and so be prepared to reduce those aspects of their military capabilities that each perceived as threatening. Once this second stage had been achieved, the final stage would involve the adoption of a purely defensive force structure, thus further reducing any fear of attack. The similarity with Etzioni's gradualist approach clearly highlights how such a proposal could ameliorate the security dilemma.

Once the plan had been announced, Gorbachev began to initiate a number of proposals and actions to induce the necessary reciprocation from the West in order to mitigate the security dilemma. In July the Warsaw Pact emphasised that vigorous verification procedures would be needed before the plan could be implemented and suggested the establishment of an international body to supervise the procedures.[79] In December 1988, at the UN, Gorbachev announced a very significant unilateral initiative in which 500,000 troops – 240,000 of which would be from the European theatre – would be cut by the end of 1989. If the Warsaw Pact cuts are included, there was to be a reduction of 106,000 troops and 7,000 tanks in eastern Europe. The cuts amounted to a 12% reduction in Soviet strength – 20% more than NATO's highest demands in the MBFR talks – and the reduction in the number of tanks was exactly what US Senator Samuel Nunn had proposed in March 1987. In January 1989 Gorbachev announced a cut in the secret defence budget by 14.2% and a reduction in procurement by 19.5%.[80] Shevardnadze announced at the on-going CSCE meeting that the Soviet Union would withdraw its forces from eastern Europe, including its nuclear forces.[81] In May Gorbachev announced that 500 tactical nuclear weapons would be withdrawn from the territories of its allies in 1989, and that the Soviet Union was prepared to withdraw all its nuclear weapons from its allies 'on [the] condition that the US take an analogous step in reply'.[82] In addition to these unilateral initiatives, Gorbachev proposed reductions in the alliance's forces so that they would be of identical strength by 1996–7.[83]

The western reaction to these proposals was largely cautious. While welcoming the Soviet commitment to reducing their overwhelming conventional superiority, the West tended to focus on the remaining imbalances between the two alliances to justify their lack of reciprocation. General Galvin, SACEUR, noted that, after the December initiative had been implemented, 'the Warsaw Pact will continue to outnumber NATO 2.5 : 1 in tanks, 2.4 : 1 in artillery and nearly 2 : 1 in combat aircraft'.[84] Simon Lunn, Deputy Secretary-General for the North Atlantic Assembly, described the initiative announced at the UN as something that NATO had feared would happen: 'This is about the scale of Soviet reductions that everyone in NATO worried about. It's more than symbolic, but it's not enough. It's just what we didn't need ... [T]he Warsaw Pact still has superiority.'[85] Yet, despite these concerns, the tide had changed in favour of reducing tension by reciprocating the Soviet initiatives.[86] According to Lehne, the December initiative:

convinced even the most hard-line Western governments that the CFE negotiations had a much better prospect of success than the MBFR.

They therefore entered the negotiations determined to make full use of the unique opportunity to eliminate the Soviet conventional superiority and to establish a stable balance of forces.[87]

In May 1989 President Bush responded to Gorbachev's attempts to gain an agreement on reduced conventional forces. Bush proposed accelerating the negotiations in the CFE talks so that an agreement could be reached by the end of 1990. Bush also proposed a ceiling of 275,000 on US/Soviet troops stationed outside national boundaries in Europe.[88]

By 1989 there would appear to be ample evidence that Gorbachev was pursuing a GRIT-type strategy, as both Bitzinger and Goldstein/Freeman suggest. His promotion of new thinking can therefore be seen as a strategy for mitigating the security dilemma. However, this does not prove that Gorbachev's attempt to implement a common security policy was the most important reason for the mitigation of the security dilemma. Before an examination of 1989–90, the crucial years during which the Cold War ended, can be undertaken, it is necessary to examine new thinking in the defence field. It was suggested in Chapter 3 that mitigation of the security dilemma is more likely if a common security approach is combined with the adoption of NOD and a minimum deterrence strategy; common security, by improving political relations, and force posture change, by enabling defence to hold the advantage in times of war.

Soviet Force Posture

The importance of the Soviet force posture in reducing tension and mitigating the security dilemma has been captured by Michael MccGwire, when he writes that in 1988:

Soviet forces continued to be deployed in Eastern Europe, superior in numbers to the NATO forces ranged against them, and clearly configured for a blitzkrieg offensive. Until that offensive overhang was removed, Western political-military establishments would remain unconvinced that the Soviet threat, which for forty years was perceived to dominate the international landscape, had changed in any substantive way.[89]

Thus, to appreciate Gorbachev's new thinking as a means of mitigating the security dilemma, it is necessary to examine its impact on Soviet military doctrine. For new thinking to be considered a mitigator, the Soviet Union would need to adopt a minimum deterrence strategy for its nuclear forces and reorganise its conventional forces into a defensive, or non-provocative, force posture. The approach to examining this hypothesis is to focus on the nuclear and conventional debates in turn. The nuclear debate fell within the enigmatic notion of 'reasonable sufficiency', while the conventional debate fell within the equally enigmatic notion of 'defensive defence'.[90]

Reasonable sufficiency

Gorbachev introduced the notion of 'reasonable sufficiency' in his political report to the 27th Party Congress, since when it has been coined by both reformers and conservatives as they sought to give substance to the term.[91] The result was that 'reasonable sufficiency' became an ambiguous term, meaning different things to different people.[92] According to Stephen Meyer, this suited Gorbachev; the term's ambiguity enabled him 'to call into question any defence programme that the general secretary perceive[d] as superfluous to Soviet security'.[93] While this may have been true, it obscured the impact that reformers were to have on the direction of Soviet doctrine. Obscuring the changes can only make security dilemma mitigation that much harder, since the western powers would remain uncertain of the Soviet Union's real intentions.

Reasonable sufficiency as a minimum deterrence concept

The theoretical underpinnings of this debate were examined in Chapter 3. In brief, it is argued that if states procure unambiguously defensive weapons and defence is perceived to hold the advantage in time of war, then the security dilemma can be ameliorated; states need not feel threatened by another's weaponry. According to Jervis, the reality of mutual assured destruction (MAD) is the equivalent of the primacy of defence. So long as both states possess a secure second-strike capability, then they can both threaten costs that patently outweigh any benefits that either could accrue from initiating hostilities. In other words, attack makes no sense; this has the effect of raising the primacy of the defence. The logic of MAD as the equivalent to the primacy of the defence leads Jervis to claim that the 'common-sense' definitions of offence and defence need to be turned on their heads. Offence should be regarded as anything that seeks to undermine the other state's assured destruction capability, while defence refers to anything that strengthens the reality of MAD. The concept that supports this notion is minimum deterrence. A minimum deterrence strategy requires only those forces necessary to threaten assured destruction credibly; such strategies therefore deliberately forego weapons that are designed for other functions which could undermine MAD. Minimum deterrence therefore complements Jervis's argument that nuclear weapons mitigate the security dilemma. Minimum deterrence also mitigates the security dilemma because it breaks the action–reaction phenomenon of the arms race, and it can help to allay fears of a surprise attack during a crisis because the weapons it requires lack a first-strike capability.[94]

The relevance of the minimum deterrence concept to the reasonable sufficiency debate was seized upon by analysts working in various research centres. These analysts are referred to as 'civilians' in the literature.[95] During 1987–8 a number of articles appeared proposing the establishment of a Soviet minimum nuclear deterrence (MND) strategy.[96] Our interest in this debate is in the importance attached to the 'defensiveness' of the systems envisaged in these proposals – that is, whether they support MAD by being counter-value and secure from a first strike.

The first article was a report produced by the Committee of Soviet Scientists for Peace against the Nuclear Threat (CSSPANT) in April 1987. CSSPANT was co-chaired by Roald Sagdeyev and Andrei Kokoshin of ISKAN.[97] The report detailed the type and number of nuclear weapons that both superpowers should maintain to acquire a stable MND strategy. On the Soviet side, the report prescribed that all nuclear delivery systems should be ICBMs; these systems were regarded as the best for crisis stability because they possessed the best C³I facilities. The report claimed that communication between command and ICBMs was more reliable than that between command and SSBNs. In addition, it was argued that the state subjected to a nuclear attack would gain an earlier warning from an ICBM, because such missiles are launched along relatively predictable trajectories. Bombers were discounted, because they could increase the risk of escalation from conventional to nuclear use. How do these ideas relate to Jervis's prescription outlined in Chapter 3?

The reliance on ICBMs is not shared by Jervis; he regards ICBMs as ambiguous because they are capable of fulfilling counter-force roles. An ICBM can be used to destroy another ICBM. Instead, he places the emphasis on SLBMs as the delivery vehicles; they are secure platforms (SSBNs) and are not seen as threats to one another.[98] Jervis would approve, however, of the crisis stability reasoning behind the report's emphasis on ICBMs.[99] Given this difference in delivery vehicles, how relevant was CSSPANT's scheme to mitigating the security dilemma?

The report explained that the reliance on ICBMs rather than SLBMs represented the Soviet attitude towards nuclear weapons. First, the Soviet Union had traditionally sought strict centralised control over their nuclear forces and this negated the development of a large SSBN fleet. Second, they were sceptical about the invulnerability of their SSBN fleet to western ASW capabilities. Third, the USSR was a land power with little access to open sea and few warm-water ports. This geographical fact ensured that the USSR had invested in ICBMs; to have developed a SLBM fleet would simply have been too expensive. Aleksi Arbatov made this point when he said: 'to be equal to the US in SSBN capabilities, the Russians would probably need three times as many submarines as the Americans, which would be very expensive, and anyhow unacceptable to the US'.[100] The Soviet reliance on ICBMs can be explained, therefore, by the different

Soviet approach towards nuclear deterrence. Pirani was right to note that: 'by American standards, [ICBMs] are the most destabilizing weapons. By Russian standards, they are the most reliable retaliatory weapons.' [101]

For the report to be regarded as a minimum deterrence strategy capable of mitigating the security dilemma, the proposed use and deployment of the ICBMs would need to match Jervis's reasons for choosing SLBMs – namely, that they are invulnerable and lack a first-strike capability. The report does seek to place these limitations on Soviet ICBMs, by envisaging de-MIRVing and placing all ICBMs on mobile platforms. By returning to single-warhead ICBMs, the report sought a limitation on Soviet and US warheads of 600 on each side, which represented a cut of 95%; this meant that there would be more strategic targets than ICBM warheads. This would negate the ability to launch a first strike. The use of mobile platforms would increase the survival rate of the missiles, thus providing a secure second strike.[102] According to Garthoff, 'such a greatly reduced strategic nuclear force on both sides was found to provide both with assured retaliatory capability, thus serving as a minimum deterrent, on a basis of strategic stability, representing reasonable sufficiency'.[103] Interpreted in this manner, reasonable sufficiency is synonymous with mitigating the security dilemma.

The CSSPANT report was criticised in March 1988 by three diplomats within the Ministry of Foreign Affairs (MFA).[104] These diplomats – Sergei Vybornov, Andrei Gusenkov, Vladimir Leontiev – focused on two aspects of the report. First, they challenged the use of ICBMs as the best means of assuring a secure second-strike capability. They claimed that techno-logical improvements would render mobile ICBMs vulnerable to a first strike.[105] Second, they highlighted the 'problem' of third nuclear powers. The diplomats claimed that, by reducing the size of their nuclear forces, the superpowers would move from a bipolar nuclear world to a multipolar nuclear world. The relevance of this criticism to MND and security dilemma mitigation is twofold. First, the diplomats were not criticising the concept of MND; their criticism was directed at the type of delivery system chosen by CSSPANT and at CSSPANT's concentration on a bipolar world. Second, the diplomats proposed a MND regime of their own which emphasised the use of SSBNs as delivery vehicles.[106] The regime was highly complex – indeed, two of the diplomats admitted later that a multipolar world was too complicated for nuclear modelling[107] – but the importance of this for mitigation is that the diplomats were supporting the MND concept and putting forward hypothetical models. These two articles produced a plethora of discussion amongst the civil-ians.[108] The important point for the security dilemma was that the crucial ingredients of assured destruction remained undisputed requirements; the only criteria were the number and type of weapons and their survivability in the face of a nuclear attack.

Soviet interest in minimum deterrence

The CSSPANT report, the diplomat's MND regime and the other schemes elucidated during the late 1980s were not intended to be options for the policy-makers to accept or reject. These schemes were designed to explore the practical implementation of reasonable sufficiency and provide the military with an alternative for defence ideas. Garthoff is right to caution that, while CSSPANT's report included a 95% reduction in nuclear weapons, 'this [did] not mean that the Soviet government was considering, or even the committee of scientists was proposing, that deep a reduction'.[109] However, if minimum deterrence is to be considered as a mitigator of the security dilemma, then the USSR would need to be seen to be adopting the concept for their nuclear forces.

Stephen Shenfield has provided an account of a lecture that Professor Baranovskiy gave in London in December 1988 which placed MND in the context of the broader implementation of Gorbachev's new thinking. Baranovskiy began by highlighting a number of problems with the implementation of MND. He noted the perennial difficulty of determining how much destructive capability constituted 'unacceptable damage', and whether, in a multipolar world, the USSR would require more weapons than just those necessary to retaliate against an American attack. His main concern, however, was the viability of MND in those circumstances where military confrontation continued to exist. He argued that state concern over limited war would continue to apply pressure on the development of war-fighting nuclear weapons; even weapons that were intended to perform a second-strike role would be modernised with the potential to fulfil a first-strike role. In other words, not only would MND fail to provide long-term stability, but it would also fail to halt the arms race. Baranovskiy suggested that MND could only be viable if it was part of a process that would relax political tensions. Such an improvement in relations would:

> reduce the perceived threat of war to such an extent that the pressures to re-create warfighting capabilities would become manageable. Ulti-mately 'deterrence' would lose meaning, for in such a world there would no longer be military threats to deter, and there would therefore be no purpose in retaining any nuclear weapons at all. MND would be just one aspect of the penultimate stage of constructing a comprehensive system of international security.[110]

In other words, MND should be considered as one aspect towards a mutual security regime. The lecture is pertinent because Baranovskiy's concerns regarding the viability of a MND regime mirrored the concerns of the Palme Commission and the SIPRI study outlined in Chapter 3. Indeed, his conviction that MND should be considered as *part* of the solution, as opposed to *the* solution, mirrors the analysis in Chapter 3 that minimum deterrence should be considered as a complementary measure within a common security approach towards mitigating the security dilemma. Baranovskiy's emphasis on MND as a stage towards nuclear disarmament was certain to appeal to Gorbachev.

In 1989 the USSR adopted the concept of MND as a means of moving towards a nuclear-free world and a mutual security regime. In July Gorbachev introduced minimum deterrence within his broader aims of implementing new thinking.[111] While he reaffirmed his belief that nuclear weapons undermined stability, he acknowledged that Soviet and western positions were different on this issue. He suggested that minimum deterrence may hold the key as a compromise. Gorbachev wrote that, 'without their having to abandon their positions', the two sides could reach agreements on reductions, with the USSR remaining 'true to its nuclear-free ideals and the West to the concept of "minimal deterrence"'.[112] He called upon experts from both East and West to discuss when 'the potential for nuclear retaliation turns into the potential for attack'. In other words, while not abandoning his wish for a nuclear-free world, Gorbachev was prepared to enter into a temporary compromise. Stephen Kux is right to state, therefore:

> Gorbachev's willingness to consider the concept of 'minimum deterrence' suggests a departure from his abolitionist line, indicates acceptance of nuclear weapons *for the time being* as a reality of East–West relations and opens room for compromise [emphasis added]'.[113]

Throughout 1989 MND was to be reiterated by senior policy-makers as the Soviet Union sought a compromise on nuclear deterrence. In August Deputy Foreign Minister Vladimir Petrovsky reaffirmed the Soviet objective 'of replacing nuclear deterrence with a mutual security regime'; as a means towards this, the two sides should 'examine quietly what lies behind the concept of minimum deterrence'.[114] Shevardnadze likewise noted in September at the UN that the Soviet Union wanted a nuclear-free world, but MND was possible as an interim solution:

> Proponents of nuclear deterrence do not believe [a nuclear-free world] can be done in the foreseeable future. In response they offer the ideas of so-called minimal nuclear deterrence. In our view, this is a step forward – albeit a modest one – and something that can be done.[115]

The approach chosen by the Soviet Union was to seek an agreed minimum level with the United States for both of their nuclear forces. There were some Soviet analysts who advocated a unilateralist approach, but they were heavily criticised by the military.[116] According to Garthoff, 'the debate over unilateral reductions to minimum deterrence has abated. Whether it is resumed or not, while the advocates have not prevailed they may have succeeded at least in making pursuit of reciprocal minimum deterrence seem a moderate course.'[117] The preferred Soviet approach was through arms control negotiations.

It would appear that, by 1989, the USSR was prepared to move towards a minimum deterrence strategy, but would only adopt such a strategy in conjunction with the USA. The reasonable sufficiency debate clearly highlighted a Soviet understanding that minimum deterrence could help to reduce tension and, as such, play an important role in mitigating the security dilemma; it does not prove, however, that these ideas did mitigate the security dilemma. If Soviet thinking in the nuclear field can be seen as relevant to security dilemma mitigation, is this also true for the conventional field?

Defensive defence

To determine if the Soviet pronouncements on defensive defence would mitigate the security dilemma, it is necessary to compare it to the ideas elucidated in Chapter 3. It was suggested that the security dilemma could be mitigated if states believed that defence held the advantage in time of war and if the deployment of forces was unambiguously defensive. If defensive defence is synonymous with these ideas, therefore, it can be considered a mitigator of the security dilemma. To be synonymous, Soviet conventional forces would need to be perceived by the West as incapable of invading their territory.

Defensive defence as a non-offensive defence (NOD) concept

In 1990 a collaborative work by Andrei Kokoshin and Major-General Valentin Larionov outlined four possible models for the conduct of war.[118] The similarities between these models and the four worlds that Jervis created in his matrix are quite striking. In the first model, the belligerents will seek to seize the initiative and launch an offensive against each other. This is similar to Jervis's first world, where offence holds the advantage and both sides procure weapons with offensive potential. The same relationship can be seen between the second model and Jervis's second world. In this model, both states adopt a defensive posture and, when attacked, initially defend. Only after this defensive engagement do they launch a counter-offensive into the enemy's territory in order to defeat the opponent; defence is perceived to hold the advantage in times of war, but both sides procure weapons with an offensive potential.[119] Since these two models correspond to Jervis's first two worlds, the security dilemma is likely to occur if these models are the basis for military doctrine.

The third model envisages defence again holding the advantage, but this time the counter-offensive is more limited and is only intended to recapture lost territory.[120] In Chapter 3 it was suggested that offensive forces that could only protect territory and lacked the ability to invade another state's territory could be called *necessary* offence. Those forces that could do both were known as *optional* offence; these terms belong to Charles Glaser.[121] This third model has no obvious counterpart in Jervis's worlds. Depending upon the capabilities of the counter-offensive forces, this model probably lies between Jervis's second and fourth worlds. For instance, if the opposing state perceives the counter-offensive potential as larger than is required to recapture lost territory (i.e., as optional offence), then it will appear little different from the second model. If the forces do not appear capable of invading the state (i.e., necessary offence), however, then it will appear less threatening and the model will be similar to Jervis's fourth world. The opposing state's perception is important, therefore, because the security dilemma can be mitigated in the fourth world.

Kokoshin and Larionov's fourth model envisages both sides as adopting purely defensive postures and forgoing the capability to launch a counter-offensive.[122] This is the same as Jervis's fourth world, where defence holds the advantage and status quo powers can discern the difference between defensive and offensive weapons. The adoption of the fourth model would be concomitant with the adoption of an NOD strategy. This model is therefore the most likely to mitigate the security dilemma. However, the adoption of a third-model strategy should not be regarded as irrelevant to security dilemma mitigation. A strategy with an offensive capability that is limited to recapturing lost territory would nevertheless be a substantial step towards mitigating the Cold War security dilemma. Thus, from the security dilemma perspective, a military doctrine based on the third model would still represent a move towards mitigation. Our interest here is whether model 4 or model 3 represented Soviet thinking on the military-technical aspect of military doctrine.

Soviet interest in NOD

In 1987 General Yazov captured the ambiguity of the counter-offensive function when he stated:

> Soviet military doctrine considers the defence as the main form of military actions in repulsing aggression. It must be reliable and steadfast, tenacious and active, calculated to stop the enemy's offensive, to bleed him, not to permit the loss of territory, and to defeat the invading hostile field forces. By defence alone, however, it is not possible to defeat the aggressor. Therefore after repulsing the attack, the troops and naval forces must be capable of conducting a decisive offensive. The tradition will take the form of a counteroffensive.[123]

Yazov's statement clearly signals the notion of engaging the enemy 'and defeating the invading forces' with defensive actions, hence underlining a movement away from the traditional Soviet objective of seizing the initiative early. However, once the invading forces were defeated, he then suggests that the Soviet forces should engage in a decisive offensive. Since the invading forces have already been defeated, Yazov would appear to imply that Soviet forces should take the battle on to enemy territory. If this is correct, then Yazov's statement would fall within the second model and would not be applicable to mitigating the security dilemma. Yazov's statement was important because many of the proposals that followed were based upon this statement.[124]

In June 1990 Yazov appeared to be supporting a strategy that fell within the third model. He stated:

> In the event of aggression against the USSR, the main type of operations of our Armed Forces will be defensive. Questions concerning defence on strategic, operational and tactical scales now occupy the foreground in the training of our troops. This does not of course mean carrying out only passive operations. As he attacks, the aggressor must be stopped, and groupings of his armed forces that have effected *penetration* must be smashed. And so, in order to complete the destruction of *invading* enemy groupings and to restore the *status-quo*, counter-attack actions and operations are envisaged [emphasis added].[125]

Yazov's use of counter-attack action as opposed to counter-offensive, together with his objective of restoring the status quo, suggest strongly that the offensive element was to be limited, as in Kokoshin and Larionov's third model. Thus, by 1990 Soviet military doctrine appeared to fit somewhere between model 2 and model 3.[126] While this may indicate a movement towards a NOD concept, it is certainly not conclusive evidence and patently does not provide evidence that such a movement mitigated the security dilemma. However, it does indicate a Soviet interest in altering the military-technical aspect of doctrine towards a less threatening stance.

While it may be claimed that Gorbachev's new thinking was an attempt to introduce a combined common security and minimum deterrence approach to acquiring security, this does not mean that it explains why the security dilemma was mitigated. The final part of this chapter is concerned with the extent to which new thinking can be said to have mitigated the security dilemma.

The End of the Cold War: 1989–1990

Did Gorbachev mitigate the Cold War security dilemma?

Did Gorbachev's implementation of new thinking via GRIT and the establishment of institutionalised security regimes, plus the Soviet debate on defensive force postures, mitigate the Cold War security dilemma, or was it simply coincidence that, by the end of 1990, over forty years of hostility came to an end? If it was more than coincidence, then Gorbachev's pursuit of common security and force posture change may be considered important elements in mitigating the security dilemma. According to Bitzinger, however, Gorbachev failed to induce western reciprocation and, therefore, the end of the Cold War was due to other reasons. He writes:

> Gorbachev's unilateral initiatives and invitations to cooperate were universally rejected. Also, it is not apparent that swift and dramatic progress in arms control and East–West *rapprochement* beginning in 1989 can necessarily be linked to Gorbachev's GRIT strategy ... It could even be argued that a steadfast NATO stance regarding the Soviets, backed up by nuclear deterrence – 'peace through strength' – actually 'won' the cold war. Finally, the 1989 revolutions in Central–East Europe and the subsequent collapse of the communist bloc and the USSR itself were certainly critical in ending the cold war [emphasis in original].[127]

Bitzinger's claim highlights four reasons that cast doubt on Gorbachev's role in mitigating the Cold War security dilemma: the lack of western reciprocation; the irrelevance of GRIT to the plethora of arms control agreements at the end of the Cold War; the success of western resolve in forcing the Soviet Union to make concessions; the divorce of the revolutions of 1989 from GRIT. If Bitzinger is correct, then, while Gorbachev did pursue policies that could have mitigated the security dilemma, the reason for its actual mitigation must be found elsewhere. To what extent is this argument correct?

The lack of western reciprocation

The late 1980s appear to contain a lack of western reciprocation to Gorbachev's initiatives, but this is not entirely true. Ken Booth divides reciprocation into positive and negative categories and this formulation suggests that his initiatives were not 'universally rejected'.[128] By 'positive' reciprocation, Booth means that the initiator receives something tangible for the action that they take. It was suggested earlier that those states which recognised new thinking as a common security policy may have reacted more quickly to Gorbachev's call for reciprocation than those that did not. The country that responded most positively to Gorbachev's new thinking was West Germany. The German response, which gained the label 'Gorbimania', was not unexpected given the similarities between new thinking and common security.[129] Barry Buzan points to West Germany's history and its development of common security ideas to explain why their reaction was expected.[130] Buzan writes:

> It should come as no surprise that Germans have been thinking longer and harder about these transformations than others ... In addition to

the immediate dangers, costs and inconveniences of sharing a small area with large foreign military forces, the Germans have lived with the knowledge that if deterrence failed, many of them, and most of their carefully reconstructed country, would be among the first casualties.

One consequence of this situation was that there developed in West Germany a tradition of thinking about alternative defence arrangements that stretches well back into the 1970s.[131]

With a convergence of thinking about security, it is not at all surprising that Germany was the first western state to respond in a favourable and constructive fashion to Gorbachev's initiatives.[132] Thus it was West Germany that took the lead in offering financial loans to the USSR and halting the modernisation of NATO's tactical nuclear weapons.[133] This latter issue involved a public disagreement with the United Kingdom over the modernisation of the Lance missile (the follow-on to Lance (FOTL) debate). The Germans were successful in persuading the Bush administration that modernisation was not required, and Bush cancelled the Lance replacement in May 1990. The debate over tactical air-to-surface missiles (TASMs) was not as polarised, but it also highlighted the differences between those members of the alliance who wanted to maintain a nuclear deterrent *vis-à-vis* the USSR and those who sought a more cooperative approach. Shevardnadze reaffirmed the Soviet position when he announced at the CSCE meeting in 1989 that modernisation was regarded as a backward step by the Soviet Union.[134] It would appear that, far from his initiatives being rejected, Gorbachev gained a valuable ally in West Germany. Hence Risse-Kappen's assertion:

> Gorbachev's overtures tapped into the German domestic consensus on security policy and, consequently, fell almost immediately on fertile ground in Bonn ... From about mid-1986 on, while most of its allies were still sceptical, the German government promoted a positive Western response to the new Soviet foreign policy ('Genscherism'). Germany became the first and only Western state to commit substantial amounts of financial assistance to the Soviet economic reform process. In sum the cold war was over for the Germans before it was over in reality, that is, about two years before the Berlin Wall came down.[135]

This German attitude stands in marked contrast to the American attitude. With little impact on US decision-making, common security was not familiar and, 'as a result, the Reagan administration reacted rather cautiously to the changes in Moscow, even though Reagan developed a friendly personal relationship with Gorbachev'.[136] This cautious approach was evident during the early months of the Bush administration, when the American views were markedly more reserved than those of the West Germans. Indeed, even British Prime Minister Thatcher, a recognised supporter of the 'hard line' approach, expressed concern at the hesitant American approach when dealing with the Soviet Union.[137] The more cautious American response was clearly expressed by Bush's National Security Advisor, Brent Scrowcroft. Scrowcroft referred to Gorbachev as a more effective version of the 'clever bear syndrome', by which he meant the perceived Soviet practice of pursuing expansionist goals while lulling the West into a false sense of security (the US feared Soviet defection). He simply regarded Gorbachev as a more formidable opponent than his predecessors, because he was reassuring. Appearing on US television on 22 January 1989, Scrowcroft stated that Gorbachev seemed:

> interested in making trouble within the Western Alliance. And I think he believes that the best way to do it is a peace offensive, rather than to bluster, the way some of his predecessors have.
>
> Until we have better evidence to the contrary, we ought to operate on that expectation ... I think the Cold War is not over. There may be, in the saying, light at the end of the tunnel. But I think it depends partly on whether the light is the sun or an oncoming locomotive.[138]

However, even this cautious and sceptical approach contained elements of what Booth categorises as negative reciprocation. 'Negative' reciprocation occurs when other states forgo the opportunity to take advantage of the initiator's unilateral initiative. Such reciprocation is not manifest by an identical gesture, therefore, but by the avoidance of actions which would make the initiator less secure. In essence, negative reciprocation entails supporting the initiative by not subverting the initiator. It was this type of reciprocation that the USA provided. During 1989, when eastern Europe was undergoing such a dramatic transformation, James Baker, the US Secretary of State, 'reassured the Soviet leader that the United States would not seek to take advantage of the situation to the security disadvantage of the Soviet Union' so long as the Soviet Union did not resort to the use of force.[139] This willingness to support, rather than subvert, Gorbachev's initiatives in eastern Europe – in this case, repealing the Brezhnev Doctrine – was also manifest during the Malta Summit of 1989, when the Bush administration informed Gorbachev that as long as violence was not used in the Baltic states, the USA would reciprocate by showing restraint in what it said about the subject.[140] Such reciprocity, while not as encouraging as the positive variety, is still valuable for the initiating state, since it lessens their fear of defection.

It would appear that, while Bitzinger is right to raise doubts regarding positive US reciprocation, there is evidence that, in Osgood's phrases, West Germany and the USA reciprocated in other 'spheres of action' and 'geographical loci'. This conclusion gains strong support from Richard Ned Lebow and Janice Gross Stein when they assert:

Gorbachev could not have succeeded in transforming East–West relations and ending the Cold War if the West had not become his willing partner ... Gorbachev met a receptive audience when he attempted to end the division of Europe. Disenchantment with the Cold War, opposition to the deployment of new weapon systems, and a wide-spread desire to end the division of Europe, given voice by well-organised peace movements, created a groundswell of support for exploring the possibilities of accommodation with the Soviet Union.[141]

The irrelevance of GRIT to the superpower arms control agreements

This claim against the value of GRIT is that the plethora of arms control agreements reached by the superpowers could have been accomplished without Gorbachev's unilateral initiatives. However, such reasoning often misinterprets the value and role of GRIT. GRIT is designed to improve relations and create the conditions for a reduction in arms that will lead to a more stable and safer world. The cooperation needed for a reduction in arms, though, is the reserve of 'bargaining' strategies. That is, the agreement to limit or reduce levels of arms in a treaty format requires a different form of cooperation to that of GRIT. Hence, Osgood regards GRIT as a complementary approach to formal negotiations, and Etzioni's PGRIT strategy requires the final stage to be conducted via negotiated agreements.[142] Thus, while GRIT may not be used within formal negotiations, its successful implementation in the broader context of the states' relationship will help to speed along those negotiations. In other words, unilateral initiatives are likely to create the conditions in which negotiated agreements could prove fruitful in eliminating or reducing those weapons that exacerbated the Cold War security dilemma. This is the implication behind the following comment by Jonathan Dean and Watson Forsberg:

> the pre-treaty reductions and withdrawals in the East, along with the radically changed political circumstances, have done far more to build confidence and reduce the risk of a major war in Europe than will be accomplished by the CFE-mandated destruction [from the East] of another 33,268 weapons.[143]

Indeed, the argument that GRIT could mitigate the security dilemma without formalised agreement is circumspect. GRIT may help to improve relations, but meaningful actions to reduce the forces that create the unintentional fear of attack result from written agreements. Once this has been achieved, then, as a complement to institutionalised security regime formation, GRIT could achieve a reciprocal response. An example of the latter was the Bush initiative in September 1991 to withdraw and dismantle some strategic and tactical nuclear weapons.[144]

Western resolve (peace through strength) ended the Cold War

The argument that the West won the Cold War by forcing the Soviet Union to respond to the West's military build-up and thereby crippling its economy has already been examined in Chapter 6. It is only necessary, therefore, to reiterate briefly that while the stagnation of the Soviet economy was the primary reason for perestroika, the cause of Gorbachev's concern was the inefficiency of the command economy rather than its inability to compete with the West in the military field. As Richard Ned Lebow and Janice Gross Stein assert: 'there is no evidence that Soviet defence spending rose or fell in response to American defence spending'.[145] Indeed, these authors claim the opposite; seeking peace by remaining resolute, 'American policy... likely prolonged the Cold War'.[146] At present it is impossible to state with confidence exactly what impact the West's military build-up, or its initial cautious response to Gorbachev's initiatives, had on the end of the Cold War. It is a contentious debate, but the existing evidence seems to suggest that the 'peace through strength' argument is far from proven.

The revolutions of 1989 were the sole cause of the end of the Cold War

It is beyond doubt that the revolutions in central and eastern Europe during 1989 were critical in ending the Cold War. The most visible sign to the western world that Soviet decision-makers had intended to orchestrate a westward communist expansion was their occupation of the eastern European states. According to Michael Beschloss and Strobe Talbott, 'in the spring of 1989, as one "test" of Gorbachev's sincerity, the Bush administration had demanded the repeal of the Brezhnev Doctrine'.[147] This was confirmed by the end of the year with the removal of communist leaderships throughout central and eastern Europe.[148] If Gorbachev's implementation of new thinking did not provide the 'green light' for these events, then Bitzinger's point is valid; mitigation occurred despite Gorbachev's efforts. However, it is untenable to assume that these events were orchestrated in isolation from the improving East–West relationship. This does not necessarily mean that Gorbachev sought such a transformation; rather that, given his foreign policy approach, it was extremely unlikely that he would prevent such actions. It was this realisation that Gorbachev would not invoke the Brezhnev Doctrine, a realisation built upon his previous actions, that enabled the revolutions of 1989 to occur.[149]

While it is not possible to assert with any assurance that Gorbachev's implementation of a common security approach via GRIT and institutionalised security regimes was essential in mitigating the security dilemma, it is difficult to imagine that mitigation if Gorbachev had not appreciated the futility of seeking unilateral security and the necessity of de-demonising the Soviet image. Since the impetus for change came from the USSR – from the initial unilateral initiatives to the crucial breakthroughs in treaty negotiations – Gorbachev appears to be the decisive figure. Josef Joffe writes that Gorbachev:

> triggered [the end of the Cold War] in 1987 by signing away the USSR's superiority in intermediate-range nuclear forces, which had been a prime factor in the outbreak of Cold War II, circa 1979–1985. He continued the process by offering, and then initiating, unilateral conventional disarmament. He finally took the process of 'deimperialism' past the apparent point of no return in the autumn of 1989 by declaring open season on Messrs Honecker, Jakes, Zhivkov and Ceausesceu, the pillars of the *ancien regime* in Eastern Europe. By the end of the year, the USSR had announced that it intended to bring back all of its foreign troops based abroad by the year 2000.[150]

Indeed, even Bitzinger, who concludes that while 'we may well be on the way to realizing Osgood's end-goal, but more despite GRIT than because of it', also notes that 'one should not write off Gorbachev's attempts at GRIT as a total failure'.[151] Mitigation of the security dilemma occurred, at least in part, because of Gorbachev's implementation of a common security policy. If this is the case with common security, what of his minimum deterrence approach for the superpowers' nuclear forces as a means of mitigating the security dilemma?

Adoption of MND?

The Strategic Arms Reduction Treaty (START I), which was the nuclear arms control pillar that marked the end of the Cold War, was signed in July 1991. The outcome of the negotiations did not lead to a treaty that would support the adoption of a MND strategy. While the treaty encompassed a number of issues, the one of particular importance for minimum deterrence was the limit placed on MIRVed warheads.[152] Shenfield writes:

> the level of MIRVing of ballistic missiles ... is the single most important technical indicator distinguishing between force structures designed for counterforce nuclear warfighting and those designed for minimum retaliatory deterrence.[153]

The treaty was disappointing in this regard, however. While it did address some destabilising elements, 'it [did] not directly address, or deliberately defer[red] addressing, the more potentially destabilizing force developments'.[154] The agreement limited the number of strategic delivery vehicles to 1,600, but limited the number of warheads to 6,000. The agreement could be interpreted, therefore, as encouraging the development of MIRVed weapons. The START Treaty can be seen as encompassing a reduction in nuclear forces, but little movement from traditional military doctrine. Hence Erick Graben writes:

Since the Soviet Union continued to deploy as many hard-target-kill-capable weapons under Gorbachev as it was allowed by treaty, it can be assumed that the military view of 'reasonable sufficiency' was the one actually implemented, and that the Soviet Union continued to strive to maintain a favourable counterforce balance to deter a potentially hostile West.[155]

While it would be correct to note that START I did not support the adoption of an MND strategy – and, indeed, by the end of the Cold War neither superpower had adopted such a strategy – the follow-up to START, START II, did signal an interest in minimum deterrence.[156] Events outside the military field acquired a momentum of their own in 1989–90 which overtook the more conservative changes occurring in Soviet military thinking. By the time the Cold War ended, neither superpower had adopted a minimum deterrence strategy for its nuclear forces; therefore, mitigation of the security dilemma did not occur as a result of Gorbachev's force posture changes.

Mitigation of the Cold War security dilemma

With the collapse of Soviet-appointed regimes in eastern Europe throughout 1989, the changes that Gorbachev was introducing were overtaken as developments took on a momentum of their own. Thus, western suspicions of Soviet duplicity, which were reduced with the collapse of the USSR's 'security buffer' in Europe, were further reduced throughout 1990 as the Soviet Union began to withdraw troops from eastern Europe and the Warsaw Pact grew increasingly moribund. The eastern half of the Cold War alliance system came to an end in February 1991. Western suspicions continued to wane with the signing of the CFE Treaty in late 1990, the turning-point for the security dilemma's mitigation.[157] In addition to reducing the forces on each side so that they 'balanced', the treaty also limited the number and type of weapons that each could deploy in Europe. For example, where the opposing forces were closest (the central zone), there was a limit of 7,500 tanks; on the flanks, the limit was 4,700. Combined with the withdrawals from eastern Europe and the collapse of the Warsaw Pact, this treaty led the West to regard the Soviet threat as perceived during the Cold War as notably reduced. According to *Strategic Survey*, 'the CFE Treaty makes a significant contribution to European security by going a long way towards eliminating the Soviet capability for launching a surprise attack against NATO territory, and to some extent it even constrains the USSR's ability to conduct large-scale offensive actions.'[158] Can the principles of common security and non-offensive defence be found in these changes?

Although the CFE Treaty did reduce the equipment necessary for offensive action (e.g., tanks, artillery, armoured combat vehicles, aircraft, combat helicopters) and, therefore, was concerned with those forces that are mostly responsible for giving rise to the misperception of threat, it did not support the adoption of NOD. However, this does not mean that these alternatives ideas were irrelevant – as noted above, Soviet military thinking was changing – rather, they were overtaken by other events. Interestingly, these other events do indicate the adoption of common security principles. In June 1989 a joint communiqué by Bonn and Moscow stated:

> The Federal Republic of Germany and the Soviet Union declare that one cannot accomplish security for one-self at the expense of the security of others ... Both sides seek to ... reduce the military potentials to a stable balance at a lower level, which is sufficient for defence, but not for attack.[159]

In October 1990 the Cold War adversaries reached an agreement on the unification of Germany within NATO. This agreement was important not only because the division of Germany had been a manifestation of the Cold War, but because the West was aware that the agreement required the safeguarding of Soviet security concerns. This sensitivity to Soviet security was epitomised by the proposed reduction of German troop levels to 370,000 and by the fact that, while Soviet troops remained in the former GDR, those German troops also in the GDR would not be under NATO command. For the Western Alliance to think in these terms is evidence of a new cooperative approach towards achieving security. The endorsement of this new approach was announced in NATO's London Declaration in July. In this declaration the western powers announced that the two blocs were 'no longer adversaries' and that the alliance would fundamentally change its force structure and strategy and 'profoundly alter the way we think about defence'.[160] The alliance signalled its new approach towards security by recognising that 'the security of every state is inseparably linked to the security of its neighbours' – in other words, security is an interdependent concept and, as a result, NATO should 'extend to [the East Europeans] the hand of friendship'.[161] NATO, whether wittingly or not, was replacing the paradoxical strategy that it had pursued vis-à-vis the USSR and was engaging in methods that were mitigating the Cold War security dilemma.

Conclusion

This chapter has sought to accomplish three goals. The first is to highlight the dangers and difficulties for states when they try to mitigate the security dilemma and to look at the way in which these can be overcome by the establishment of institutionalised security regimes via a GRIT-type strategy. The dangers lay not only in mistaking a status quo power for a revisionist power, but in suffering a pre-emptive attack from another status quo power. In order to overcome these dangers, it is necessary to overcome two difficulties: to determine trustworthiness and to convince others of one's good intentions. It is noted that new thinking was a common security policy and, as such, could have overcome these difficulties. To achieve this outcome, new thinking was aided by the West German recognition of it as a common security policy. The final element of this first goal illustrated how a GRIT-type strategy can create the conditions necessary for the formation of institutionalised security regimes.

The second goal is to determine if new thinking in Soviet foreign policy and force postures complemented the theoretical constructs that were noted in Chapter 3 for the mitigation of the security dilemma. It is highlighted that Gorbachev did appear to be implementing a common security approach via a GRIT-type strategy and, despite initial calls for nuclear disarmament, he also appeared to be moving towards a minimum deterrence strategy and the advocacy of a NOD approach for conventional forces. By the end of 1988, Gorbachev had initiated an approach towards achieving security that could have mitigated the security dilemma.

The final goal is to ascertain to what extent new thinking was responsible for mitigating the security dilemma. It is suggested that the Soviet debate on force posture, while indicating a willingness to explore NOD concepts, had not been translated into policy implementation. The CFE Treaty, for instance, was an example of transparency between the Cold War adversaries, not an example of the adoption of NOD. Thus, by the end of the Cold War the West remained sceptical of Soviet declarations of defensiveness. In March 1990 the British Secretary of Defence, Tom King, commented that Soviet modernisation did not indicate a NOD approach.

> We believe that [in 1989] the USSR completed ten submarines, six major surface warships, 50 bombers, 600 fighters, at least 1700 tanks and 450 ballistic missiles. Soviet tank production, even at half the previous level, is still more than double the annual output of the whole of NATO ...
>
> That is not to try and re-stir the embers of the Cold War; but these are the facts on which we need to base out future actions and judgements.[162]

In the nuclear field, the START I agreement did not codify a superpower adoption of minimum deterrence; it was only when their relationship had improved that the two moved in this direction in START II. If these results were largely disappointing, then the changes in foreign policy were more encouraging. While it is too early to determine the precise role of new thinking in mitigating the security dilemma, the Soviet awareness of this concept, and Gorbachev's persistence in implementing unilateral initiatives, certainly had a role, perhaps an initiating and sustaining one, in mitigating the Cold War security dilemma. The final chapter will examine whether these ideas have continued to mitigate and even escape the security dilemma or whether, in post-Cold War Europe, the security dilemma is re-emerging.

Notes

1. Robert Jervis, *Perception and Misperception in International Politics* (New Jersey: 1976), p. 82.
2. In Charles Osgood's hypothetical example, the US Senate sought to impeach the President for pursuing a conciliatory policy: see Charles E. Osgood, *An Alternative to War and Surrender* (Chicago: 1962), p. 11.
3. Jervis, *Perception*, p. 77.
4. Herbert Butterfield, *History and Human Relations* (London: 1951), p. 19.
5. Jervis, *Perception*, p. 86.
6. Mikhail Gorbachev, *Perestroika: new thinking for our country and the world* (London: 2nd edn, 1988), p. 140.
7. Ibid., pp. 140–1.
8. Compare the Independent Commission on Disarmament and Security Issues under the chairmanship of Olaf Palme, *Common Security: a programme for disarmament* (London: 1982), p. 7, with Gorbachev, ibid., p. 138.
9. Gorbachev, *Perestroika*, p. 142.
10. Ibid.
11. Ibid., p. 141.
12. Wheeler and Booth claim that the ideas of the North American and West European peace movements 'spread to Moscow where they were placed on the superpower agenda by President Gorbachev': Nicholas J. Wheeler and Ken Booth, 'The Security Dilemma', in John Baylis and N. J. Rengger (eds), *Dilemmas of World Politics: international issues in a changing world* (Oxford: 1992), p. 45.
13. Thomas Risse-Kappen, 'Ideas Do Not Float Freely: transnational coalitions, domestic structures, and the end of the cold war', *International Organization*, 48/2 (1994), p. 194.
14. Janice Gross Stein, 'Political Learning by Doing: Gorbachev as uncommitted thinker and motivated learner', *International Organization*, 48/2 (1994), p. 186.
15. Those academics who agree with the view that the western peace community influenced Soviet thinking tend to favour the existence of 'epistemic communities'. For detail on this phenomenon, see the special issue of *International Organization*, 46/1 (1992). A contradictory opinion which highlights the bureaucratic model is given by Stuart Kaufman in 'Organizational Politics and Change in Soviet Military Policy', *World Politics*, 46/3 (1994), pp. 355–82.
16. Gorbachev noted the similarity of the Palme Commission to the Soviet concept of security and admitted Brandt and Bahr's ideas 'were close or identical' to his own. What is interesting about these revelations is that Gorbachev had little or no clear idea of his foreign policy before he became General Secretary. Shevardnadze has stated that, in 1979, 'although it was clear to both of us that if we did not change our foreign policy by removing the main sources of distrust – the use of force and rigid ideology – we could never create a zone of security around our country ... At that time those ideas had not crystallized for Gorbachev.' In an interview with Janice Gross Stein, Alexander Yakovlev recalled that in 1983 Gorbachev 'did not know what he wanted to do but our idea was to stop the Cold War before it led to catastrophe. We had to do something.' Indeed, there appears to be widespread agreement that Gorbachev knew

that he had to change Soviet foreign policy but had no plan of how to do so. As such, contacts abroad with common security proponents like Egon Bahr could well have had a great influence upon him. For Gorbachev, see *Perestroika*, pp. 206–7; for Shevardnadze, see *The Future Belongs to Freedom* (London: 1991), p. 26; for Gross Stein, see 'Political Learning', p. 174.

17. The most obvious point of contact between common security ideas and the Soviet leadership was Georgii Arbatov, who had been the Soviet representative on the Palme Commission. Arbatov, who also headed the United States of America and Canada Institute (ISKAN), was one of Gorbachev's closest advisers. He has claimed: 'the Palme commission was significant in changing the political thinking in the Soviet Union and introduced the concept of common security to officials'. Arbatov also stated: 'We do not claim to have invented all the ideas of the new thinking. Some of them originated outside the Soviet Union with people such as Albert Einstein, Bertrand Russell, and Olaf Palme. We are developing them, along with our ideas, into a full program for international conduct.' These comments clearly support the notion that new thinking was influenced by western common security proponents. Arbatov's comments are quoted from Risse-Kappen, 'Ideas', pp. 201 n52, 202.

18. According to this view, there was widespread disillusionment during the 1970s due to the failings of Marxist-Leninist analysis to explain developments in the Third World. Since writings on the Third World attracted little attention from decision-makers, the authors could raise concerns that would otherwise have been censored. Michael MccGwire has suggested that such concerns 'must have raised questions about the validity of [Marxist-Leninist] analysis in other spheres of international relations': Michael MccGwire, *Perestroika and Soviet National Security* (Washington: 1991), p. 157. For details on the origins of new thinking and the Third World writings in the 1970s, see Peter Shearman, 'New Political Thinking Reassessed', *Review of International Studies*, 19/2 (1993), p. 143. For the failings of the socialist model for the Third World, see Alexi Kiva, 'The Third World's Illusions and Realities', *International Affairs (Moscow)*, 10 (October 1991), pp. 30–9.

19. Two such influential advisers included Alexander Yakovlev and Yevgeniy Primakov. While Yakovlev had served in the USA and Canada, his writings implied that such thinking had little to commend it. Jeff Checkel describes them as 'vitriolic, propagandistic, and extremely anti-American'. Primakov clearly favoured a common security approach, as is evident from his 1987 article. Yet, according to Risse-Kappen, 'there is not much evidence that transnational contacts were important to' either Primakov or Yakovlev: Jeff Checkel, 'Ideas, Institutions, and the Gorbachev Foreign Policy Revolution', *World Politics*, 45/2 (1993), p. 284 n52. For Primakov's article, see 'New "Flexibility" in Soviet Foreign Policy', *Pravda*, 10 July 1987, p. 4, trans. in *Current Digest of the Soviet Press*, 39/28, pp. 1–4. Hereafter known as *CDSP*. For Risse-Kappen, see 'Ideas', p. 193.

20. Janice Gross Stein, 'Detection and Defection: security "regimes" and the management of international conflict', *International Journal*, 40/4 (1985), p. 604.

21. Robert E. Axelrod and Robert O. Keohane, 'Achieving Cooperation under Anarchy', *World Politics*, 38/1 (1985), p. 234.

22. GRIT and its relevance to the security dilemma has been implied by Alexander George. George notes that Osgood regarded the Cold War conflict as one in which mutual interests existed, but the relationship was contaminated by acute distrust of motives. It was this distrust, therefore, that lay at the heart of the conflict. As a result, GRIT was only applicable to relaxing tensions, not achieving cooperative agreements where conflicts of interest were concerned. This implies relevance to the security dilemma, since the dilemma results from an inadvertent conflict, not a conflict in which the states deliberately threaten one another. Joshua Goldstein and John Freeman are explicit in linking GRIT to the security dilemma for the reasons that George noted. They write:

'under the assumptions of the spiral model, a strategy such as GRIT ... is most appropriate': See Alexander George, 'Strategies for Facilitating Cooperation', in Alexander L. George, Philip J. Farley and Alexander Dallin (eds), *US–Soviet Security Cooperation: achievements, failures, lessons* (New York: 1988), p. 706; Joshua S. Goldstein and John R. Freeman, *Three Way Street* (Chicago: 1990), p. 16.

23. Osgood, *An Alternative*, pp. 88–9.

24. The title supports Osgood's assertion that GRIT requires persistence and fortitude. For reference to Osgood, see Amitai Etzioni, *The Hard Way to Peace: a new strategy* (New York: 1962), p. 84.

25. Ibid., p. 14.

26. Ibid., p. 99.

27. Ibid., p. 102.

28. Goldstein and Freeman, *Three Way Street*, p. 154.

29. Richard A. Bitzinger, 'Gorbachev and GRIT, 1985–1989: did arms control succeed because of unilateral actions or in spite of them?, *Contemporary Security Policy*, 15/1 (1994), p. 69.

30. Gorbachev, *Perestroika*, p. 225.

31. 'Gorbachev Announces Nuclear Test Moratorium', *Pravda* and *Izvestia*, 30 July 1985, p. 1, trans. in *CDSP*, 37/30, p. 8.

32. If the Soviet Union had already completed its testing, then clearly the moratorium would only affect the United States and could not be seen as a sincere attempt to reduce tension. Likewise, if the test ban could not be verified, then the USA would not be able to determine if the Soviet Union was actually complying with the initiative.

33. The USSR completed only 7 tests in 1985, compared with 20–30 annual tests since 1978. For more on this, see Goldstein and Freeman, *Three Way Street*, p. 116.

34. Quoted from Bitzinger, 'Gorbachev and GRIT', p. 73.

35. Quoted from Goldstein and Freeman, *Three Way Street*, p. 121.

36. Indeed, the USA continued to test their SDI project throughout 1986 and to make the Soviet Union fearful that the USA was extending the arms race into space.

37. Bitzinger, 'Gorbachev and GRIT', p. 75.

38. Quoted from Goldstein and Freeman, *Three Way Street*, p. 116.

39. Ibid., p. 121.

40. Gorbachev has stated that while 'we failed to find a solution to the fundamental problem of halting the arms race and strengthening peace ... we got to know each other better, clearly saw the nature of our differences, and started dialogue': Gorbachev, *Perestroika*, p. 227.

41. Given that, in his first term in office, Reagan had made statements about 'prevailing' in a nuclear war and had embarked upon a massive build-up of military hardware, it is not surprising that the Soviet Union attached considerable importance to the Geneva Accords.

42. MccGwire, *Perestroika*, p. 194.

43. Quoted from ibid., p. 195.

44. Stefan Lehne, *The Vienna Meeting of the Conference on Security and Cooperation in Europe, 1986–1989* (Boulder: 1991), p. 26.

45. Quoted from ibid., p. 27. For more on this, see Sverre Logaard, 'The Stockholm CSBMs and the Future of the CDE', *Arms Control*, 8/2 (1987), pp. 155–68. See also Volker Pittberger, Manfred Efinger and Martin Mendler, 'Toward an East–West Security Regime: the case of confidence- and security-building measures', *Journal of Peace Research*, 27/1 (1990), pp. 55–74.

46. Logaard, 'The Stockholm CSBMs', p. 161.

47. Lehne, *The Vienna Meeting*, p. 27.

48. Gorbachev said: 'the Reykjavik meeting greatly facilitated, probably for the first time in many decades, our search for disarmament'. At an impromptu press conference at

Keriavik Airport, Donald Reagan, the White House Chief of Staff, lashed out at the Soviet negotiators, saying that 'they finally showed their hand; it showed them up for what they are'. These quotes, along with the 'strange interlude' description, can be found in Michael Mendelbaum and Strobe Talbott, 'Reykjavik and Beyond', *Foreign Affairs*, 65/2 (1986/7), pp. 216, 230–1, 235.

49. Gorbachev linked the two issues together when he wrote: 'A nuclear test ban is a touchstone. If you sincerely wish to eliminate nuclear weapons, you will agree to ban tests because such a ban will lead to a reduction of the existing arsenals and an end to their modernization': Gorbachev, *Perestroika*, p. 228.

50. Gorbachev believed that the US inertia was largely the result of a 'militarist group' within the USA. This group was comprised of leading members from the military-industrial complex and some politicians. Hence Gorbachev's statement that, with this opportunity to talk one-to-one with Reagan, he would be able to 'wrench arms control out of the hands of the bureaucrats': Strobe Talbott, *The Master of the Game: Paul Nitze and the nuclear peace* (New York: 1988), p. 315.

51. Osgood, *An Alternative*, p. 99.

52. See Talbott, *Master*, p. 315.

53. MccGwire, *Perestroika*, p. 199.

54. Gorbachev commented 'that the Americans came to Reykjavik completely empty handed. The impression was created that they had come there only to gather fruit into their basket with empty hands': ibid., p. 199 n73.

55. Taubman was writing about the meeting in Vienna between Shultz and Shevardnadze at which they tried unsuccessfully to clarify what had been agreed at Reykjavik: see Philip Taubman, 'A Time of Mistrust', *New York Times*, 7 November 1986, p. 1.

56. 'I think the Soviets convened that summit, proposed the summit, allegedly for discussion, in order to spring on the President a series of proposals for which he would then be condemned publicly if he refused to accept': Zbigniew Brzezinski, in Bernard Gwertzman, 'The Road Ahead', *New York Times*, 14 October 1986, p. 11. See also Anthony Lewis, 'Reagan's Dream', *New York Times*, 16 October 1986, p. 31.

57. Gorbachev, *Perestroika*, p. 240. Gorbachev also referred to Reykjavik as 'a major event. A reappraisal [had taken] place. A qualitatively new situation [had] come about. Nobody [could] now act in the same way as he had acted before': Gorbachev's address on Moscow Television Service (MTS), 'Vremya', quoted from MccGwire, *Perestroika*, p. 202.

58. Talbott, *Master*, p. 325. After this meeting, the Americans insisted that Reagan had not endorsed a nuclear-free world within 10 years, but was expressing his long-standing desire that a nuclear-free world would be achieved some time in the future. The Reykjavik negotiations were to break down, as Gorbachev was insistent that Reagan forgo his SDI dream, and Reagan was just as determined that SDI would be implemented. With both failing to reach a compromise, Reagan literally picked up his papers and walked out.

59. The impression was that 'Reagan had thrown away the promise of a nuclear-free world by clinging to his version of a space-based defence – even if there might be no missiles to defend against'. It was an impression that was largely accurate. Poindexter, the National Security Advisor, stated: 'If they really want to kill SDI, which it appears is their motivation, there is no way we can come to an agreement on that': see 'Forward Spin', *Time*, 27 October 1986, pp. 7, 24.

60. David Buchan and Patrick Cockburn, 'NATO Chiefs Concerned at Arms Plan', *Financial Times*, 17 October 1986, p. 44.

61. Jonathan Dean, *Meeting Gorbachev's Challenge: how to build down the NATO–Warsaw Pact confrontation* (London: 1986), p. 30.

62. 'The net effect of the Reykjavik plan looks like a Europe decoupled from America and at the mercy of the Soviet Union': Ian Davidson, 'NATO Cannot Survive Another Triumph', *Financial Times*, 20 October 1986, p. 17.

63. Jane M. O. Sharpe, 'After Reykjavik: arms control and the allies', *International Affairs*, 63/2 (1987), p. 250.
64. David Buchan, 'UK Sees Risk if "Zero Option" Leaves NATO Troops Outnumbered', *Financial Times*, 22 October 1986, p. 48.
65. David Shipler, 'Kohl, in Washington, Meets with Reagan to Discuss Iceland Talks', *New York Times*, 22 October 1986 p. A10.
66. Anthony Bevins, 'Thatcher Stresses Distrust of Soviets', *Independent*, 11 November 1986, p. 1.
67. Andrew McEwen, 'United Front on a European Deterrent', *Independent*, 21 November 1986, p. 20.
68. The need to reduce the Soviet conventional forces was not only for this reason. Gorbachev also sought a reduction in force for financial reasons. During this period he introduced the concepts of 'reasonable sufficiency' and 'defensive defence'. These were important initiatives in mitigating the security dilemma and are the subject of analysis in section 2.
69. The figures are from Dean, *Meeting Gorbachev's Challenge*, p. 20.
70. Hella Pick and Martin Walker, 'Superpowers Hail INF Treaty as a Turning Point in Arms Race', *Guardian*, 9 December 1987, p. 1., R. W. Apple, Jr., 'Optimistic and Wary', *New York Times*, 9 December 1987, p. A20.
71. Bitzinger, 'Gorbachev and GRIT', p. 77.
72. Daniel Druckman, 'The Psychology of Arms Control and Reciprocation', in Bennett Ramberg (ed.), *Arms Control without Negotiation: from the Cold War to the new world order* (Boulder: 1993), p. 28.
73. The formulation of cooperation can broadly be divided into two types. These are 'bargaining' strategies and strategies that require 'reciprocity'. 'Bargaining' strategies are concerned with facilitating an agreement over conflicts of interest and are used in formal negotiations. 'Reciprocity' strategies are conceived as means of reducing tension and improving relations. Both strategies require responses from the participants (i.e., cooperation) to succeed. The former often takes the form of mutual concessions, and the latter unilateral initiatives.
74. Thomas Risse-Kappen, 'Did "Peace through Strength" End the Cold War?', *International Security*, 16/1 (1991), p. 186.
75. On 5 June 1987 Reagan had called for an increase of spending on conventional forces by the European allies in response to a US–Soviet agreement: see Alex Brummer, 'Europe Told to Spend on Conventional Armaments', *Guardian*, 6 June 1987, p. 8. For details on NATO's concerns regarding the INF Treaty's impact on its strategy, see Lewis A. Dunn, 'NATO after Global "Double-Zero"', *Survival*, 30/3 (1988), pp. 195–209.
76. In order to prevent the NATO Alliance replacing INF weapons with 'smart' conventional systems, the Rumanians proposed an arms-spending moratorium by both alliances. Although it gained endorsement by the Warsaw Pact in May 1987, it was rejected by the Western Alliance.
77. Nicholas Beeston, 'Cut in Forces Could Follow Missile Deal', *The Times*, 13 March 1987, p. 8.
78. Roy Allison, 'Current Soviet Views on Conventional Arms in Europe', *Arms Control*, 9/2 (1988), p. 139.
79. 'Statement by the Warsaw Treaty Member-States', *Pravda*, 17 July 1988, pp. 1–2, trans. in *CDSP*, 40/29, p. 24. The Committee of Senior Officials (CSO) and the Conflict Prevention Centre (CPC) were established within the CSCE framework as independent bodies designed to meet, amongst other things, these requirements.
80. Quoted from General John R. Galvin, 'Some Thoughts on Conventional Arms Control', *Survival*, 31/2 (1989), p. 100.
81. 'Toward a New Scope and Quality of the All-European Dialogue', *Pravda*, 20 January

1989, p. 5, trans. in *CDSP*, 41/3, p. 20. For confirmation by General Yazov, see 'In the Interests of General Security and Peace', *Izvestia*, 27 February 1989, p. 3, trans. in *CDSP*, 41/9, p. 18.

82. 'Baker Hears New Soviet Arms Cut Plans', *Pravda* and *Izvestia*, 12 May 1989, pp. 1–2, trans. in *CDSP*, 41/19, p. 3.

83. The proposals included reductions of over a million troops. For details of the proposals, see ibid.

84. Galvin, 'Some Thoughts', p. 100.

85. Quoted from Bitzinger, 'Gorbachev and GRIT', p. 75.

86. An important initiative which confirmed for many in the West that Soviet policy-makers were sincere in their desire for better relations was the decision to withdraw from Afghanistan. Announced in February 1988, the last Soviet troops left a year later.

87. Lehne, *The Vienna Meeting*, p. 141.

88. In January 1990 Bush proposed a further reduction of US and Soviet troop levels in central Europe to 195,000.

89. MccGwire, *Perestroika*, p. 296.

90. Dividing the Soviet debate into reasonable sufficiency and defensive defence, creates an artificial divide. The two terms were closely related – indeed, 'inextricably tied', according to Roy Allison – and this closeness led to hybrid notions such as 'defensive sufficiency' being used to describe Soviet doctrine. Yet dividing the debate in this fashion enables a coherent examination of the different methods required to mitigate the security dilemma at the nuclear and conventional level. The Allison comment is from Roy Allison, 'New Thinking about Defence in the Soviet Union', in Ken Booth (ed.), *New Thinking about Strategy and International Security* (London: 1991), p. 222.

91. Gorbachev said: 'our country is in favour of withdrawing weapons of mass destruction from circulation and confining military potential to the bounds of reasonable sufficiency'. He then added the caveat: 'but the nature and level of these bounds continue to be limited by the positions and actions of the US and its bloc partners': see 'Gorbachev's Political Report', *Pravda* and *Izvestia*, 26 February 1986, pp. 2–10, trans. in *CDSP*, 38/8, p. 28.

92. The ambiguity of the reasonable sufficiency debate was not to be overcome. This was largely due to the lack of agreement on such crucial issues as what constituted sufficiency and how that sufficiency was to be determined. With no agreed formula, the debate remained an enigma.

93. Stephen M. Meyer, 'The Sources and Prospects of Gorbachev's New Political Thinking on Security', in Sean M. Lynn-Jones, Steven E. Millar and Stephen Van Evera (eds), *Soviet Military Policy* (Massachusetts: 1989), p. 130.

94. The latter point is explained by appreciating the increased perception during a crisis that an attack is imminent. If this perception is illusory, then the security dilemma is acting at its highest pitch and Butterfield's tragedy could occur. For more on this, see Robert Jervis, 'Arms Control, Stability, and Causes of War', *Political Science Quarterly*, 108/2 (1993), p. 249.

95. For a thorough examination of this debate, see Stephen Shenfield, *Minimum Nuclear Deterrence: the debate among Soviet civilian analysts* (Brown University: Center for Foreign Policy Development, 1989). It is important to note that the military and the civilians had a different interpretation of reasonable sufficiency. The critical issue that divided them was the link between sufficiency and parity. The military considered sufficiency to codify the maintenance of quantitative parity with the western states, but at lower levels. In May 1987 Marshal Akhromeyev stated: 'Our principal is to maintain the armed forces and our military potential at the level of approximate military balance and sufficiency for a reliable defence of the Soviet Union and the countries of the Warsaw Pact.' The civilians, however, considered parity to mean something different. Primakov (IMEMO) wrote in July 1987: 'When we talk about reasonable sufficiency

in this period, what comes to the fore, despite the great importance of the quantitative aspects of strategic parity, is its qualitative aspect: the inability of either side to avoid a devastating retaliatory strike.' This is an extremely important difference, since Primakov's criterion does not require the USSR to match the force levels of its opponents in order to maintain a credible deterrence. Instead, Primakov's criterion provides a means of escaping the arms race and maintaining deterrence through a force that is large enough to threaten assured destruction with credibility in the event of a nuclear attack; it is similar to the western conception of minimum deterrence. An article by Vitaly Zhurkin of the European Studies Institute which attracted much western comment supported Primakov: 'Reasonable sufficiency presupposes that for the prevention of aggression by the other side it is not so much necessary to equal his forces as to deter its leadership from unleashing war. In other words, a reasonable approach considers not only an estimate of hypothetical capabilities of a possible adversary, but also a dialectical analysis and account of his realistic intentions and, the main thing, his interests.' For the Akhromeyev quote, see Raymond L. Garthoff, 'New Thinking in Soviet Military Doctrine', *The Washington Quarterly*, 11/3 (1988), p. 139; for the Primakov quote, see 'New "Flexibility" in Soviet Foreign Policy', *CDSP*, 39/28, pp. 1–4; for Zhurkin, see Garthoff, 'New Thinking', p. 143. Zhurkin's article can also be found in Christoph Bluth, *New Thinking in Soviet Military Policy* (London: 1990), pp. 85–7; Meyer, 'The Sources and Prospects', pp. 131–3; and Allison, 'New Thinking', pp. 220–3.

96. The concept of minimum nuclear deterrence (MND) was also to suffer from ambiguity in its interpretation. However, there was general agreement that the Soviet definition was 'essentially identical to the concept used by Western theorists'. Thus Shenfield asserts: 'MND may be said to pertain when one or more states deploy nuclear armaments at a level and in a structure that are sufficient, but not substantially more than sufficient, to permit that state or those states to inflict an "unacceptable" amount of retaliatory damage after suffering any feasible nuclear attack.' Shenfield is supported by Christoph Bluth who comments: 'to arrive at a concept of minimum deterrence, the Soviet arms control community has taken up a Western concept – namely, the potential to inflict unacceptable damage in a retaliatory strike.' Both authors note the Soviets' usage of the McNamara index, thus implying the similarity between the US and Soviet interpretation of minimum deterrence.

The western conception of minimum deterrence, however, specifically refers to strategic nuclear weapons, whereas the Soviet interpretation has also been used to refer to tactical nuclear weapons. According to Stephen Kux, this signified confusion in Soviet circles about minimum deterrence. He writes: 'a limitation to "assured retaliatory capabilities" would exclude any form of extended deterrence. Yet most Soviet references to "minimum deterrence" relate mainly to Europe, more specifically to tactical nuclear weapons, and not to strategic weapons ... While the Soviet usage of "minimum deterrence" might be politically expedient, it confuses traditional meanings of the term.' It is this reference to tactical nuclear weapons that causes the ambiguity in the Soviet use of the term. Raymond Garthoff, however, suggests that the references to tactical nuclear weapons indicated the Soviet perception that MND was a temporary measure designed to bring about a nuclear-free world. Thus, in 1989, with the Soviets beginning to regard the elimination of tactical nuclear weapons in Europe as unlikely, they began to use the term 'a minimum nuclear deterrent in Europe' as a means of reaching a compromise. This, Garthoff suggests, explains the following rather confusing comment made by General Chervov at the CSCE multilateral seminar on military doctrine held at Vienna in early 1990. Chervov 'explained that the Soviet conception of "minimum nuclear deterrence" was a response to NATO's lack of support, "at this stage", for the Soviet preference of eliminating tactical nuclear weapons from Europe'. The Soviet conception of MND for strategic weapons was, therefore, the same as the western conception; the ambiguity arose because it was used to refer to a temporary state of affairs concerning all nuclear weapons. For the Shenfield quote, see Shenfield, *Minimum Nuclear Deterrence*, p. 3; for Bluth, see *New Thinking*, p. 43; for Stephen Kux, see 'The Soviet Debate on Strategic Nuclear Arms', in Roy Allison (ed.), *Radical Reform in Soviet Defence Policy* (London: 1992), p. 137; for Raymond L. Garthoff, see *Deterrence and the Revolution in Soviet Military Doctrine* (Washington: 1990), p. 144.

97. The report is translated in Shenfield, *Minimum Nuclear Deterrence*, pp 7–10.

98. Jervis's favouritism for submarines reflects the western priority of these as secure second-strike systems.

99. See Jervis, 'Arms Control', pp. 239–53.

100. Quoted from Felix Pirani, 'The Dark Side of Glasnost', *New Statesman and Society*, 1/27 (9 December 1988), p. 20.

101. Ibid.

102. A revised edition of the report, published in February 1988, placed a majority of ICBMs in silos. This new position reflected the belief that communication with mobile ICBMs might become disabled during a crisis (electromagnetic pulses (EMP)) and that hardened silos did provide a substantial source of protection against a nuclear attack. The silo-based ICBMs did not therefore reflect a change of thinking over the need to have a secure second strike.

103. Garthoff, *Deterrence*, p. 140.

104. Sergei Vybornov, Andrei Gusenkov and Vladimir Leontiev, 'Nothing Is Simple in Europe', *International Affairs (Moscow)*, 3 (March 1988), pp. 34–41.

105. At present, there appears to be agreement that a counter-force capability against mobile ICBMs is not feasible. The vulnerability of mobile missiles is discussed in William J. Holland, 'The End of the Triad? why SSBN advances make a dyad possible', *Arms Control Today*, 19/7 (1989), p. 10, and Michael Brower, 'Targeting Soviet Mobile Missiles', *Survival*, 31/5 (1989), pp. 433–45.

106. Shenfield has produced an interpretation of the diplomats' regime: see Shenfield, *Minimum Nuclear Deterrence*, pp. 16–18.

107. Sergei Vybornov and Vladimir Leontiev, 'The Future of the Old Weapon', *International Affairs (Moscow)*, 9 (September 1988), pp. 81–9.

108. In July Ivan Tyulin and Andrei Zagorsky of the Moscow State Institute of International Relations (MGIMO) commented on the two articles. They did not regard the two European powers as constituting a multipolar problem and thought it would remain bipolar, with the Europeans siding with America. They preferred the use of ICBMs, because they provided greater strategic stability. In March 1989 Ednan Agayev of the MFA also proposed a MND regime, though he used the term 'defensive nuclear deterrence'. While the use of 'defensive' was not evidence of any influence from Jervis, it nevertheless reveals the similarity of the thinking. See Ivan Tyulin and Andrei Zagorsky, 'Dimensions of a "Near-Zero" Nuclear Balance', *International Affairs (Moscow)*, 7 (July 1988), pp. 111–14; Ednan Agayev, 'Towards a New Model of Strategic Stability', *International Affairs (Moscow)*, 3 (March 1989), pp. 96–103.

109. Garthoff, *Deterrence*, p. 140.

110. Shenfield, *Minimum Nuclear Deterrence*, p. 20.

111. 'Gorbachev Addresses the Council of Europe', *Pravda*, 7 July 1989, pp. 1–2, trans. in *CDSP*, 41/27, pp. 6–8.

112. The West, of course, did not subscribe to minimum deterrence, but, according to Garthoff, 'Gorbachev opened the door for negotiation on how much nuclear weaponry is enough for a deterrent, rather than perpetuating an impasse over the very concept of deterrence': Garthoff, *Deterrence*, p. 138.

113. Kux, 'The Soviet Debate', pp. 138–9.

114. Quoted from Garthoff, *Deterrence*, p. 138.

115. 'The fortunes of peace are inseparable from the fortunes of our restructuring': *Pravda*, 27 September 1989, pp. 4–5, trans. in *CDSP*, 41/39, pp. 20–1.

116. The unilateralist approach was first advanced by Aleksandr Bovin in December 1988 and by Igor Malashenko of the ISKAN in January 1989. These proposals were expounded upon by Aleksi Arbatov (IMEMO) in April 1989 and then by Professor Radomir Bogdanov in June 1989. For an examination of these proposals, see Igor Malashenko, 'Non-Military Aspects of Security', *International Affairs (Moscow)*, 1 (January 1989), pp. 40–51; Alexi Arbatov, 'How Much Defence Is Sufficient', *International Affairs (Moscow)*, 4 (April 1989), pp. 31–44; Radomir Bogdanov and Andrei Kortunov, 'On the Balance of Power', *International Affairs (Moscow)*, 8 (August 1989), pp. 3–13. The unilateralists were subjected to a barrage of criticism from the military. In July 1989 Bogdanov's views were criticised by Colonels Vladimir Dvorkin and Valeriy Torbin and then by retired Lieutenant-General Volkov in September. Major-General Lyubimov criticised Arbatov in August 1989. For details, see Shenfield, *Minimum Nuclear Deterrence*, pp. 22–5, and Garthoff, *Deterrence*, pp. 145–7.
117. Garthoff, *Deterrence*, p. 147.
118. A collaborative piece of work between civilians and the military was unusual and perhaps represented the fluidity of the debate in military circles. These two authors produced a number of articles, with the four models originally being published in 1988 in an article entitled, 'Opposing General Purpose Forces in the Context of Providing Strategic Stability': see MccGwire, *Perestroika*, p. 329 n75.
119. Kokoshin and Larionov were fond of using the Kursk battle during the Second World War as an example of a successful defensive operation. Such a battle would be categorized as belonging to this second model.
120. The Soviet term for a counter-offensive at this level (operational) was 'counter-strike'.
121. See Charles Glaser, 'Political Consequences of Military Strategy', *World Politics*, 44/4 (1992), p. 509.
122. Offensive actions in this model were at the tactical level and known in Soviet jargon as 'counter-attacks'.
123. Quoted from Garthoff, *Deterrence*, p. 162.
124. Many statements, such as those by Vladimir Lobov, Chief of Staff of the Warsaw Pact forces, and Chief of General Staff Moiseyev, kept the option of invading enemy territory open. Others, though, such as Marshal Viktor Kulikov, Commander-in-Chief of the Warsaw Pact forces, and Major-General Stepan Tyushkevich, omitted the word 'counter-offensive', which implied a model 3 approach. For more, see ibid., pp. 162–5.
125. Dimtri Yazov, 'Soviet Military Doctrine', *RUSI Defence Yearbook 1990* (London: 1990), p. 38.
126. Garthoff supports this by claiming that, prior to 1990, 'Soviet doctrine seem[ed] to be in transition from the second to the third variant': see Garthoff, *Deterrence*, p. 166.
127. Bitzinger, 'Gorbachev and GRIT', p. 77.
128. See John Baylis and Ken Booth, *Britain, NATO and Nuclear Weapons: alternative defence versus alliance reform* (London, 1989), pp. 204–7.
129. New thinking and common security shared the same core assumptions about the way in which long-term security could be achieved. New thinking adopted the idea that state security is interdependent, largely as a result of the global consequences of a nuclear war. This assumption led Gorbachev to proclaim, firstly, that security could not be attained via the use of military force, and, secondly, that states should not seek security at the expense of each other. The implementation of new thinking was the implementation of common security. For details, see Gorbachev, *Perestroika*, pp. 140–2.
130. Common security and the related concept of non-offensive defence were born in West Germany. Since then the concepts have spread, most notably to those countries neighbouring West Germany (Denmark and other Nordic countries). This resulted in the development of a community of western European peace researchers in various institutes: Stockholm International Peace Research Institute; the Peace Research

Institute in Oslo; the Centre for Peace and Conflict Research in Copenhagen; the Institute for Research and Security Policy in Hamburg; and the Peace Research Institute in Frankfurt. These proponents of common security used forums such as the Pugwash Conferences to promulgate their ideas. In keeping with the 'epistemic community' approach, Thomas Risse-Kappen suggests that, through meetings such as Pugwash, the western peace community was able to influence Soviet thinkers. He notes that 'Andrei Kokoshin, deputy director of ISKAN and one of the most prominent "new thinkers" in Soviet foreign policy, participated regularly' at these conferences: see Risse-Kappen, 'Ideas', p. 199.

131. Barry Buzan, 'Foreword', in Bjorn Moller, *Resolving the Security Dilemma in Europe: the German debate on non-offensive defence* (London, 1991), p. xvi.

132. The Social Democrats (SPD) were the greatest exponents of a common security approach, but even the other main parties adopted approaches that differed little in substance. The Christian Democrats (CDU)/Christian Social Union (CSU) spoke of 'reciprocal security', by which they meant 'the willingness on the part of both parties to allow each other the same measure of security. It requires the abstention from trying to solve political problems by military means. The concept of reciprocal security rests on the balance of mutually secured defence capability, on a system of reciprocal confidence-building measures, as well as on *détente* and disarmament.' For quotation, see Moller, *Resolving the Security Dilemma*, p. 190.

133. Robert Mark Spaulding, Jr., notes: 'upon conclusion of the Polish round table agreement in April 1989, the Federal Republic took the lead in promising increased Western support ... One year later, the same thoughts and identical rhetoric reappeared with regard to the role of Western aid in securing the future of the reform movement in the Soviet Union': Robert Mark Spaulding, Jr., 'German Trade Policy in Eastern Europe, 1890–1990; preconditions for applying international trade leverage', *International Organization*, 45 (Summer 1991), pp. 365–6.

134. For more details on the modernisation controversy, see Hans Binnendijk, 'NATO's Nuclear Modernization Dilemma', *Survival*, 31 (March/April 1989), pp. 137–55.

135. Risse-Kappen, 'Ideas', p. 207.

136. Ibid., p. 206.

137. Evidence of her 'hard line' attitude can be witnessed in the following comments made by Thatcher in February 1988. She warned that the 'Russian bear was easier to deal with when it looked like a bear than it does now', and that 'the nicer the Russians get, the more dangerous they are'. Quoted from Richard Ullman, *Securing Europe* (London: 1991), p. 158 n23. Despite these remarks, by early 1989 she was warning the Bush administration not to act too slowly: see Michael Beschloss and Strobe Talbott, *At the Highest Levels: the inside story of the end of the Cold War* (Boston: 1993), pp. 29–31.

138. Quoted from Beschloss and Talbott, *At the Highest Levels*, pp. 17–18. By April Scrowcroft was referring to the West as having won the Cold War, but he still emphasised that there should be no change in US policy.

139. Raymond L. Garthoff, *The Great Transition: American–Soviet relations and the end of the Cold War* (Washington: 1994), p. 400.

140. For more on this, see Beschloss and Talbott, *At the Highest Levels*, p. 164.

141. Richard Ned Lebow and Janice Gross Stein, *We All Lost the Cold War* (Princeton: 1994), p. 375.

142. For instance, Osgood testified to the US House Committee on Foreign Affairs in 1973 that a successful implementation of GRIT, as a parallel process to the MBFR talks, could provide the means of achieving a successful treaty: see Druckman, 'The Psychology of Arms Control', p. 22.

143. Jonathan Dean and Randall Watson Forsberg, 'CFE and Beyond: the future of conventional arms control', *International Security*, 17/1 (1992), pp. 87–8. This comparison

is not intended to imply that CFE was unnecessary or unimportant. After all, the creation of this institutionalised regime acted as a catalyst for the formation of others.

144. This unilateral initiative received a quick reciprocal response from the USSR. For details, see *NATO Review*, 39/5 (1991), pp. 11–12.

145. Lebow and Stein, *We All Lost*, p. 371.

146. Ibid., p. 376.

147. Beschloss and Talbott, *At the Highest Levels*, p. 134. The Brezhnev Doctrine initially referred to the Soviet repression of the Czech coup in 1968. Since then, it has become synonymous with the Soviet policy of maintaining a 'right of interference' in their sphere of interest.

148. At the Warsaw Pact Summit in December 1989 all of the east European members, bar one, was represented by a 'self-styled reformer'. The exception was Romania; within three weeks of the meeting, communist rule here too was brought to an abrupt end: see ibid., p. 169.

149. In July 1989, while in Paris, Gorbachev had implied that the Brezhnev Doctrine was no longer Soviet policy. In an answer to a question about democratisation in Poland and Hungary, Gorbachev had replied that 'how the Polish people and the Hungarian people arrange things is their business'. In Helsinki in October he publicly stated that the Soviet Union had 'no right, moral or political', to interfere in the states of eastern Europe: see 'In Paris Gorbachev Meets the Press', *CDSP*, 41/27, p. 5.

150. Josef Joffe, 'Once More: the German question', *Survival*, 32/2 (1990), p. 131.

151. Bitzinger, 'Gorbachev and GRIT', p. 77.

152. MIRVed warheads enabled a single missile to destroy a large number of targets. The ability of one missile to hit many targets, combined with the great accuracy of the warheads, led the West to regard the Soviet MIRVed ICBM fleet as the most destabilising weapon in the USSR's arsenal.

153. Shenfield, *Minimum Nuclear Deterrence*, p. 31.

154. 'A Vintage Year for Arms Control', *Strategic Survey 1989–1990* (London: 1990), p. 199.

155. Erick K. Graben, 'Superpower Nuclear Minimalism in the Post-Cold War Era?', *Arms Control*, 13/3 (1992), pp. 355–6.

156. The START II Treaty, signed in January 1993, with its elimination of all MIRVed ICBMs and reduction in total warheads on each side to between 3,000 and 3,500, can be seen as supporting the movement towards a MND strategy. The following articles examine the possibility of minimum deterrence in the future in a positive light: Jan Kalicki, Fred Chernoff, Eric Mlyn, Sergei Fedorenko, Andrei Kortunov and Aleksandr Pisarev, 'Fundamental Deterrence and Mutual Security beyond START', in Smoke and Kortunov (eds), *Mutual Security: a new approach to Soviet–American relations* (London: 1991), pp. 249–68; Michael J. Mazarr, 'Military Targets for a Minimum Deterrent: after the Cold War how much is enough?', *The Journal of Strategic Studies*, 15/2 (1992), pp. 147–71; Graham Barral, 'The Lost Tablets: an analysis of the concept of minimum deterrence', *Arms Control*, 13/1 (1992), pp. 58–84; Michael E. Brown, 'The "End" of Nuclear Arms Control', *Arms Control*, 14/1 (1993), pp. 38–68; Sergei Rogov, 'The Evolution of Strategic Stability and the Future of Nuclear Weapons', *Arms Control*, 14/2 (1993), pp. 5–22.

157. For details of the CFE Treaty, see Dean and Forsberg, 'CFE and Beyond', pp. 80–98. It could be argued that because the CFE Treaty placed such limitations on Soviet offensive forces that it made a Soviet attack extremely unlikely, it actually escaped the security dilemma. Therefore, instead of being a turning-point in the *mitigation* of the security dilemma, this was when the Cold War security dilemma was *escaped*. However, escape can only occur once the treaty has been successfully ratified and implemented.

158. 'Old Problems, New Challenges', *Strategic Survey 1990–1991* (London: 1991), p. 249.

159. Quoted from Moller, *Resolving the Security Dilemma*, p. 193.

160. *London Declaration on a Transformed North Atlantic Alliance* (Brussels: NATO Information Service, 1990), paras 6, 11, 14.

161. Ibid., para 4. The new alliance strategy was announced at the NATO Summit in Rome on 7–8 November 1991. See *NATO Review*, 39/6 (1991).

162. Tom King, 'Defence and Security in a Time of Change', *RUSI Journal*, 135/2 (1990), p. 6.

Conclusion:
Post-Cold War Re-emergence?

> In ... a [security] community peace is predictable; the security dilemma has been escaped.[1]

It is postulated in Chapter 3 that if states create a security community through cooperation, the dynamics of the security dilemma will no longer plague their relationship. The existence of a security community can be demonstrated by the absolute certainty amongst its members that none of them will resort to military force to solve their differences. In essence, the acquisition of an enhanced military capability by one member of a security community does not generate fear in the other members that it intends them harm. Although it may seem self-evident that the end of the Cold War saw the end of the Cold War security dilemma, it is also self-evident that Russia and the West do not conduct their relations in a security community. Although the Cold War is over, this does not mean that the security dilemma which lay at its core – the western fear of Soviet/Russian expansion and Moscow's fear of western expansion – has been escaped.

The objective of this final chapter is to determine whether the security dilemma that bedevilled East–West relations during the Cold War can be witnessed in the post-Cold War relationship between Russia and the Western Alliance. If it still exists, does the post-Cold War relationship between the old adversaries indicate a continuing amelioration and eventual escape of the security dilemma, or is the security dilemma re-emerging? The chapter is not concerned with the possible emergence of new security dilemmas throughout Europe due to the uncertainties created by the collapse of the bipolar system.

With the removal of the superpower rivalry in Europe, the 1990s has seen the emergence of a myriad of security issues. According to Barry Buzan, Europe is experiencing the removal of a superpower overlay which has suppressed the local dynamics of European security for the last forty years. He argues that as 'the superpower overlay of Europe breaks up, it is obvious that what is emerging is much changed from the pre-1945 dynamics. Indeed, what the character of the European security complex will be in the twenty-first century is one of the great speculative questions of the day.'[2] It is certainly true that the emerging dynamics of this European security complex have produced an array of issues which will dominate the local security agenda for years to come. The most prominent of these issues are: a possible residual threat from the former Soviet Union; the potential for ethnic rivalry and the collapse of statehood; economic deprivation in central and eastern Europe (CEE); the future of many European institutions and their ability to manage the new security environment; the development of a common foreign and security policy (CFSP) for the European Union; and the continuing interest and presence of the United States in Europe. While not all of these are directly relevant to an examination of the security dilemma between Russia and the West, their diversity does indicate that the primary focus of European security is no longer based solely on the relationship between Moscow and the Western Alliance.

Richard Ullman recognises the continuing vitality of the security dilemma between the old Cold War adversaries by noting that the 'effect of arms control has been to soften the impact of the security dilemma, not to enable states to escape it'.[3] He goes on to to claim that a 'primary function of a new security regime in Europe will be to continue the process of removing from the continent the weight of the security dilemma', a process begun by Gorbachev.[4] It was noted in the previous chapter that while unilateral initiatives could help to improve relations by reducing suspicions and distrust, the establishment of institutionalised security regimes was required to mitigate and possibly provide an escape from the security dilemma. There are two crucial areas of the relationship between Moscow and its old adversaries that are relevant to the establishment of such regimes: arms control and NATO expansion. The former is a good barometer for assessing the continued mitigation of the security dilemma, while the latter provides the prospect of escape. The previous chapter also noted the way in which Gorbachev's ideas on defensive defence and reasonable sufficiency were adjusting the Soviet force posture to a stance that helps to ameliorate security dilemmas. The continuing presence or rejection of such ideas will also be a good gauge for assessing the vitality of the security dilemma.

This final chapter will examine the relationship between Russia and the Western Alliance from the point of view of three issues which are of crucial importance to a study of the security dilemma. The first is the ratification and implementation of arms control agreements signed immediately after the Cold War; the second will focus on the question of NATO expansion and the former Warsaw Pact members; the third will examine the force postures of the two Cold War antagonists. This examination should provide an answer to whether the security dilemma that lay at the heart of the Cold War is being laid to rest or is being resurrected. However, before these issues can be examined, it is necessary to analyse the impact of Gorbachev's removal from office. Gorbachev was the driving force behind the changes in the USSR; since he is no longer at the helm, it is important to ascertain if his successor, Boris Yeltsin, is also sensitive to the security dilemma. If he is not, this could have serious implications for the continuing amelioration of the security dilemma.

With the collapse of the Soviet Union in December 1991, Boris Yeltsin, the Russian President elected in June 1991, became the leader with whom the West would have to work if the Cold War security dilemma was not to re-emerge.[5] Much depends, therefore, upon whether there is a continuity between the ideas that directed Gorbachev's foreign policy and those influencing Yeltsin. Gorbachev surrounded himself with reformers and encouraged the input of civilian analysts into foreign and defence thinking – all of which made him aware of the security dilemma. If such reformers are prevalent in the Yeltsin government, then this bodes well for the continuing mitigation of the security dilemma.

Although a number of reformers in Gorbachev's government joined the Yeltsin bandwagon in 1991 – as the USSR began to lose its legitimacy in the eyes of the people – the influence of these civilians on the development of Soviet/Russian military thinking and on relations with the West in general has declined.[6] According to Jennifer Mathers, the 'perception among institute analysts with expertise in national security issues [is] that their golden age of power, prestige and influence has come and gone'.[7] Evidence of this declining influence can be found in the limited impact of research institutes on policy-making and the corresponding increase in the impact of the military. This increase in military influence at the expense of the civilians was given tangible evidence by the appointment of General Pavel Grachev to the Defence Ministry; it had been widely expected that Russia would have a civilian Defence Minister. Charles Dick confirms this declining civilian input, noting that in the 1993 Russian military doctrine 'there is little sign of civilian influence', which, he claims, 'attests to the fact that the Armed Forces still retain their all-but exclusive grip on the formulation of defence policy'.[8] It is also notable that the ability of the Russian Foreign Ministry to influence policy, which was considerable during Gorbachev's period in office, has declined markedly. The close relationship between Shevardnadze and Gorbachev which was the source of this influence was not evident between Yeltsin and the prominent radical Andrei Kozyrev, the former Russian Foreign Minister. In the month before Kozyrev's replacement by Yevgeniy Primakov, Mathers is proved right when she warns:

> Kozyrev ... is apparently struggling to maintain his position in a political atmosphere characterized by the rise to greater prominence and power of those, such as Defence Minister Pavel Grachev, who hold considerably more conservative views on both foreign and domestic political issues.[9]

This decline in civilian influence, and the corresponding rise of military thinking, does not automatically indicate that the East–West security dilemma will be resuscitated, but it is certainly not an encouraging development. If the military's influence should denote a movement for the return of dominance that Moscow enjoyed during the Cold War, then the security dilemma's mitigation could be reversed. It is the attitude that Russia has towards the West, and their perception of western intentions, which will dictate the workings of the security dilemma. This will now be examined by analysing the ratification and implementation of the arms control treaties signed by the Cold War adversaries; Russia's attitude towards NATO expansion; and, finally, Russia's post-Cold War military doctrines.

Arms Control

The end of the Cold War produced a plethora of arms control agreements which, if implemented, would make escape from the security dilemma a distinct possibility. The 1990s have aptly been referred to as the 'arms control implementation era', and it is the success of these measures that will help to determine the extent to which the security dilemma has been mitigated.[10] In the previous chapter three arms control agreements were noted as having a significant value in mitigating the security dilemma – the Confidence- and Security-Building Measures (CSBMs) agreed at Stockholm (1986) and Vienna (1990), the Conventional Armed Forces Treaty (CFE, 1990), and the Strategic Arms Reduction Treaty (START I, 1991). Since 1990, two further CSBM regimes have been agreed at Vienna. While these measures have continued to build on the previous regimes by increasing transparency and thereby reducing the chances of misinterpretation, the mitigation of the Cold War security dilemma has proceeded to a further stage. Thus, while additional CSBM regimes perform a useful role, it is the success of the CFE and START treaties, and the extent to which they have been built upon, that will provide an insight into the continuing vitality of the East–West security dilemma.

It was noted in the previous chapter that the CFE Treaty marked a turning-point in the mitigation of the Cold War security dilemma. By placing limits on the number of weapons that could be deployed, the treaty was reducing those forces that were mainly responsible for giving rise to the misperception of threat. In 1990 it was noted that:

> If they fully materialize, these developments will together totally eliminate the possibility of a massive, short preparation Soviet attack from forward positions which would smash through NATO's shallow defences to reach the English Channel and North Sea, the Chief fear of NATO governments over the past four decades.[11]

While this had a very significant political impact in further reducing Cold

War suspicions – and was thus of great value in reducing the bugbear of uncertainty – it is the story of the treaty's implementation that will reveal much about the degree to which the security dilemma has been mitigated. After all, it is only when the treaty has been implemented that the reductions agreed in 1990 will actually occur.

The treaty was designed to reduce the conventional forces between the Cold War alliances, but the revolutions in eastern Europe in 1989 made an anachronism of it when it was signed in late 1990. With the resulting disbandment of the Warsaw Pact and the USSR, the ratification and implementation process appeared problematic. A treaty designed to be a cornerstone of the Cold War's conclusion had to adjust to being the framework around which the new European security order would emerge. Hence the comment by Dean and Forsberg that 'the CFE Treaty may not be viable over the longer term since it was intended to be implemented by two alliances, not by NATO on one side and, on the other, thirteen disparate and sometimes quarrelling states'.[12] This has not been the case, however with both western, CEE and republics of the former Soviet Union (FSU) emphasising throughout the two-year ratification process and the continuing implementation process that the CFE Treaty is of great importance to the future of European stability.[13] The driving force behind this attitude is the belief that, by cooperating with the West, their own security is enhanced. Hence Jane Sharp's claim that:

> [for] the former Soviet republics who want good relations with the Western democracies, especially for those that aspire to membership in Western institutions ... adherence to the CFE Treaty thus offered an important opportunity to emerge from the shadow of Russian domination and to participate in a serious enterprise with their Western partners.[14]

It is not surprising, therefore, that Ukraine was initially one of the more ardent supporters of the treaty. The treaty has assumed great importance in enabling the newly independent states to engage in a cooperative venture over the types of weapons that can easily, by generating fear about other states' intentions, create a security dilemma. The ratification of the CFE Treaty on 17 July 1992 and its continuing implementation has not only maintained the mitigation of the East–West security dilemma, but it has also helped to dampen those dynamics which could create new security dilemmas amongst CEE and FSU states. In order to focus on the security dilemma between Moscow and the Western Alliance, however, it is necessary to examine Russia's attitude towards the treaty during the ratification and implementation process.

The collapse of the Soviet Union has ensured that, for Moscow, the CFE Treaty will produce an unwelcome outcome. Even with the treaty's 'sufficiency' rule and flank limits, the Soviet Union would have retained a formidable military capability in comparison to its former Warsaw Pact allies.[15] However, the Tashkent Agreement of May 1992 divided the USSR's entitlements amongst eight republics, which, according to Sharp, 'has codified a humiliating loss of status and military power' for Russia.[16] If Sharp's comment is a fair assessment of Moscow's perception of the CFE Treaty, then its willingness to implement such a vital element in mitigating the security dilemma must be questioned. Such a perception may not be the result of the security dilemma, but if it is allowed to prevent the treaty's implementation, this could enable the dilemma's dynamics to worsen other aspects of the Russian–Western Alliance relationship.

Support for the CFE Treaty in Russia does indeed appear to be slight. Richard Falkenrath claims that while the 'Russian political leadership still expresses support for the CFE Treaty ... this has less to do with any perceived merits of the treaty itself than with the fact that the West has linked economic assistance and good political relations to Russia's compliance with its arms control commitments'.[17] Signed during the heyday of the Soviet reformers, the implementation process is being conducted by the increasingly influential Russian military, a body which Falkenrath asserts would shed few tears 'if the CFE Treaty were to be cast aside'.[18] The military have begun to cast doubts on its applicability to the new security issues facing Russia, particularly with respect to the flank constraints.[19] The Russian concerns regarding the flank constraints centre around two broad issues. First, the flank ceilings are an anachronism of the Cold War and should be adjusted to meet the realities of Russian security in the post-Cold War world. In particular, altering the ceiling will allow the Russians to deploy forces in the North Caucasus region, where they perceive a security threat, rather than having to concentrate their forces in the West along the old East–West line. The second issue concerns the difficulties that the Russians are having in re-housing their troops. They argue that they have adequate facilities in the well-developed Leningrad Military District (MD) and in the warm North Caucasus MD, but, because of the flank limitations, they cannot make full use of them. Instead, they will need to construct facilities elsewhere, which would add a further burden to an already struggling economy. However, given that the CFE Treaty is concerned only with equipment, it would appear that this second reason is a clandestine attempt by the military to enable the deployment of treaty-limited equipment (TLE) with the troops. The key point for the East–West security dilemma is that these flank concerns do not appear to be generated by the fear that the Western Alliance is seeking to take advantage of Russian vulnerability. Instead, they appear to be a direct result of the new security problems facing Russia (e.g., Chechnya, civil war in Georgia, and the protracted conflict between Armenia and Azerbaijan); the remnants of the Cold War security dilemma are not behind the CFE flank problem. However, should Russia use this issue to circumvent the treaty – 'the cornerstone of European security' – this could act as a harbinger of western suspicion and mistrust.

The first sign that Russia was dissatisfied with the flank constraints surfaced after Grachev inspected military units in the Caucasus in March 1993.[20] In September Russia announced that it would 'consider the possibility of taking adequate unilateral measures to ensure its own security, including those that wouldn't respond fully to the spirit of the Treaty'.[21] A year later, Grachev announced the TLE increases that he thought were necessary in the flanks – 1,100 tanks, 3,000 ACVs and 2,100 artillery pieces. Throughout 1994, some of the forces returning from central Europe were deployed in the northern and southern flanks, increasing the TLE above the CFE constraints and, therefore, making Russian compliance with the implementation deadline problematic. Since 1993, the Russians have sought to alter the treaty's provisions. While the West does have some sympathy with the Russian position, they appear unwilling to: (a) endanger the treaty by embarking upon a process that could unravel it, especially given the reaction of Ukraine, Turkey and Greece to Russian increases in the Caucasus; (b) enable Russia to project military power vis-à-vis its 'near abroad'; and (c) appear to condone Russia's actions in its southern territory (Chechnya and North Ossetia).

Failure to gain an alteration to the CFE Treaty has led Russia to link the implementation of the treaty to the issue of NATO expansion. Grachev warned on 3 April 1995 that if NATO expanded, Russia might not only suspend CFE implementation, but also create 'new groups of armed forces on the most threatened fronts and closer security ties among CIS countries would be other possible countermeasures'.[22] 'Closer security ties' could include the deployment of tactical nuclear weapons in Belarus or Kaliningrad.[23] This has very serious implications for the continuing mitigation of the East–West security dilemma and will receive analysis in the section on NATO. Now, however, it is pertinent to look at what European security will lose if the CFE Treaty collapses and at the implications of this for the East–West security dilemma. By reducing the forces that are required for launching attacks and by placing limits upon the numbers that can be deployed in forward positions, the treaty clearly has a valuable role to play in reducing statesmen's fears about the likelihood of attack. The treaty does even more than this, though, by also providing a CFE verification regime which enables on-site inspections and obligates each party to provide detailed information concerning command structures and force deployments. In both reducing offensive forces and generating transparency between old adversaries, the CFE Treaty is a vital cog in the security dilemma's mitigation; it is a cog that is in danger of being lost. Should the CFE Treaty become a victim of increasing distrust and tension between Russia and the Western Alliance – over the issue of NATO expansion, for instance – not only would the task of mitigation become harder, but there would be a very real danger of the security dilemma re-emerging. Before examining this issue, it is necessary to determine if the other arms control agreements of import to mitigation (START I and II) have also encountered difficulties during their implementation.

The value of arms control to security dilemma mitigation is twofold. First, it fulfils a political role in symbolising improved relations and in providing the impetus for those relations to continue to improve. This can be witnessed in the number of CSBM agreements reached since the Helsinki Final Act. Second, arms control can fulfil a purely military role in mitigating the security dilemma by reducing those weapons that give rise to the greatest fear in others of the existence of malign intent. The CFE Treaty performs both roles by reducing forces which were deemed as indicating an aggressive intent and also by paving the way for the CFE–1A agreement. The nuclear arms control agreement reached at the end of the Cold War (START I) performed the political role which was manifested in the signing of START II in January 1993. START II, unlike START I, also performs a military role by reducing those nuclear weapons that are referred to in security dilemma literature as offensive. Thus, while the implementation of START I is important, it is the implementation of START II that has the greater impact on security dilemma mitigation.

The implementation of START I, much like the CFE Treaty, was complicated by the collapse of the Soviet Union. In this case, however, the demise of the USSR created four nuclear republics – Belarus, Kazakhstan, Russia, and Ukraine. In May 1992 the four republics and the USA signed the Lisbon Protocol, which committed the three former Soviet republics to comply with the Non-Proliferation Treaty (NPT) as non-nuclear states in the shortest possible time. Substantial progress was made throughout 1994 towards ratification of the treaty, when Ukraine's demands for financial compensation and security assurances paved the way for Ukraine's accession to the NPT in November and the implementation stage of START I came into force in December.[24] The treaty allows the parties seven years to implement its provisions from the date of ratification. At the time of writing, all the parties are proceeding with their objectives and are progressing on schedule.[25]

It was noted in the previous chapter that START I did not support the adoption of a minimum deterrence strategy and, therefore, did not provide for the change in nuclear force posture that is required for security dilemma mitigation. However, it did encourage the two superpowers to engage in negotiations which resulted in a treaty that did support the adoption of a minimum deterrence strategy. It was noted in Chapters 3 and 7 that highly accurate nuclear weapons capable of destroying counterforce targets, thereby providing the potential for a decapitating first strike, undermined mutual assured destruction (MAD). By undermining MAD, these nuclear weapons could be considered offensive and are likely to exacerbate a security dilemma. The advent of multiple independent re-entry vehicles (MIRVs) is regarded as highly destabilising because they have the potential capacity to inflict such a decapitating strike. The START II Treaty is so vital to mitigating the security dilemma because it is specifically designed to de-MIRV the superpowers' nuclear arsenals. The treaty will eliminate all land-based MIRVed strategic ballistic missiles, and each party will be limited to no more than 3,000–3,500 deployed warheads. It is evident that the successful implementation of START II would support the ideas of minimum nuclear deterrence that were advocated by the various civilian analysts outlined in the previous chapter. The treaty's successful implementation is thus a valuable yardstick by which to determine the vitality of the East–West security dilemma.

A combination of foreign and domestic factors within both Russia and the United States have affected the progress of START II and, in so doing, have made the ratification and implementation of the treaty problematic.[26] A domestic factor that is causing problems is the expense involved in carrying out the treaty's denuclearisation provisions. There is a growing perception in Russia that START II is very burdensome; this is making ratification and implementation look increasingly unlikely. The perception that START II is not in Russian interests is an extremely worrying development for the continued mitigation of the security dilemma. It is certainly true that START II does place greater demands on Russia than on the USA. Soviet nuclear forces had emphasised the deployment of MIRVed ICBMs, and the treaty's provisions do 'require a substantial shift on the part of Russia ... in the emphasis placed on force components'.[27] The treaty's emphasis on de-MIRVing calls for the elimination of the important SS-18, with its ten accurate warheads, the 'downloading' of the SS-19s to one warhead each, and an increase in the single warhead SS-25s. The actual number and type of missiles that are planned for the deadline in 2003 are unknown, but there are many projections.[28] From the security dilemma perspective, the danger is that if altering Russia's land-based force proves too expensive, then Russia might stop the transition to the SS-25 and maintain its MIRVed SS-24s, SS-18s or not download its SS-19s.[29] In other words, Russia might not 'incorporate one of the most important features of START II: the elimination of MIRVed ICBMs'.[30]

The debates in Russia in 1994 on the future of their nuclear force structure indicated that Russian compliance with the START II provisions could not be taken for granted. While Lieutenant-General Lev Volkov contends that de-MIRVing is the correct path for the future of Russia's strategic nuclear forces – 'ratification or non-ratification of START II will not change the main direction of development of the SRF (Strategic Rocket Force) – the transition from MIRVed missiles to single-warhead missiles' – his opinion is not shared by all.[31] One of the most vocal critics is Colonel Petr Belov who 'advocates ignoring the START II treaty and updating and maintaining silo-based MIRVed missiles and SSBNs'.[32] At present, the restructuring of the SRF towards single-warhead ICBMs is continuing, but if alternative, MIRVed, force structures are advocated, these may be seen as providing the strategic rationale for halting what is seen as an economically burdensome process.

While economic and strategic considerations could prevent the continuing de-MIRVing of the SRF, the maintenance of good relations between Russia and the West would probably overcome such factors. However, these factors are coinciding with a changing attitude in Russia towards the West, and the effect of this can be seen in the treaty's stuttering ratification progress. Initially caught in a power struggle between Yeltsin and Ruslan Khasbulatov, Chairman of the former Supreme Soviet, the treaty is now in the hands of the increasingly conservative-thinking State Duma.[33] According to John Lepingwell, the increase in conservatives indicates a growing disillusionment with the reform process and this 'new dynamic has hastened the transition in Russian foreign policy from a strongly pro-Western stance to one based more directly on a realist view of geopolitics and the advocacy of Russian interests'.[34] This assertion of Russian interests has led to increased tensions in US–Russian relations, most notably over NATO expansion, but also over Russian action in Chechyna and the Russian–Iranian nuclear reactor deal. The summit between Clinton and Yeltsin in May 1995 failed to make any progress on outstanding security issues.[35] It would appear that, as with the CFE Treaty, changing perceptions in Russia about its relationship with the West and how its interests can best be achieved could signal the end for START II. If neither the CFE Treaty nor START II are implemented, this does not bode well for the continuing mitigation of the security dilemma. If it is a deterioration in relations between Russia and the West that is behind the failure to implement these valuable treaties, this suggests that not only is the security dilemma not being mitigated, but that it is actually re-emerging.

The progress of the arms control treaties signed at the end of the Cold War reveal a great deal about the security dilemma between Moscow and the Western Alliance. The new CSBM measures, combined with the continuing implementation of the CFE Treaty and the two START Treaties, provide positive signs that the security dilemma is being mitigated. The process has proved to be more troublesome than was hoped would be the case, but, at least in the first instance, this was not due to the security dilemma. Instead, the problems lay with a changing security environment due to the collapse of the USSR and the economic difficulties that Russia has encountered in its transition to a market economy. However, whilesoever the security dilemma remains, albeit in a mitigated fashion, it can always re-emerge. What is particularly worrying is that the latest difficulties encountered by both the CFE and START II Treaties indicate that relations between the old Cold War adversaries are deteriorating. In such a circumstance, the security dilemma could easily re-emerge. We shall now examine the relationship between Russia and the Western Alliance in order to determine the condition of the security dilemma.

NATO Expansion

It was noted earlier that the security dilemma cannot exist within a security community, where the members have absolute certainty that military force will not be used to settle disputes amongst them. In the immediate aftermath of the Cold War, one of the European security debates focused on the type of architecture that would replace the confrontationalist two-bloc system. Numerous proposals were raised in policy-making and academic circles for the evolution and creation of a number of interlocking institutions to safeguard the security of post-Cold War Europe. Although they differed on the roles that NATO, the West European Union (WEU), the CSCE, or even a new European Security Organisation (ESO) could perform, the emphasis, with a few notable exceptions, was on the stability that the correct 'mix' of these institutions would produce[36] – a stability that would enable the creation of a security community within Europe. With the European Union (EU) and the CSCE tainted with failure over the peace process in the former Yugoslavia and with the west Europeans supporting and developing their victorious Cold War alliance, NATO has emerged as the institution which most CEE states see as providing the security they desire.[37] In January 1994 the members of the Western Alliance stated that they expected 'and would welcome NATO expansion that would reach to the democratic states to our East'.[38] Since then, the United States President, Bill Clinton, has affirmed that it is a question of 'when' not 'if' NATO offers membership to the former members of the Warsaw Pact.[39] While the CSCE has continued to evolve in the 1990s – and, indeed, became the Organisation for Security and Cooperation in Europe (OSCE) in January 1995 – it has done so by complementing, not replacing, NATO. It has become increasingly evident that if all of Europe is to become a security community, this will involve, in part, the expansion of NATO.[40] Hence Philip Gordon's assertion that NATO provides, 'the foundation of a "pluralistic security community"', and Stanley Sloan's suggestion that NATO can be an element within a 'Transatlantic Cooperation Community'.[41] The key to this outcome is the affect that NATO expansion will have on Russia.

If Russia perceives that, far from creating stability in Europe, NATO enlargement will undermine what Russia deems necessary for its own security, then the security dilemma between Moscow and the Western

Alliance could be rekindled. In this instance, Russia's perception of that enlargement would not be that it indicated benign intent by the West, but that it is part of a western strategy either to subjugate Russia or encircle and exclude it from European security. If this is Russia's perception, then it is likely that NATO's attempts to create stability in the East will have the paradoxical effect of generating Russian insecurity. Such insecurity might be manifested by the rise of conservative (hard-line) politicians in the Federal Assembly or the Yeltsin administration, or the election of a conservative (communist) President; a Russian desire to dominate its near abroad; and/or a growing suspicion and mistrust of the western powers. These dangers have been recognised by Charles Glaser. He warns:

> policies that increase Russian insecurity could be self-defeating. If Western policies for guaranteeing Central European security appear threatening to Russia, then these policies could pressure the Russians to pursue the very actions they were designed to prevent. Extending the West's military sphere of influence into the East could raise Russian concerns about Western intentions, increasing the value it sees in controlling additional territory.[42]

Is the security dilemma continuing to be mitigated or is it re-emerging between Moscow and the West?

It was claimed in Chapter 3 that cooperation between states can have a cumulative effect. With the benefits accrued through limited cooperation, they may be more willing to cooperate on more significant issues and achieve even more. It was suggested that, given the fear of defection, this cumulative effect can be helped by institutionalising the cooperation and thereby creating rules, procedures and forms of punishment should defection occur. In Chapter 3 this was discussed in relation to security regimes and common security and the ways in which they could mitigate the security dilemma. In July 1990 NATO's London Declaration recognised that the security of European states was inseparably linked and, in so doing, adopted the 'objectives and terminology formulated in the Palme Report'.[43] Since then, NATO has sought to institutionalise its cooperative relations with the CEE states, first through the North Atlantic Cooperation Council (NACC) and then the Partnership for Peace (PfP) programme. Does this indicate that the foundations of a security community are being laid by NATO, and does this mean the security dilemma's mitigation is continuing?

There are reasons to be optimistic that the NACC and PfP could complete the mitigation of the East–West security dilemma. Both are designed to create greater transparency in defence matters, thus reducing uncertainty amongst statesmen about the intentions of their neighbours and, therefore, lessening the possibility of the pursuit of paradoxical policies. The two processes are concerned with similar aspects of state relations, but while NACC is a forum for dialogue, the PfP is a 'practical programme of cooperation, rather than [a] generalised consultation and information exchange'.[44] Through NACC Work Plans, the member states have organised numerous seminars on such issues as defence conversion, defence budgets, and the implementation of the CFE Treaty, and they have also created an ad hoc group on peace-keeping.[45] The PfP, created two years after the NACC, is designed to go 'beyond dialogue and cooperation to forge a real partnership', which it does by building on six aspects of the NACC process:[46] (1) ensuring transparency in national defence planning and budgeting processes; (2) ensuring democratic control of defence forces; (3) maintaining the capability and readiness to contribute to operations under the authority of the UN or CSCE; (4) developing cooperative military relations with NATO in order to undertake joint missions in peace-keeping, search and rescue, and humanitarian operation; (5) developing forces better able to operate with NATO members; and (6) consulting with NATO in the event of a partner perceiving a threat to its security. Such programmes are clearly relevant to security dilemma mitigation. Not only is transparency highlighted, but the pooling of resources envisaged in (4) and (5) makes it much harder for states to threaten one another, a point that gains support from Joseph Lepgold when he writes:

> the military structures of NATO states have become exceptionally transparent to one another, which makes it hard for them to threaten a treaty ally. Gradually extending similar integration through practical PfP programs would help to reassure other members of a country's benign intentions.[47]

According to Nick Williams, an analyst in NATO's Political Affairs Division, the PfP broadens and deepens the 'integrative process represented by the NACC'.[48] Indeed, the PfP would appear to represent the progression of cooperation which, it was envisaged in Chapter 3, could mitigate the security dilemma. With successful cooperation at the NACC stage, those 'partners' who have sought greater cooperation with NATO have done so through their Individual Partnership Programme (IPP). IPPs are created by the partners themselves, who choose from a menu of activities that NATO offers, thereby allowing each partner to cooperate with NATO at its own pace. Lepgold agrees that this cumulative, or incremental, approach can lead to the creation of a 'pluralistic security community among ... many countries'.[49] It is certainly the belief of the CEE partners that they are engaged in a process which will result in their eventual membership of NATO. While the actual relationship between PfP and NATO enlargement has been an ambiguous one, in September 1995 NATO published its 'Study on Enlargement', which confirmed CEE expectations that their membership of NACC and PfP was necessary for full NATO membership.

NATO's evolution from a collective defence alliance to an all-encompassing European security body is a major step towards escaping the security dilemma. However, the way in which this process affects the relationship between the alliance and Russia is what will determine whether the security dilemma between Moscow and the West continues to be mitigated. If Russia should perceive NATO expansion as a threat to its security, then, far from being mitigated, the security dilemma could re-emerge.

In mid-1993 the signs were good. Yeltsin had declared an interest in joining NATO in December 1991, and then in August 1993 Russia declared that Polish membership of NATO 'would not be counter to Russian interests nor to the pan-European integration process'.[50] Since the failed coup in 1993, however, Russia has adopted a different attitude towards NATO expansion. Yevgeniy Primakov, who recognised the Cold War security dilemma during Gorbachev's period in office, warned in November 1993, while Head of Russian Intelligence, that NATO expansion would result in a 'substantial reassessment of the Russian defence concept and a redeployment of armed forces, a change in operative plans'.[51] Although Russia did sign the PfP Framework Document on 22 June 1994, Moscow's interpretation of this process is very different from that of the CEE states. Rather than an instrument for expansion, PfP is viewed by the Russians in much the same way as it is viewed by western critics: it is an alternative to, not an instrument for, NATO expansion.[52] Indeed, former Russian Foreign Minister Andrei Kozyrev claimed that it was NATO's possible enlargement that prevented Russia from signing an IPP in December 1994. He stated that 'a speedy and unjustified expansion of the Alliance does not suit' Russia.[53] With enlargement continuing to remain on NATO's agenda, Russia has continued to voice its concerns. After NATO's study on enlargement was published, Vitalii Churkin, the Russian Ambassador to Belgium, stated that 'we are still opposed' to NATO expansion.[54] In March 1996 NATO's Secretary-General, Javier Solana, failed to calm Russian fears concerning NATO enlargement when he returned from Moscow. According to an article in *Nezavisimaya Gazeta*, 'the planned process of the alliance's enlargement is being taken by the majority of Russian politicians not simply as a threat, but as a collapse of partner relations with the West'.[55] With Russia seemingly unable to stop NATO's desire to expand, the future of the CFE and START II Treaties has come under threat. Vladislav Chernov of the Ministry of Foreign Affairs has declared: 'one thing is predictable – the CFE treaty will vanish the day the first country of Eastern Europe joins NATO, and no possible concessions on the flank issue would save it'.[56] Vladimir Shumeiko, the Federation Council Chairman, 'told US Defence Secretary William Perry

... on 3 April 1995 that the Russian parliament will not ratify START II unless questions over NATO's expansion eastward are resolved'.[57] Linking the future of these arms control treaties to NATO's expansion has made this subject the key to the vitality of the East–West security dilemma. Can NATO expansion, which could aid the creation of a security community and thus escape the security dilemma, be achieved without creating fear in Russia that its security interests are being threatened and, thereby, revitalising the security dilemma?

There appear to be two main reasons why Russia is antagonistic towards NATO expansion. First, they are concerned at what they perceive as an 'open-ended' approach by the West, which could conclude with the NATO membership of FSU republics such as the Baltic States and even Ukraine. Second, NATO expansion is seen as symbolising a Russian perception that, since the end of the Cold War, the West has betrayed Moscow by exploiting not cooperating with the new democracy. This perception of betrayal has been seized upon by the more extreme Russian politicians, who accuse the reformers of failing to safeguard Russian interests and present the Western Alliance as a threat to Russian security. Combined with the growing domestic resentment towards the failing reforms in Russia, and the consequent growth in support for the more extremist views, even moderate politicians are opposing NATO's expansion. Thus, while it is easy to dismiss the extremist views of Vladimir Zhirinovsky when he claims that NATO's 'only goal is to destroy and dismember Russia', it is not so easy when the more moderate Vladimir Lukin warns against NATO expansion by stating that if 'the blind selfishness of shortsighted politicians to the west of our borders prevails, we will turn to the means that are still in our hands. Those means are a kind of desperation, but they are effective.'[58] Lukin's 'means' are tactical nuclear weapons being deployed in Belarus and Kaliningrad.

Russian concern about NATO's open-ended approach is centred around the likelihood of the Baltic States or Ukraine joining NATO. Thus, while Clinton's assertion that NATO enlargement should not create a division in Europe is laudable, it does, by its very nature, make NATO membership possible for FSU republics.[59] Indeed, the idea of Ukrainian membership in either a first or second phase of NATO expansion has been suggested by US Deputy Secretary of State, Strobe Talbott.[60] However, it is evident that such an outcome is unacceptable to the Russians. An unnamed senior Russian foreign policy adviser has said that, if Ukraine joined NATO:

> We would have to consider using their dependence on our oil and gas to do the greatest possible damage to the Ukrainian economy, causing destabilisation by stirring up the Russians in Ukraine, and especially the Crimeans, and greatly increasing military pressure over Sevastopol. This would lead to an international crisis of the first order.[61]

The situation is similar with regard to other FSU republics. According to a report in *Komsomol'skaya Pravda* (29 September 1995), translated by the *Conflict Studies Research Centre* (*CSRC*), the Russian General Staff have composed a new doctrine to meet the perceived threat from NATO expansion. According to the *CSRC*, because Russian military strategy dictates that the 'potential adversary should be counterbalanced every-where', tactical nuclear weapons will be deployed in:

> the West (the border with Poland and Russian territorial waters in the Baltic Sea), in the North (the border with Norway and Russian territorial waters of the Barents Sea) and in the South (Russian territorial waters of the Black Sea, Russian military bases in the Crimea, Abkhazia, Georgia and Armenia).

With regard to the Baltic States, the 'draft doctrine envisages the immediate deployment of Russian troops in the Baltic States if NATO grants membership to Estonia, Latvia and Lithuania. Any attempt on the part of NATO to resist this will be considered by Russia as a prelude to a global nuclear catastrophe.'[62] Russia also views the membership of CEE states in NATO with some trepidation. The difficulty for Russia is not that CEE membership of NATO will in itself pose a threat to Russian security, but that, once started, NATO enlargement might be difficult to stop. Hence Alexi Arbatov's claim that 'once NATO frontline runs along the borders of Ukraine, Belarus and Lithuania, these countries would ask whether the Alliance is not directed against them. And if not, why not include them as well?'[63] Indeed, Lieven suggests that it is because of this possibility that, should NATO expand 'as far as Poland [Russia] will ... force Ukraine to accept a full military alliance ... and Ukrainians are acutely aware of this danger'.[64] This perhaps explains the Minister of Ukrainian Foreign Affairs, Hennadiy Udovenko's, assertion that while 'Ukraine understands the aspirations of Central and Eastern European states to become members of NATO', Ukraine 'has not put the issue of NATO membership on [its legislative] agenda'.[65]

The second reason for Russia's antagonism towards expansion lies within the steady deterioration of relations between Moscow and the West. The perception in Russia is that, during 1991 and 1992, the western powers pocketed Russian concessions in negotiations and gave little in return. The START II negotiations and Russia's acquiescence to western policies against Iraq and in relation to the former Yugoslavia are criticised by conservatives and moderates as Russia 'giving' and the West 'taking'. Even Alexi Arbatov believes that the Russian negotiators should have gained more concessions from the USA in the START II talks, which, he says, adopted a tough bargaining stance reminiscent of the Cold War days.

The START II negotiations ... suggest that trust goes only so far. In spite of the end of the Cold War, and in spite of a lot of nice words said recently about the two powers no longer being adversaries, the US attitude will not be lost on the treaty's Russian critics – whether they are moderates or extremists.[66]

Perhaps the crucial issue to confirm the Russian view that the West had double standards came in 1992 and 1993, when Latvia and Estonia disenfranchised their Russian immigrants. Not only did the West appear to betray their own ideals by not supporting Russia, but the West also insisted upon the continued withdrawal of Russian troops. According to Lieven, 'the image of Western powers as mendacious hypocrites, using the language of democracy and partnership to trick Russia into strategic concessions, has grown steadily since then'.[67] This helps to explain Sergei Karaganov's attitude towards NATO expansion:

> For Russians, NATO expansion is a psychological question as much as a strategic one: it involves mutual trust and Western recognition of Russia's status. Expansion would result in a shift in the whole Russian perception of the West and of developments of the past five years. It would confirm a feeling of having been if not defeated, than at least tricked and framed. In 1990, we were told quite clearly by the West that the dissolution of the Warsaw pact and German unification would not lead to NATO expansion. We did not demand written guarantees because in the euphoric atmosphere of that time it would have seemed almost indecent – like two girlfriends giving written promises not to seduce each other's husbands.[68]

According to Arbatov, the cooperative ideas of the late 1980s, referred to in the previous chapter as part of a GRIT-type strategy, 'have begun to suffer a loss of interest in the West, and have become tainted by their association with the never-ending concessions in Russia'.[69] The trust necessary for a cumulative deepening of cooperation which could lead to the eventual escape of the security dilemma no longer appears to exist and, as a result, the cooperative process is slowing down. Indeed, Pavel Felgengauer, commenting on the May 1995 summit, writes: 'the Russian–American summit in Moscow was very different from previous summits; it was more like another round of fruitless talks from the Cold War era than a meeting between new strategic partners'.[70]

It is too early to state that the security dilemma between Moscow and the Western Alliance is re-emerging, but it is evident that efforts to mitigate the security dilemma and create a security community have lost their momentum. It has been suggested that the West should sign a treaty with Russia in order to placate their fears about NATO's intentions.[71] However, Yury Baturin, the former National Security Adviser to the Russian President, claims that 'hopes of combining NATO expansion with the establishment of a special partnership with Russia are quite dim. NATO would undermine the basis for such a partnership, since Russia could only regard such a step as unfriendly.'[72] Lieven adds that 'any such treaty would ... have implicitly at least to rule out NATO membership for Ukraine. On this, the Russians say, they will never compromise.'[73] There is clearly a danger that when NATO admits its first, new members, Europe will again become divided between the Western Alliance and a Russian-dominated CIS.[74] It could be that two such blocs, which do not intend harm to each other, might avoid the security dilemma. It is just as plausible, however, as Baturin claims, that NATO expansion:

> could lead, sooner or later, to a feeling of Russian military and political isolation, to stronger anti-Western sentiment in our country and to a revival of militarist thinking. Under these conditions, one cannot rule out the possibility of a resumption of confrontation and a new division of Europe that would ultimately undermine, not strengthen, the security of all countries.[75]

Whether the security dilemma will re-emerge as the Western Alliance and Russia seek a mutually acceptable approach to European security after the Cold War will also depend on the way in which they react to each other's new force deployments. If, during this deterioration in relations, they also interpret each other's military forces as offensive, then the security dilemma could easily re-emerge.

Force Posture

In the previous chapter it was shown that Gorbachev sought to move Soviet military doctrine towards a non-offensive stance; as a result, the 1990 draft of the military doctrine contained no references to the offensive or counter-offensive when describing the actions of the Soviet armed forces. While this draft was not adopted, it clearly indicates that the type of force posture that would aid security dilemma mitigation was prevalent in Soviet political thinking. In the aftermath of the collapse of the USSR, the rejection of a unified CIS command and the inheritance of some three million troops, Russia produced its own military doctrine in late 1993, and drafts of a new doctrine are currently being reported in the Russian press and western research centres. It is the degree to which Russian military doctrine has moved away from the intrinsic 'defensiveness' of the Gorbachev era that is of interest. A move towards old-style Soviet thinking, which exacerbated the Cold War security dilemma, could not only hinder the security dilemma's mitigation, but also exacerbate the worsening East–West relations, noted above, which could cause it to re-emerge.

The draft of the Russian military doctrine was published in May 1992 and indicated a departure from the non-offensive defence thinking of the

Gorbachev period. While defence remained the objective at the military-political level, it was removed at the military-technical level. In essence, this meant that the counter-offensive was reinstated, though it was unclear whether this was designed to recapture lost territory or launch an attack on enemy soil. For instance, while it was clear that any large-scale counter-offensive would require the build-up of additional forces, the draft doctrine stated that the defeat of the enemy, as opposed to the repulsion of the aggressor, was the main task. This departure from the Gorbachev line does not indicate that Russia was becoming more aggressive; rather, it reveals that the military, who had now regained their position of dominance over the direction of Russian strategic thought, had remained unconvinced of the merits of defensive defence. In addition, the allied attack against Iraq in the 1990 Gulf War appeared to reveal an inherent weakness with non-offence defence.[76] According to three Soviet military officers, the Iraqi experience revealed that a 'defence incapable of creating the necessary conditions for launching a decisive offensive will not fulfil its mission'.[77]

Debates on the draft doctrine ensued, with Colonel General Rodionov, Head of the General Staff Academy, arguing that the 'new Russian military doctrine must precisely, clearly, and unequivocally reflect the proposition that if an opponent has begun aggression and armed conflict, the laws of warfare immediately take effect: state borders cease to exist'.[78] This line of argument, that the new doctrine must enable unrestricted offensive action, was also articulated by General Gareev when he argued that, once war had 'broken out it is irrelevant what sort of operations – offensive or defensive – are conducted by the country's armed forces'.[79] In November 1993, when the doctrine was adopted, the offensive had been fully reinstated. The doctrine states that in 'the event of aggression against Russia or its allies, the tasks of the Armed Forces will be to repulse the enemy, defeat him and create conditions for the restoration of peace on terms satisfactory to the Russian Federation'.[80] In other words, the ability to launch a decisive counter-offensive on enemy territory is required. Hence Charles Dick's comment on the doctrine:

> Regardless of how war comes about, operations will be conducted decisively, using an appropriate mix of offensive and defensive action to destroy the enemy. Traditional emphasis on strategic and operational manoeuvre and the execution of deep operations continues: so, too, logically, does the maintenance of a major counteroffensive (which is the same thing as an offensive) capability.[81]

With the offensive reinstated in the military-technical side of doctrine, a dynamic is emerging which could exacerbate a deterioration of East–West relations and ultimately drive a rekindled Cold War security dilemma. The emphasis on offensive military capabilities can undermine attempts to portray an inoffensive image of Russia; their very 'offensiveness' can appear threatening. This danger has been recognised by Stuart Kaufman, who notes that if:

> the West reacts with suspicion to such rearmament, it would prove (in Russian military eyes) that the West is hostile and must be deterred – with more modern weapons. Those additional weapons would have to be justified to the Russian public by promoting the idea of a Western threat. Since the idea of a direct threat from the West is an obsolete bogeyman, a new one would have to be invented: perhaps a Western plot to oppress ethnic Russians in the Baltic states or Ukraine. In any case, such a security dilemma spiral is not impossible.[82]

Although it would be premature to assert that a security dilemma between Moscow and the West is re-emerging, exacerbated by the military doctrines of the two sides, there are warning signs. While it is true that both sides have drastically reduced the size of their military forces, it is also true that both have indicated a preference for offensive postures. Thus, while the Russians have reinstated the counter-offensive in their military doctrine, NATO has replaced its Cold War linear line of defence with an emphasis on mobility and the creation of rapid reaction forces. These are designed to deploy, at short notice, a force of sufficient strength to defend a member's territory, receiving substantial military support from reserve units as necessary.[83] The forces available to NATO, as the Gulf War illustrated so dramatically, are capable of decisive offensive action. This has not been ignored by the Russian military. While admitting that these forces pose no threat to Russia at the present time, military officers note that, in the event of NATO enlargement, their mobility could pose a security threat in the future. They highlight that, through the PfP, NATO is achieving operational and technical compatibility between its forces and those of its former adversaries in CEE states. Should NATO expand to include these states, it would be able to deploy its forces on their territory. Accordingly, the military warn:

> By 2000 a favourable and compatible operational environment enabling large offensive airmobile and air units from the NATO countries (including the US) to move thousands of kilometres in a few hours' time, while maintaining their capability to inflict powerful and decisive strikes at a moment's notice, is supposed to span Europe from the Atlantic to the Russian border near Pskov and Narva. In the worst-case scenario, it would essentially be impossible to defend Pskov, Kaliningrad and St. Petersburg.[84]

The offensiveness of force postures can also explain the growing Russian concern with the US interest in ballistic missile defence. It was shown in Chapter 3 that area-wide anti-ballistic missile (ABM) sites can be considered offensive because they undermine the basis of mutual assured destruction (MAD). With Russia and the United States committed under START II to the de-MIRVing of their ICBMs, an attempt by either to erect such defences could be perceived as seriously undermining the credibility of the other's second-strike capability. It is this reasoning that explains Russia's unease at the US interest in theatre missile defences (TMD) and at the possibility that the United States will abrogate the ABM Treaty.[85] These Russian concerns have adversely affected the ratification of START II. According to Lepingwell, 'if the United States were to proceed with testing and deployment of extensive TMDs or territorial defences, Russia would almost certainly retain a substantial number of MIRVed ICBMs as a countermeasure'.[86]

While it is unlikely that the offensiveness of Russian and western force postures will, on their own, revitalise the security dilemma, it is the concern that these types of force postures creates that could exacerbate a deterioration of relations for other reasons. What is certain is that these developments do not aid security dilemma mitigation and, as such, should be viewed with some trepidation.

Conclusion

It is apparent that, in the years since the end of the Cold War, Europe has not become a pluralistic security community and, in so doing, escaped the East–West security dilemma. It is also apparent that the new security environment, with its different security risks, has required Moscow and the Western Alliance to re-evaluate their relationship. It is too soon to know whether this re-evaluation will continue to mitigate the security dilemma or whether the security dilemma will re-emerge and create a 'Cold Peace'. What is certain is that the process of mitigation begun by Gorbachev has slowed significantly, and the uncertainty of intent caused by suspicion and mistrust has grown steadily.

The ratification and implementation of the CFE Treaty and its nuclear counterparts – START I, II – best exemplify the state of the East–West security dilemma. The successful implementation of the treaties will finalise Gorbachev's effort to mitigate the security dilemma; while progress towards this outcome is continuing, the prospect of mitigation remains. However, it has been indicated that although such progress is continuing, problems are arising in the relationship between Moscow and the Western Alliance which are threatening the implementation of the treaties. This deterioration in relations – referred to as the 'end of the honeymoon' – is most manifest in the issue of NATO expansion.[87]

Since late 1993, it has become increasingly evident that Russia views NATO enlargement as detrimental to its interests and a possible security threat for the future. This Russian perception can be explained by at least two factors. The first is the Russian feeling of western betrayal or, in prisoner's dilemma terms, western defection. With the collapse of communism, the Russian government embraced the twin concepts of democracy and the free market and looked forward to enjoying the benefits that these would bring as Russia became a partner in the world economy. The results have been somewhat different; the economic costs of adopting a capitalist system have been prohibitively high and western economic assistance has been modest. In foreign policy, the Russians have found that their acquiescence to western polices has been taken for granted, while weapon modernisation and plans for NATO expansion continue to proceed. Rather than being a partner in a new world order, Russia still appears to be the potential threat. Gorbachev captures this feeling of betrayal (i.e., defection) and the dangers that it could bring when he claims that, after the break-up of the Soviet Union:

> the West, especially the United States, decided to take advantage of Russia's temporary weakness and started a new geopolitical game whose aim was to alter Russia's status as a world power ... This policy will yield nothing but confrontation between East and West. These approaches must be abandoned immediately; if not, the threat of a new cold war could become a reality.[88]

The perception of betrayal has led to conservative attacks on the Russian reformists and the reversal of pro-western policies by the Yeltsin administration. Indeed, support for the communist candidate, Gennady Zyuganov, in the 1996 presidential election reveals the widespread Russian disillusionment with the 'partnership years'. In military circles, this disaffection is revealed by the increasing number of articles that identify the West as a threat.[89] The West, as defectors, can no longer be trusted; efforts to enlarge their military alliance are treated with apprehension in Russia.

The second Russian concern about NATO expansion focuses on its open-ended nature and on the danger that, once membership is granted to one former adversary, others, most notably the Baltic States, will intensify their demands for membership. NATO may find itself forced either to reject these demands and create a new division in Europe, or grant them and extend the alliance's border to Russia. It is the latter scenario that is creating the greatest fear in Russia and lies behind the warnings that such an eastward expansion would culminate in the deployment of Russian troops in the Baltic States.

With NATO enlargement continuing to remain high on the alliance's agenda, Russia has begun to use the implementation of the arms control treaties as a means of leverage. The West is faced with a dilemma: it either extends NATO membership and risks a new Cold War with Russia, or it refuses membership and creates a perception of insecurity in CEE states. The former is most likely to introduce a re-emergence of the old East–West security dilemma, the dynamics of which can already be seen in operation; the latter could germinate the seeds of new security dilemmas, ready to exacerbate the fears that exist in a power vacuum. The dilemma is fully appreciated by western policy-makers, but their preference for the continued existence of NATO is making expansion the most likely outcome and, with it, the likely re-emergence of the Cold War security dilemma.[90]

Notes

1. Nicholas J. Wheeler and Ken Booth, 'The Security Dilemma', in John Baylis and N. J. Rengger (eds), *Dilemmas of World Politics: international issues in a changing world* (Oxford: 1992), p. 54.

2. Barry Buzan, *People, States and Fear: an agenda for international security studies in the post-Cold War era* (Hemel Hempstead: 2nd edn, 1991), p. 198.

3. Richard H. Ullman, *Securing Europe* (London: 1991), p. 39.

4. Ibid., p. 40.

5. The collapse of the Soviet Union was announced officially by Mr Afanassievsky, the Soviet Ambassador to Brussels, at the inaugural meeting of the North Atlantic Co-operation Council (NACC) on 20 December 1991.

6. According to John Morrison, Yeltsin's election as Russian President in June 1991, 'by cementing the position of the Russian republic and helping it shed its "ghost" image, further weakened the legitimacy of the Soviet Union as a state and strengthened that of Russia': John Morrison, *Boris Yeltsin: from Bolshevik to Democrat* (London: 1991), p. 268.

7. Jennifer G. Mathers, 'Déjà Vu: familiar trends in Russian strategic thought', *Contemporary Security Policy*, 16/3 (1995), p. 384.

8. Charles J. Dick, 'The Military Doctrine of the Russian Federation', *The Journal of Slavic Military Studies*, 7/3 (1994), p. 494.

9. Mathers, 'Déjà Vu', p. 385. Grachev has subsequently been replaced by presidential candidate General Alexander Lebed after the first round of voting in the June 1996 presidential elections.

10. Zdzislaw Lachowski, 'Conventional Arms Control and Security Dialogue in Europe', *SIPRI Yearbook 1995: armaments, disarmament and international security* (Oxford: 1995), p. 761.

11. Jonathan Dean, 'The CFE Negotiations, Present and Future', *Survival*, 32/4 (1990), p. 313.

12. Jonathan Dean and Randall Watson Forsberg, 'CFE and Beyond: the future of conventional arms control', *International Security*, 17/1 (1992), p. 77.

13. NATO's 'Study on NATO Enlargement', produced in September 1995, affirmed that the CFE was 'the cornerstone of European security' and, therefore, 'it is of fundamental importance to preserve the Treaty's integrity and to ensure its full and timely implementation': *Study on NATO Enlargement*, para. 21.

14. Jane Sharp, 'Conventional Arms Control in Europe', *SIPRI Yearbook 1993: world armaments and disarmament* (Oxford: 1993), p. 599.

15. The sufficiency rule allows one state to retain approximately one third of the holdings of each alliance. Sheehan and Durward claim that the rule 'was designed to prevent any single state from possessing sufficient residual forces so as to enable it to dominate the continent'. The flank limits place restrictions on the forces deployed in northern and southern Europe. For the West, this applies to Iceland, Norway, Greece and

Turkey; for the East, it applies to Bulgaria, Romania and the Soviet Union's Leningrad, north Caucasus, Odessa and Transcaucasus Military Districts: Michael Sheehan and Rosemary Durward, 'Conventional Arms Control and Security in Europe', *Defense Analysis*, 12/1 (1996), p. 9.

16. The 8 republics are Armenia, Azerbaijan, Belarus, Georgia, Kazakhstan, Moldova, Russia and the Ukraine: Sharp, 'Conventional Arms Control', p. 593.

17. Richard A. Falkenrath, 'The CFE Flank Dispute: waiting in the wings', *International Security*, 19/4 (1995), p. 121.

18. Ibid., p. 122.

19. The flanks are limited to 700 tanks, 580 armoured combat vehicles (ACVs), and 1,280 artillery pieces.

20. Barbara Starr, 'Russia Still Looking to Amend CFE Treaty', *Jane's Defence Weekly*, 20/12 (18 September 1993), p. 7.

21. Falkenrath, 'The CFE Flank Dispute', p. 129.

22. *Open Media Research Institute (OMRI) Daily Digest*, 1/67 (4 April 1995).

23. The deployment of such weapons has been suggested by Vladimir Lukin, Head of the Duma's Foreign Affairs Committee and member of the liberal Yabloko movement. See James Meek, 'NATO Chief Fails to Sway Russia', *The Guardian*, 22 March 1996.

24. Ukraine proved to be the largest obstacle to START I ratification, with the combination of security fears *vis-à-vis* Russia and the costs involved in destroying the ICBMs delaying the process. The breakthrough occurred with the Trilateral Statement signed in Moscow on 14 January 1994. Even so, the Ukrainian Parliament (Rada) only acceded to the NPT, thereby allowing START I to be ratified, after Ukrainian President Leonid Kuchma 'launched an aggressive lobbying campaign': James E. Goodby, Shannon Kile and Harald Müller, 'Nuclear Arms Control', *SIPRI Yearbook 1995*, p. 639.

25. Ibid., pp. 639–41.

26. START II was ratified by the US Congress in January 1996.

27. Stephen J. Cimbala, 'From Deterrence to Denuclearization: US and Russian nuclear force reduction options', *The Journal of Slavic Military Studies*, 7/3 (1994), p. 421.

28. In Goodby, Kile and Müller the Russian force is projected to comprise of 605 SS-25s (rail-mobile); 90 SS-25s (based in converted SS-18 silos); 105 SS-19s downloaded to 1 warhead each: See Goodby *et al.*, 'Nuclear arms control', p. 643. In Cimbala, 'From Deterrence to Denuclearization', there are ten force projections, with the most plausible basing the ICBMs solely on SS-25 missiles.

29. The START II Treaty does contain denuclearisation assistance for Russia, but it is likely that the USA would tie such financial assistance to the full implementation of the treaty. The Russian military may prefer to cut costs their own way and have a greater influence on the development of Russia's strategic nuclear forces. It was for economic reasons that Russia violated START I by using modified SS-25 missiles to launch satellites: see Martin Fletcher, 'US Accuses Russia of Arms Violations', *The Times*, 10 May 1995.

30. John W. R. Lepingwell, 'START II and the Politics of Arms Control in Russia', *International Security*, 20/2 (1995), p. 86.

31. Quoted from ibid., p. 74.

32. Ibid.

33. In April 1993 Khasbulatov linked the treaty's ratification to the dismissal of Foreign Minister Andrei Kozyrev.

34. Lepingwell, 'START II', p. 77.

35. See 'US–Russian Summit Focuses on Iran Nuclear Deal', *The Current Digest of the Post-Soviet Press (CDPSP)*, 47/19 (7 June 1995), pp. 1–4.

36. The notable exceptions can be found amongst realist writers, who emphasise the declining value of institutions when no immediate threat exists for their members. John Mearsheimer is an eloquent advocate of this position. See 'The False Promise of

International Institutions', *International Security*, 19/3 (1994/5), pp. 5–49. For critical replies, see 'Promises. Promises: can institutions deliver?', *International Security*, 20/1 (1995), pp. 39–93.

37. The future of NATO as the premier western military alliance was – and, to a much lesser extent, still is – precarious. In the early 1990s pretenders to the NATO crown emerged in the guise of the revitalised WEU, the development of a EU Common Foreign and Security Policy (CFSP), and the creation of a joint Franco-German brigade, which at the time was seen as the embryo of a future European army. However, NATO has remained the preferred alliance for its key members. The USA, while uncertain of the extent to which it should remain committed to European security after the Cold War (an issue that may be resolved one way or the other by the accomplishments of IFOR), provided the impetus for NATO's evolution with the Partnership for Peace proposal. Britain considers NATO as 'vital [for] ensuring European security and stability', while Germany views the transatlantic link as 'indispensable for security'. Equally important to the maintenance of NATO's status is that France, the main protagonist for the other challengers, decided in December 1995 to rejoin NATO's Military Committee, a decision that, even if unintended, is a major endorsement of NATO's status as the premier western military alliance. For an overview of the theoretical debates and some empirical matters, see David G. Haglund, 'Must NATO fail?: theories, myths, and policy dilemmas', *International Journal*, 50/4 (1995), pp. 651–74; for British quotation, see Douglas Hurd, 'Developing the Common Foreign and Security Policy', *International Affairs*, 70/3 (1994), pp. 421–8; for Germany, see Lothar Gutjahr, 'Global Stability and Euro-Atlantic Cooperation: the new Germany's national interests', *European Security*, 3/4 (1994), pp. 639–63.

38. North Atlantic Council, 'Partnership for Peace: invitation', *NATO Review*, 42/1 (1994), p. 28.

39. On 7 July 1994 Clinton told the Polish Parliament that NATO enlargement 'is no longer a question of whether, but when and how': quoted from Adam Daniel Rotfeld, 'Europe: the multilateral security process', *SIPRI Yearbook 1995*, p. 267.

40. Since a security community is defined in military terms (i.e., no use of force to settle disputes), the role of a military alliance is clearly essential to its establishment. However, this certainty that another member will not resort to the use of force is rooted in much more than military cooperation. The very essence of a security community is that the members share common political, economic and social aspirations. And, while they may disagree about the manner in which these aspirations are realised, they know that force is not a viable tool with which to settle any disputes. To create such a community in Europe, therefore, can only be accomplished *in part* by NATO expansion. The enlargement of the EU or the continuing evolution of the OSCE is also required. Some commentators believe that NATO is already a security community, but, given the relationship between Greece and Turkey, who have resorted to force *vis-à-vis* one another (Turkish invasion of Cyprus in 1974, and the show of force in the eastern Aegean Sea over conflicting territorial claims in January 1996), this seems inaccurate: see Coral Bell, 'Why an Expanded NATO Must Include Russia', *Journal of Strategic Studies*, 17/4 (1994), pp. 31–2.

41. Philip H. Gordon, 'Recasting the Atlantic Alliance', *Survival*, 38/1 (1996), p. 44; Stanley Sloan, 'US Perspectives on NATO's Future', *International Affairs*, 71/2 (1995), pp. 230–1.

42. Charles L. Glaser, 'Why NATO is Still Best: future security arrangements for Europe', *International Security*, 18/1 (1993), p. 14.

43. Adam Daniel Rotfeld, 'Europe: towards a new regional security regime', *SIPRI Yearbook 1994* (Oxford: 1994), p. 205 n2.

44. Nick Williams, 'Partnership for Peace: permanent fixture or declining asset', *Survival*, 38/1 (1996), p. 102.

45. For NATO and partners' CFE implementation, see Necil Nedimoglu, 'NATO and Partner Countries Cooperate in Implementing the CFE Treaty', *NATO Review*, 42/3 (1994), pp. 18–20; for initial contacts, see *NATO Review*, 40/1 (1992). pp. 12–22; for more details on NACC, see Guido Gerosa, 'The North Atlantic Cooperation Council', *European Security*, 1/3 (1992) pp. 273–94; Daniel George, 'NATO's Economic Cooperation with NACC Partners', *NATO Review*, 41/4 (1993), pp. 19–22; for details on NACC documentation, including its Work Plans, see *NATO Review*, 40/1 (1992), pp. 29–30, *NATO Review*, 40/2 (1992), pp. 33–5, *NATO Review*, 40/3 (1992), pp. 32–4, *NATO Review*, 41/1 (1993), pp. 28–32, *NATO Review*, 41/3 (1993), pp. 33–4, *NATO Review*, 41/4 (1993), pp. 30–5, *NATO Review*, 42/3 (1994), pp. 29–32; for details on PfP, see *NATO Review*, 42/1 (1994); Lennart Meri, 'Estonia, NATO and Peacekeeping', *NATO Review*, 42/2 (1994), pp. 7–9; Gebhardt von Moltke, 'Building a Partnership for Peace', *NATO Review*, 42/3 (1994), pp. 3–7.
46. North Atlantic Council, 'Partnership for Peace', p. 28.
47. Joseph Lepgold, 'The Next Step Toward a More Secure Europe', *Journal of Strategic Studies*, 17/4 (1994), p. 13.
48. Williams, 'Partnership for Peace', p. 102.
49. Lepgold, 'The Next Step', p. 12.
50. Yeltsin sent an address to the NACC inaugural meeting on 20 December 1991 in which he states: 'Today we are raising a question of Russia's membership in NATO': See *NOD and Conversion*, 21 (March 1992), p. 19. The quote on Polish membership is from Rotfeld, 'Europe', p. 212.
51. Rotfeld , 'Europe: the multilateral security process', p. 274.
52. US Republican Senator Richard Lugar referred to PfP as a 'policy for postponement', while Peter Corterier, North Atlantic Assembly Secretary-General, regarded PfP as establishing 'a no-man's land of permanent instability and insecurity ... among nations who cannot by themselves provide for their own security': quoted from John Borawski, 'Partnership for Peace and Beyond', *International Affairs*, 71/2 (1995), pp. 238–9.
53. Rotfeld, 'Europe: the multilateral security process', p. 278. In May 1995 Russia did sign an IPP, but the Russian Presidential Aide on International Affairs, Dmitry Ryurikov, stated that Russia would continue to resist NATO enlargement, because it 'conforms neither to Russia's interest nor to those of Europe': see Haglund, 'Must NATO fail?', pp. 671–2, and *OMRI Daily Digest*, 1/105 (31 May 1995).
54. *OMRI Daily Digest*, 1/190 (29 September 1995).
55. Quoted from Martin Walker and David Fairhall, 'Christopher Promises Bigger NATO', *The Guardian*, 21 March 1996.
56. Vladislav Chernov, 'View from Russia: the expansion of NATO and the future of the CFE Treaty', *Comparative Strategy*, 14/1 (1995), p. 89.
57. *OMRI Daily Digest*, 1/67 (4 April 1995).
58. The Zhirinovsky quote is from Strobe Talbott, 'Why NATO Should Grow', *The New York Review of Books*, XLII/13 (10 August 1995), p. 29; Vladimir Lukin, 'Lukin to NATO: don't move East and isolate Russia', *CDPSP*, 47/20 (14 June 1995), p. 9.
59. President Clinton, on 10 January 1994, said: 'why should we draw a new line through Europe just a little further East? Why should we now do something which could foreclose the best possible future for Europe?'
60. Talbott, 'Why NATO Should Grow', p. 30.
61. Quoted from Anatol Lieven, 'Russian Opposition to NATO Expansion', *The World Today*, 51/10 (1995), p. 198.
62. Alexander Lyasko, 'Although the Doctrine is New, It Resembles the Old One', *CSRC* 178. This information is based on a leak of a draft military doctrine and, therefore, should not be considered official policy. However, the CSRC does note that: 'while it is not possible to verify the existence of a new draft military doctrine, the excerpts referred to in this KP article appear entirely in keeping with the hard and

uncompromising line being adopted by senior Russian political and military figures over the past year concerning NATO.' See also Richard Beeston, 'Russia has a Nuclear Answer to Wider NATO', *The Times*, 30 September 1995.

63. Alexi Arbatov, 'NATO and Russia', *Security Dialogue*, 26/2 (1995), p. 143.

64. Lieven, 'Russian Opposition', p. 198.

65. Hennadiy Udovenko, 'European Stability and NATO Enlargement: Ukraine's perspective', *NATO Review*, 43/6 (1995), pp. 15–18.

66. Alexi Arbatov, 'START II, *The Bulletin of the Atomic Scientists* (April 1993), p. 18.

67. Lieven, 'Russian Opposition', p. 199.

68. Ibid., p. 198.

69. Alexi Arbatov, 'Russia's Foreign Policy Alternatives', *International Security*, 18/2 (1993), p. 24.

70. Pavel Felgengauer, 'New Assertiveness in Russian Foreign Policy Seen', *CDPSP*, 47/21 (21 June 1995), p. 1.

71. See Zbigniew Brzezinski, 'NATO – Expand or Die?', *New York Times*, 28 December 1994. See also Henry Kissinger, 'Expand NATO Now', *The Washington Post*, 9 December 1994.

72. Yury Baturin, 'Russia and NATO: dangerous games being played in verbal fog', *CDPSP*, 47/14 (3 May 1995), p. 24.

73. Lieven, 'Russian Opposition', p. 199.

74. The signing of the 'Treaty on Deepening Integration in Economic and Humanitarian Spheres' by Russia, Belarus, Kazakhstan and Kyrgyzstan on 29 March 1996, the signing of the 'Treaty on Forming a Community' by Russia and Belarus on 2 April 1996, and the conducting of joint air patrols by the CIS on 1 April 1996 suggest, if not a return to the old USSR, the establishment of EU-type structures for the signatories. The military cooperation has been referred to by Grachev as an alternative to NATO. Although the documents stress the equality of the signatories, Russia's dominant position in the CIS indicates that it will become the authoritative partner. For more on this, see Roger Kangas, 'CIS Integration: a gradual approach', *OMRI Analytical Brief*, 1/5 (29 March 1996); Peter Rutland, 'Russo-Belarusian Union: new beginning, or dead end?', *OMRI Analytical Brief*, 1/46 (29 March 1996); *OMRI Daily Digest*, 2/67 (3 April 1996); *OMRI Daily Digest*, 2/66 (2 April 1996); *OMRI Daily Digest*, 2/65 (1 April 1996).

75. Baturin, 'Russia and NATO', p. 24.

76. For details of the impact of the allied offensive against Iraq on Russian military thinking, see Stuart Kaufman, 'Lessons from the 1991 Gulf War and Russian Military Doctrine', *The Journal of Slavic Military Studies*, 6/3 (1993), pp. 375–96.

77. Major-General Yu. V. Lebedev, Lieutenant-General I. S. Lyutov, Colonel V. A. Nazarenko, quoted from Charles J. Dick, 'Counter-blows in Russian Military Thinking', *The Journal of Slavic Military Studies*, 6/3 (1993), p. 397.

78. Mary C. FitzGerald, 'Chief of Russia's General Staff Academy Speaks Out on Moscow's New Military Doctrine', *Orbis*, 37/2 (1993), p. 286.

79. Quoted from Mathers, 'Déjà Vu', p. 387.

80. Dick, 'The Military Doctrine of the Russian Federation', p. 490.

81. Ibid., p. 503.

82. Kaufman, 'Lessons from the 1991 Gulf War', p. 392.

83. For details, see North Atlantic Council, 'The Alliance's New Strategic Concept', *NATO Review*, 39/6 (1991), pp. 25–32.

84. Pavel Felgengauer, 'Partners: Russian Generals aren't interested in NATO countries' good intentions', *CDPSP*, 47/25 (19 July 1995), p. 31. See also Igor Korotchenko, 'General Staff Have doubts', *CDPSP*, 47/20 (14 June 1995), p. 20.

85. Andrei Kozyrev has repeatedly warned against the unilateral curtailment of the ABM Treaty: see Vladimir Nadein, 'US Senate Strikes Blow against Missile Balance', *CDPSP*, 47/31 (30 August 1995), pp. 22–3. See also Aleksandr Sychov, 'Washington Is Not

Behaving Like a Gentleman in Preparing to Test ABM System', *CDPSP*, 47/3 (15 February 1995), pp. 29–30, and Vladimir Belous, 'ABM Talks Deadlocked', *CDPSP*, 47/11 (12 April 1995), p. 26.

86. Lepingwell, 'START II', p. 88.
87. Andrei Kozyrev uses the honeymoon simile in 'Partnership or Cold Peace?', *Foreign Policy 99* (Summer 1995), pp. 8–9.
88. 'Mikhail Gorbachev on Relations between the West and Russia', *CDPSP*, 47/37 (11 October 1995), p. 25.
89. See Mathers, 'Déjà Vu', pp. 389–90. A particularly worrying example can be found in a report entitled 'Special Institute Staff Suggests Russia Oppose NATO and the USA', which was published in *Segodnya* (20 October 1995).
90. Awareness of the dilemma can be seen in Clinton's warning that dividing Europe 'could create a self-fulfilling prophecy of future confrontation': see Henry Kissinger, 'Be Realistic About Russia', *The Washington Post*, 25 January 1994. The dilemma has produced a plethora of articles either for or against NATO expansion, with the argument in favour often linking the extension to NATO's survival. Hence the title of Michael Clarke's piece, 'NATO Must Upset Russia or Do Nothing and Die', in *The Sunday Telegraph*, 7 November 1993.

Index